What Catholics Really Believe

Dispelling the Misrepresentations and Misunderstandings
of Historic Christianity with Scripture and Tradition

DR. RAY GUARENDI & REV. KEVIN FETE

WHAT CATHOLICS REALLY BELIEVE

Dispelling the Misrepresentations and Misunderstandings
of Historic Christianity with Scripture and Tradition

Answer Guide: Dave Armstrong

Editor: Stanley D. Williams, Ph.D.

Nineveh's Crossing

www.NinevehsCrossing.com
Novi, Michigan USA

Ecclesiastical approval for publication was granted by The Most Reverend Allen H. Vigneron, Archbishop of Detroit, May 20, 2009, in accord with cannon 827§3 of the Code of Canon Law.

Unless otherwise noted, Scripture quotations (except those included in quotations from other sources) in the body of this book have been taken from *The New American Bible* with the revised Psalms and New Testament authorized by the Board of Trustees of the confraternity of Christian Doctrine and approved by the administrative board of the United States Conference of Catholic Bishops and the United States Catholic Conference. Scripture quotations in the answer key are from *The Catholic Edition of the Revised Standard Version of the Bible*, copyright © 1965, 1966 National Council of the Churches of Christ in the United States of America. Used by permission. All rights reserved. Excerpts from the English translation of the *Catechism of the Catholic Church* for the United States of America copyright © 1994, United States Catholic Conference, Inc. — Libreria Editrice Vaticana. English translation of the *Catechism of the Catholic Church: Modifications from the Editio Typica* copyright © 1997, United States Catholic Conference, Inc. — Libreria Editrice Vaticana.

Television hosts: DR. RAY GUARENDI, FR. KEVIN FETE
Television series producers: DR. RAY GUARENDI, REV. JEFF MICKLER (Director)
Production: CATHOLIC TELEVISION NETWORK, YOUNGSTOWN, OHIO
Post-production enhancement: SWC FILMS, edited by MICHAEL SROKA
Executive Producer, Editor, Design, Publisher: STANLEY D. WILLIAMS, PH.D.
Study Questions: STANLEY D. WILLIAMS
Answer Guide: DAVE ARMSTRONG
Photography: © The Crosiers/GENE PLAISTED, OSC. Used with permission.
Asst. Editors: PAMELA S. WILLIAMS, DEBORAH DAVIS
Transcriptions: MARY LYLE, JENNIFER DALLACQUA, DEBORAH DAVIS
Cover, design & layout: STANLEY D. WILLIAMS
Proofreaders: RAY GUARENDI, DAVE ARMSTRONG, DAVID THOMAS, JAN SWEDORSKE
Archdiocese of Detroit Censor: ROBERT FASTIGGI, PH.D.
Censor coordinator: MICHAEL TRUMAN, Archdiocese of Detroit Chancellery

ISBN 978-0-9824058-2-6
Library of Congress Control Number 2010930535
Printed in Malaysia for Imago.
Body font: Book Antiqua, Marker Felt
Layout: Adobe InDesign CS3 on a Mac
Second printing

CONTENTS

DEDICATION

Rev. Kevin Fete (1957-2006)

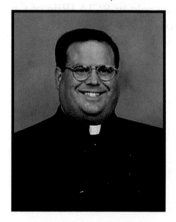

*Do not make the minimum requirement
your maximum responsibility.*

Fr. Kevin Fete went to be with his Lord July 26, 2006 at the age of 48. He was diagnosed with metastasized cancer of the kidney five weeks earlier. Here is his obituary from the *Catholic Exponent*, Diocese of Youngstown, Ohio.

Friday, August 11, 2006
Parishioners and Friends Remember Father Fete
by Joanne Malene, Staff Associate

NORTH CANTON, OHIO — There's a big hole in the heart of Little Flower Parish that will probably take some time to heal. The recent death of Father Kevin Fete has left many of his old friends and parishioners desolate and yet, at the same time, laughing as they told stories of Father Kevin, about his spirituality, his humanity and his humor.

David Schmidt, pastoral associate at Little Flower, first met Father Fete 28 years ago when the two of them were at what was then St. Gregory's Seminary in Cincinnati.

"He was a junior in the seminary when I was a freshman, but our friendship grew over the years," Schmidt said. "We became stronger friends after the seminary. In many ways, he was the same person after he was ordained as he was before he was ordained. I used to joke that he had mellowed over the years, but through and through, he was genuine. When my wife and I started having kids our friendship really blossomed. He often said if he had not been called to celibacy he would have had a dozen kids. He really liked hanging out with the kids."

"Father Fete took a very active role in RCIA [Rite of Christian Initiation of Adults]," Schmidt noted. "He was a good pastor, but he was also a great teacher. People were hungry for truth and for knowledge of the faith and he gave it to them. He was brilliant and insightful and had a great sense of humor. He saw things other people couldn't see. That made him a tremendous homilist. He would grab people with his humor and, once he had them, he would drive home the point."

Father Michael Mikstay, a Youngstown diocesan priest and an active duty U.S. Navy chaplain stationed at the Naval Air Station in Jacksonville, Fla., also got to know Father Fete in the seminary.

"He was in his first year at St. Gregory's and I was in my last year," Father Mikstay said. "Except when I have been deployed overseas or on a ship, there weren't even two or three weeks that we didn't talk. I grew up in St. Paul's Parish in Canton and he grew up at St. Joan of Arc so we had a lot in common.

"I guess the biggest thing we shared was a love of the priesthood and we had a mutual support for each other and for our unique ministries," he said. "We shared some of the same hobbies. We actually lived together in several rectories when I was home in the diocese. I have to say he was my closest and dearest priest friend."

Father Mikstay said that Father Fete had a dedication to teach what the Church teaches and a dedication to spreading the faith, not only to his parishioners but also to people with whom he crossed paths. But, he said, Father Fete's sense of humor was a key part of who he was.

"The man probably could have been a stand-up comic," Father Mikstay said. "He was extremely witty, extremely imaginative and had a tremendous sense of humor. But I would say as humorous as he was and with his ability to joke and tease, he was also deeply spiritual, caring and compassionate. The Diocese of Youngstown – and I personally – has lost a rich and wonderful benefit. I have suffered the personal loss of a once-in-a-lifetime friend, colleague, confidant, brother. I believed Kevin to be one of God's great blessings in my life. I am a better man and priest for having known and lived with him during my lifetime."

Michele Schafer was director of religious education at Little Flower for six years before becoming director of Campus Ministry at Walsh University in 2004.

"As our pastor and shepherd, he was most definitely a preacher of powerful and eloquent words and he was full of challenge," Schafer said. "Now that I look back, I see that the way he lived his life, was the living proclamation of God working through him.

"He took very seriously his vocational call to be a priest," she said. "He displayed much patience with us and he had a really beautiful balance between his pastoral ministry as a priest and his very humaneness to be with the people of God. He was always very personable. Christ is always pictured with people, eating with them, bringing them together; Father Fete was like that. He would walk into a room and just bring people together. He really lifted people up and he showed that he believed in their dignity and that they were important."

Bill Melvin and his family converted to Catholicism because of the ministry of Father Fete. Melvin came from an evangelical background, working as a Bible study teacher at a fundamentalist church before meeting the priest.

"We joined Little Flower about eight years ago and went through RCIA," Melvin said. "We were drawn to the parish because of the orthodoxy of Father Fete and his incredible way of explaining the Catholic faith. We heard about Little Flower from friends who had started going there. And, I think there were three or four couples from my Bible study who came to the Catholic faith because of him.

"You have to understand, that everything with Father Fete was to the 'nth' degree, whether it was in football or the Catholic faith," Melvin said. "Everything with him was by the book. If the Church taught it, then that was it. He had an incredible gift for homilies and for making everything seem so real. The faith just came alive under his leadership.

Barnabas
St. George Greek Orthodox
St. Paul, MN

"Father Fete had a way of making everybody feel important," he continued. "No matter who they were, he cared about everyone – whether you were a janitor or a rocket scientist – it didn't matter who you were. If he met you once, you were in his heart.

"It was an honor to learn the Faith under him. His homilies were so wonderful. We have lost a cherished gift in someone who can explain the faith as he could. He was by far the most gifted human being I have ever met in my life.

"Two things I would say personified Father Fete. First, he never said goodbye; he always said, 'Be at peace.' And, if you asked him how he was, he would always say, 'by the grace of God, brother.' We will sorely miss him."

Gloria Mitchell, a parishioner at North Canton St. Paul, first met Father Fete when he came to St. Paul's. She said there are a number of things she will remember about him.

"First, it would be his no-nonsense Catholicism," she said. "There wasn't any room to stretch the rules; I think my faith deepened from knowing him. He had a wonderful sense of humor. And, he was incredibly intelligent. He was so knowledgeable about a vast number of topics that I was always amazed. And, he was very adventurous. I think he inspired people to live their lives to the absolute max.

"Father believed in abiding by the laws of the Church and he thought that was very important," Mitchell continued. "I am a cradle Catholic and I think I learned more about the Church from him. You could ask him about anything.

"He loved things big; he did things in a big way and he liked it that way. And, he had such a wonderful sense of humor. Have you heard about the socks? He always wore bright colored socks. It was a way to express himself with his black clothing, but he loved any wild or brightly colored socks. In his casket he had bright pink socks and during calling hours, his family wore bright colored socks. And that is how he would have liked it. I feel honored, especially for the past few years and the past couple of months, to have known him and been part of his life."

Mitchell was part of a group that traveled to Tanzania. She said that wherever they went, in all of the little churches, Father Fete would preach.

"It all had to be translated, of course, but the people loved him. At his funeral, a letter was read from the people of Moshi, Tanzania and I could feel that the people were truly grieving with us from the other side of the world."

Michele Schafer noted that Father Fete was known to say, "Do not make the minimum requirement your maximum responsibility."

"He understood the preciousness of life in everything he did," Schafer said. "The people of God were definitely his passion. He proved that to the very end, in the way he died. He was a great witness to all of us as we now have to move forward without him."

The Center of All Time

PREFACE

Of the various obstacles confronting my career plans, one was my conversion to Catholicism in 1998. At the same time, I was finishing my doctoral research that ended up as a Hollywood trade book titled *The Moral Premise: Harnessing Virtue and Vice for Box Office Success*. The book explains to mainstream screenwriters, producers, and directors, how the story structure of a motion picture around a true moral premise affects box office ticket sales. It was well accepted and I planned to move to the West Coast and take the next step in my filmmaking career that had started in Detroit.

But now that I was Catholic there was a problem. No, I didn't see a moral conflict between my Christian faith and making movies. In fact, I saw the use of films to influence culture with positive, morally inspiring tales something that followed in the footsteps of Christ's parables and the Bible, 75% of which is story.

What kept creeping into my mind was one of the things I learned from my research upon which *The Moral Premise* was based—the role of valid arguments and the rejection of logical and linguistic fallacies in the search of truth. My study of fallacies in narrative film arguments opened my eyes to the problems that plagued Protestant Christianity, which had precipitated thousands of denominations, all claiming to have a corner on the true faith, but all disagreeing with each other on what that truth was. For me, Protestantism was a textbook example of relativism; and that lack of unity was the largest obstacle to Christian evangelism. (c.f. John 17:20-21)

The lack of Christian unity, I believe, is also the principal cause of Western civilization's moral decline. Putting that at the feet of Christianity haunted me. It is absolutely mind boggling that Christians claim to know the truth, and yet reject a rigorous examination of logical reasoning and critical thinking, relying instead on personal experience to interpret Scripture under the color of "faith." Gone is the "Faith of Our Fathers" (the fathers of the Early Church). In its place is "Believe in yourself."

The faith upon which Christianity is based is not blind nor based on whim, dream, or vision as some atheists claim, but rather established on physical evidence, reason, and historical record. Even pagan philosophers will acknowledge the wisdom of John Paul II revealed in his encyclical letter on the relationship between Faith and Reason

(*Fides Et Ratio*), which begins:

> Faith and reason are like two wings on which the human spirit
> rises to the contemplation of truth; and God has placed in the
> human heart a desire to know the truth—in a word, to know
> himself—so that, by knowing the loving God, men and women
> may also come to the fullness of truth and themselves.

—John Paul II, *Fides Et Ratio*

These thoughts drove me to do something concrete, didactic, and explicit. I wanted to help dispel the relativism and fallacies that separated Christianity. I say "concrete, didactic, and explicit" because such descriptors pandered to my cultural need for instant gratification. Making movies, while more accessible to the general public and buoyed by entertainment value that attracted larger audiences, are nonetheless obtuse, metaphoric, and implicit, with a "call to action" that is all but hidden. Do both, I figured. But how? And what?

Several years earlier Dr.. Ray Guarendi, noted Catholic clinical psychologist and humorist, had approached me to produce his hallmark DVD on child discipline, *You're a Better Parent Than You Think*—a stand up comedy routine that kept a standing room only audience of parents rolling in the aisles for 90 minutes. Shortly after I discovered Dr. Ray had another side. He had also become an articulate Catholic apologist by virtue of his defection to Evangelical Christianity for 10 years, where he taught a Bible class. The story of why he came back to Catholicism is told in a television/DVD project I produced in 2006 titled *Why Be Catholic?*

As we waited for the right venue in which to shoot that presentation, Ray sent me a pile of VHS tapes he had produced with Rev. Jeff Mickler, SSP, Ph.D., out of the Catholic Television Network in Youngstown, Ohio some years earlier. (Today, Fr. Jeff is an active evangellist on YouTube.) In the 13-part series Ray sat down with his priest, Fr. Kevin Fete, and talked about the misrepresentations and misunderstandings Protestants had about  Catholicism. They titled the series *WHAT CATHOLICS REALLY BELIEVE*. The hook for the series was Ray's experience in Protestant, Evangelical Christianity, and his natural petulant, although humorous demeanor. Ray asked me if there was anything we could do with this series, since it had been sitting on the shelf in Youngstown, having been aired locally only once or twice.

The programs were technically in need of renewal, but the content was astonishingly evergreen. During my 1997 journey to understand Catholic teachings, I had read dozens of books, the *Catechism of the Catholic Church,* and had re-read much of the New Testament. Yet, here, in this series, were clear, engaging arguments for Catholicism that I had never heard, and all based on good reasoning and faith in Jesus Christ.

I tried to find someone who would want to invest the money to have my production company technically update the programs and prepare them for DVD distribution. But no one seemed interested. After months of prayer and investigation, I decided to start a small distribution company with Dr. Ray's *Why Be Catholic?* and the *What Catholics Really Believe* series as our anchor products. It took us eight months of production and post-production to complete the two projects and prepare the DVDs for sale; and indeed they have become some of our best sellers.

It seems appropriate then that the DVD project that gave impetus to starting Nineveh's Crossing, also became the impetus for Nineveh's Crossing to enter book publishing, (although the book version of our hugely popular DVD *Common Ground: What Protestants and Catholics Can Learn From Each Other* was printed before this). We have tried to maintain the enlightening and spontaneous nature of the video series in this publication, even though the exchange between Dr. Ray and Fr. Fete has been significantly edited for print. Catholic apologist Dave Armstrong and I created a loose leaf Study Guide and Workbook for the video series, which has been used in many adult and teen catechism classes across the country and elsewhere in the English speaking world. The content of that guide has been incorporated into this book, with questions at the end of each chapter, and an extensive answer guide at the end.

So, here is it, (as our ad copy says) "a fabulously insightful, illuminating, and, at times, entertaining dialogue between Dr. Ray Guarendi & Rev. Kevin Fete as they explore the common misunderstandings and misrepresentations of Catholicism. With a mixture of history, doctrine, and fun debate, they mine what is often overlooked. Far from two guys' opinions, they quote extensively from Scripture, the *Catechism of the Catholic Church,* and writings from the Early Church Fathers. We call it sanctification with a smile."

Stanley D. Williams, Ph.D., Publisher

I Stand At The Door And Knock.

Revelations 3:20
Plymouth Congregational
Des Moines, IA

Publisher's Dedication

For Trudy, April, & Joshua

that faith and reason
will pierce your hearts.

St. Paul's on the Hill
St. Paul, MN

Be eager to present yourself as acceptable to God, a workman who causes no disgrace, imparting the word of truth without deviation.

—St. Paul, 2 Timothy 2:15

Ecumenical dialogue, which prompts the parties involved to question each other, to understand each other, and to explain their positions to each other, makes surprising discoveries possible.

—Pope John Paul II
"So That They May be One"
(*Ut Unum Sint*)

There are not over one-hundred people who hate the Roman Catholic Church. There are millions, however, who hate what they wrongly believe to be the Catholic Church.

—Archbishop Fulton Sheen
"Life is Worth LIving" Radio & Television Series

Substance: Body, Blood, Soul, Divinity

St. Anthony's Church
Kansas City KS

1. Jesus

DRG: (to audience) Welcome to "What Catholics Really Believe." I am Ray Guarendi – a psychologist and lay Catholic. With me is Pastor Kevin Fete. He is pastor of Little Flower Parish in Canton, Ohio.

Hello, Father Fete.

FKF: Hi Ray. How are you doing today?

DRG: Today we are going to talk about Jesus.

FKF: Great!

DRG: Your favorite topic, right?

FKF: We'd be in big trouble if we didn't want to talk about Jesus.

DRG: I want a 50 word biographical summary on who Jesus is, according to Catholic teaching.

FKF: Okay. I think one of the first things that we look at is the very question itself, "Who is Jesus?" Because, it is the question Jesus Himself poses to His own disciples.

DRG: "Who do you say that I am?"

FKF: Yes, Jesus asked His disciples, "Who do you say that I am?" And then they go through the titles to try and grasp who Christ is. Finally, Peter himself, being endowed by God with some insight says, "You are the Messiah." And Jesus gives affirmation to that. But at the same time, He tells them not to speak about it, because the titles themselves can be misunderstood by a lot of people.

So, for the Catholic Church just to say who Jesus is by listing titles doesn't do justice to who Jesus is. That's why the Church took hundreds of years, literally, to dissect and look at this person—this Savior, this Messiah. We, as Catholics, would conclude that He is both fully human and fully divine. He is the son of man, Son of God. He is the Messiah. He is the Savior through whom we find salvation.

DRG: So in that sense, we agree with the vast majority of what would be called conservative Christians, independent Bible-believing Christians, Fundamentalists,

*St. Andrew's Cathedral
Victoria, BC, Canada*

Evangelicals. Most of the non-Catholic Christian world would say, "We agree on that: Savior of the World, Son of God, God, Redeemer of the human race. He died for us." Why, then, is there so much misunderstanding among non-Catholics and maybe ex-Catholics who say things like: "I finally got a relationship with Jesus Christ when I left the Catholic Church. Not religion, but relationship is what matters. I now realize that Jesus Christ is my personal Lord and Savior, and I didn't realize that when I was in the Catholic Church"?

Where are these phrases, these beliefs, coming from, that "only when I left the Catholic Church did I find Jesus"?

FKF: I think that takes us right back to the whole issue of titles again—people getting caught up in the phraseology and the way something is worded. Catholics, who live their faith profoundly, do have a personal relationship with Jesus Christ. We may not articulate it in that fashion. But it is a matter, then, of semantics, not a matter of individuals not having Christ in their life.

DRG: What does "a matter of semantics" mean?

FKF: It means that when people say, "I have a personal relationship with Jesus Christ," there's this sense that "Jesus, He's my buddy, He's my friend." Sometimes I hear people that I know, people I love, speaking about Jesus. I hear: "He's my friend. I can turn to Jesus. I love Jesus. I talk to Jesus. He's there with me." Well, anyone who is Catholic has that sense of Christ in their life, but they don't use that same type of language to describe it. They'd say it

SEMANTICS
The study of how the meaning or interpretation of a word, sign, or sentence can change based on its use or context.

in other ways. They might say, "I come to the Church. I receive the body and blood of Christ in the celebration of the Eucharist. I welcome Christ into my life each time I take communion."

And a lot of people will say of us Catholics,

> *You know, you're a church and yet you have no altar calls. You have no altar calls.*

Well, we do have altar calls—every Mass. That is called an altar right behind us, and we are called to that altar by Christ who said,

> *Do this in memory of me. (1 Corinthians 11:24)*

As friends of Christ, Jesus laid out some conditions on that friendship. Jesus is the one who said,

> *You are my friends if you do what I command you. (John 15:14)*

Not just <u>say</u> you're my friend. But, if you <u>do</u> as I command you. And one of the things Jesus commanded is,

> *Take this bread. Take this cup. Do this in memory of me. (1 Corinthians 11:23-25)*

ALTAR CALL
The call of Christ to come bodily to Him and give ourselves totally to the work of God. In Evangelicalism the act of being called by the preacher forward to the altar rail, confessing your sins and giving your life to Christ.

DRG: We're going to have two shows on the Eucharist. But, now getting back to semantics...

My grandmother is a 92-year-old Italian Catholic. If I were to say to her, "Mama, do you have a personal relationship with Jesus Christ? If you died tonight, do you know where you're going to go? Have you accepted Jesus Christ into your heart as Lord and Savior?" Now, Fr. Fete, could you imitate for me the look that my grandmother would give me if I asked her that? Go ahead. You're good at this.

FKF: I'd probably have difficulty, but it would probably be... (Fr. Fete makes a perplexed face.)

DRG: Yes, something along those lines. You've seen my grandmother. She would just look at you and go "What?!" But if I take her over to a crucifix, and I ask, "Mama, who is that?" She'd say, "Gesù Cristo." (Italian phrase) "What did he do?" "He died on the cross." "What for?" "Well, he died for my sins." "Why Mama?" "So we could believe in Him, and do what He says, and go to heaven." Now, see, her language is different. All too often, Father, people of other denominations come up to a Catholic and say, "Have you been born again? Is Jesus Christ your personal Lord and Savior? Have you asked Jesus into your heart?" And Catholics give them that deer-in-the-headlights look.

FKF: Because it's not the language we use. It'd be like a Greek speaking to someone in Chinese and wondering why they're not answering the question.

BORN AGAIN
Accepting Christ's love into our hearts and inviting the Holy Spirit into our lives in a personal and intimate way.

DRG: Exactly! And then the conclusion by the non-Catholic is, "You see? They don't even understand the most basic thing about the Gospel. Instead they go to church on Sunday and they pray to saints. And they say this 'Roz-a-ry' or however you pronounce it, and they don't even understand the basics of the Scripture."

Let me share with you something. You know this because you're my pastor. But I was out of the Catholic Church for eight or nine years, in another denomination—in what would be called an independent, Bible-believing church, which I find a fascinating description because it implies the Roman Catholic Church doesn't believe in the Bible and yet the Catholic Church is VERY Bible-believing, as we'll get into in later episodes. In this particular church perhaps fifty-percent of the people were ex-Catholics. One day a woman in our Bible study said this, which tragically you hear too often:

> I was born a Catholic, I made my First Communion. I was educated 12 years in parochial school and went to Mass for 35 years. I never heard the words 'Jesus Christ' in a Mass.

So, I went back to my Catholic parish. I got one of our little missalettes, and I counted the number of times, in our most recent Mass, that the name Jesus as Savior, Son of God, Lord and Redeemer, Lamb of God, Savior of the World, was mentioned in the Mass for one hour. Now, this was not counting your homily or the Gospel. Take a guess how many times?

FKF: 72.

DRG: That's a good guess. That's one of those numbers you fling out Bible-speakingly, you know? "Jesus went out with 72." When in doubt say 72.

FKF: 72!

DRG: Or 3, 7, or 10.

FKF: That's right!

DRG: Thirty-seven (37) times. Thirty-seven! I went back to this lady. I just looked at her, and I said, "Where were you for thirty-five years? Why do you blame the Catholic Church for not saying what you didn't hear?"

Here's another question for you. I'm going all the way back to the basics. I heard from some children that they were asked to pray for the people in Mexico. And the reason they were asked to pray for the people in Mexico—now this was from their Sunday School teacher in another denomination—was because the people in Mexico "don't believe that Jesus Christ rose from the dead." And the reason for that is, "They still have him on the cross." Why do Catholics have Jesus on the cross? Isn't He risen?

FKF: I hear that critique a lot. And when you walk into a lot of Catholic Churches, the first thing you see is a crucifix. And some say, "Well look, you still have Jesus crucified, but not risen. You don't believe in the resurrection." A lot of people who make that criticism are people who are Bible-preaching Christians. And if you open that Bible up… St. Paul, 1 Corinthians, one of the things he says is,

> We proclaim Christ crucified, a stumbling block to Jews and foolishness
> to Gentiles. (1 Corinthians 1:23)

To people who don't understand the nature of the resurrection, the crucifixion doesn't make sense either. But the Scriptures themselves tell us, "We proclaim Christ crucified." It doesn't mean that we say, "Christ is dead." It doesn't mean that Christ has not risen. Indeed in the proclamation of the faith in the middle of the Mass,

> Christ has died, Christ is risen, Christ will come again.
> (Eucharistic Proclamation, Roman Missal)

DRG: That counts as three "Christs," by the way, when I counted them.

FKF: And, I mixed up the numbers, because I had two Masses on Sunday. So I ended up multiplying by two there when I said 72 earlier. I apologize for that.

DRG: That's Okay.

DENOMINATIONS
The organization of Protestant Christianity into thousands of sects: e.g. Lutheran, Methodist, Presbyterian, Baptist, Reformed, Assembly of God, Nazarene, et. al.

FKF: But again we have that Scripture that makes it very clear, "We proclaim Christ crucified," and yet people come to our church who say on the basis of their study of Scripture they don't understand how we can have the crucifix there.

DRG: If Jesus was not on the crucifix, in some respects, you could say that the cross is meaningless, because it represents nothing more than an ancient torture device. It is Christ who made the cross mean what it is. True?

FKF: Oh, indeed! And the cross at the time of Christ would probably be the equivalent of the electric chair today. But what makes the cross a symbol of hope for us is not just the fact that Jesus Christ Himself rose from the dead, but He rose after <u>dying</u> for our sins.

DRG: Here's another stumbling block for you to counter, and this is a stumbling block for many outside the Catholic Church, one of the prime convincers that you and I are not Christian.

> Father, are you saved? If you were to die tonight, would you know where you are going to go? And furthermore, if you go to heaven, and Jesus says, "Why should I let you in?" What would you tell Him?

FKF: Me personally?

DRG: Well, no. I mean you could use my name if you want, but some people don't think that will help.

FKF: This is a tough thing, because a lot of people want an absolute certainty that they are saved.

Grace Episcopal Cathedral
Topeka, KS

DRG: And they would say that is the Gospel. There are several verses in Scripture that say you may KNOW that you have salvation. There are multiple verses in Scripture that say, "These are written so that in believing you may have life in His name."

FKF: The problem again is that sometimes we take specific passages, and we quote those and those alone. We don't take them in the whole context of things. You've got to be very careful about quoting Scripture in a limited sense. Because Scripture — if you believe Scripture — itself tells us that even the devil can use Scripture for his own cause. I don't want to equate people who take that approach and say they're the devil. But I do want to say that you've got to be careful about taking a little piece out and saying, "This is it!"

There are so many <u>other</u> places where Christ says, you know, "If you <u>call</u> me Lord, Lord but you have not been <u>doing</u> the will of the Father, I'm going to act like I don't know who you are." Jesus is the One who said about the Father,

And He will separate them from one another, as a shepherd separates the sheep from the goats. He will place the sheep on His right and the goats on His left. (Matthew 25:32-33)

To the other ones He will say, "Because you didn't do those things, I cast you off to the everlasting pit." There's a criterion Christ gives us: "I'm looking at your <u>whole</u> life. I'm looking at <u>everything</u> you do. Yes, you need to profess Me as Lord. Yes, you must believe that I am the Way, the Truth, and the Life. But if you believe I am the Way, then you will <u>follow</u> My ways. If you believe I am telling the Truth, you have to <u>live</u> my Truth. That's how you come to <u>share</u> that Life."

SAVED & SALVATION

Within Protestantism these terms are often used interchangeably along with justification, sanctification, born again, redeemed, and "Holy Spirit baptism." The problem arises when certain sects define these terms with subtle differences but use them as if they are the same.

DRG: Whoa, whoa, whoa! You're telling me that a Catholic cannot say, "Yes! I am saved."

FKF: Well, they can say it, and I can say I am thin. Okay?

DRG: (laughing) All right. You just have to tell folks at home that the camera puts 10 pounds on you.

FKF: And ice cream did the other 80.

But, we hear in the Scriptures that we're not to be judging who finds salvation and who gets damnation. Yet, at the same time, in our hearts we want to judge ourselves favorably, and say, "I'm going to be saved." And we want to do that at zero or no cost.

I think it goes back to our crucifix issue, Ray. The cost of our salvation was the death of our Lord and Savior. And a lot of times we don't want to know about the cost. We want to have the benefits of what the Lord did without having to pay the price of discipleship.

DRG: Okay. I'm going to hang you. I'm going to hang you again. Are you saying that I, as a Catholic, cannot stand here and say, "I am saved."

FKF: Clear cut?

DRG: Clear cut. 100%, no doubt about it.

FKF: I would say you <u>cannot</u> say that.

DRG: That is what the Church teaches.

FKF: You <u>cannot</u> say, "I am saved."

DRG: Let me offer just a few Scriptures to support that, among the many.

FKF: You can BELIEVE you are saved.

DRG: I am redeemed.

FKF: Yes.

DRG: I can say, "I am redeemed"?

FKF: Yes.

DRG: But to make God's call, to say God has decided ...

FKF: To say, "I'm a saint. I am in heaven. Here I am," doesn't fly.

DRG: Now again, there are Scripture verses that seem to imply that I <u>am</u> saved.

FKF: Correct.

DRG: But, then you've got other verses here that kind of shake you up a bit. I'll read you just a few of them. These are just a couple I've picked out. These are the words of our Lord:

> *You will be hated by all, because of my name, but…by your perseverance you will secure your lives. (Luke 21:17, 19)*

Another translation of verse 19 says:

> *But, those who endure <u>to the end</u> shall be <u>saved</u>.*

Remember that part, "endure to the end." There is another Scripture here called the Parable of the Sower and the Seeds. Our Lord says,

> *The seed sown on rocky ground is the one who hears the word and receives it at once with joy. (Matthew 13:20)*

Now you've got somebody taking it in.

FKF: They're taking it in. And remember, according to John, the Word made flesh is Jesus.

DRG: Not the Bible. The Word made flesh is not the Bible.

CANONIZE
The Catholic church's process of declaring with certainty that a deceased person is in heaven. Such persons are called "Saints."

FKF: So, this is not just a matter of taking in the Word. It's not <u>just</u> taking in Jesus—also translated as, "I've accepted Christ Jesus into my life." Being saved is not just that.

DRG: **Just like Jesus continues to explain:**

> *But he has no root and lasts only for a time. When some tribulation or persecution comes because of the word, he immediately falls away. (Matthew 13:21)*

But I've got another one for you. This is a kicker: Was Judas a Christian at any time?"

FKF: I'd say yes. And, scripture supports that.

DRG: **Scripture says that. This is the first chapter of Acts. I am kind of one of those Catholics who's learning the order of the Bible. This is in the first chapter of Acts, verse 23. This is where they were replacing Judas after he died:**

> *So they proposed two, Joseph called Barsabbas who was surnamed Justus and Matthias. And they prayed and said, "You, Lord who knows the hearts of all show which of these two you have chosen to take part in this ministry and apostleship from which Judas, by transgression, fell." (Acts 1:23-25 paraphrased)*

St. Paul's Episcopal Concord, NH

It didn't say, "He never was." It said he was, and it used the word "apostleship" to describe him. But then <u>he fell</u>. That's a powerful word, by "transgression" he fell. In other words, Scripture is clear in so many spots that <u>you can walk away</u>. Is that Catholic teaching? You can walk away?

FKF: That's absolutely right. You have free will. God is love. God has to let you always be able to choose your response to God. If God forced that choice, at that point it would no longer be true love, because no longer would it be a free choice. You always have that choice.

DRG: **Let me read you one more, along with this idea of "Are you saved?" And again, this is a disagreement within the Protestant-Christian community, which is you <u>can</u> lose your salvation versus you <u>can't</u> lose your salvation once you've got it.**

FKF: "...once saved, always saved."

DRG: "Once saved, always saved. Once you've got it, you've got it, if it's legitimate," Calvinists say, "If you lose it, you never had it to begin with," and we'll talk about that in a second. So, here's the Scripture. This is Second Peter, Chapter 2, verse 20 and 21, talking about people who are Christians.

> *For if they, having escaped the defilements of the world through the knowledge of (our) Lord and savior Jesus Christ, again become entangled and overcome by them, their last condition is worse than their first. For it would have been better for them not to have known the way of righteousness than after knowing it to turn back from the holy commandment handed down to them. (2 Peter 2:20-21)*

Scripture, seems to say what the Catholic Church teaches.

FKF: Yes, it does.

DRG: Which is, at any moment, you can say, "I want to do it my way, not your way, God. I'm outta here!" Whether that's, "I don't believe in this nonsense anymore" or whether it is because, "Uh, there just happens to be a nice-looking lady over there whom I want to dump my wife and kids for. And, it feels right to me, Father, it just feels right."

FKF: We need to remember, too, there's the mercy of God, and you can come back to the Lord if you choose to do so.

First Presbyterian Mason City, IA

DRG: Whoa, hold on ....

FKF: I know, but some people don't like that.

DRG: Hold on a second! Now you're saying "I can have my salvation, I can lose my salvation, I can have my salvation, I can lose my salvation." What kind of position is this?

FKF: It's the position of Jesus Christ.

DRG: 70 by 7.

FKF: 70 times 7. And that's not a matter of just doing a mathematical equation, and saying, "490. After the 494th forgiveness of a sin, then you can be sent to hell."

DRG: On the fifth day of our marriage, my wife said to me...

FKF: You already hit 490.

DRG: (laughing) How'd you know that?

FKF: (laughing) I can't tell you.

DRG: Okay, in the first couple of centuries of the Christian Church, did they believe you could leave the community of believers, abrogate your rights as a Christian, your privileges as a Christian, and then come back?

FKF: Certainly. There are recorded instances of it. Their sense of what you need to do to reunite yourself to the community certainly called upon showing your commitment. In fact, you even find cases of people coming back after denying the Lord. Peter would be one prime example.

FREE WILL
Our ability, given to us by God, to choose our own destiny, including our reliance or rejection of God's grace.

DRG: That's a big one.

FKF: Here's Peter who knows the Lord, and who knows He is the Messiah.

DRG: Would that be apostasy? Would that be apostasy if he swears he didn't know the man?

FKF: "I don't even recognize Him, didn't see Him, don't know Him, don't want to know Him because I don't want to get killed here." Out of his fear, he chooses to reject his relationship with Christ.

DRG: Are you saying that Peter was never saved to begin with?

FKF: Well, that's the angle some would have to take. Which means then, when he says that you are the Messiah, which is where we started today, then what you'd be saying is that he really didn't know Jesus was the Messiah. When Jesus said, "Someone greater than yourself revealed this to you," we'd have to say, "Well then, Jesus didn't know what He was talking about either." We'd have to reject that. Because, again we'd have to say, "Well, if Jesus knew what He was talking about, then Peter knew what he was talking about." But then you'd have to say, "Peter DID know Jesus. He DID have that personal relationship. He DID find the one who was the Life, and out of his fear, he did reject the One."

DRG: Father — how should I put this? "Consolation" is too weak a word — give Catholics the truth of what they can say regarding their own salvation. I want some sense of security in my trust in God. I want to be able to at least feel joy and peace in knowing that I'm in God's hands.

So what does the Church teach on that? What is the Catholic Church's definition of assurance of salvation?

FKF: First of all, just in the sense of peace, when you celebrate the Mass, after the consecration, after the proclamation of the *Our Father*, the priest prays, "Lord Jesus Christ, you said to your apostles, I leave you peace. My peace I give to you." That is a reminder that Christ makes peace not as the world knows it. It's a peace inside ourselves and with ourselves. Saying we have been <u>blessed</u> with <u>the grace of God</u> and <u>this gift of faith</u>, if we choose with our free will to embrace that gift, then we share the life that comes through Christ Jesus as our Lord and Savior.

DRG: So even though I can't make the call for God—for instance, I can't say, "Ray Guarendi is 100% certain that on the Day of Judgment that God will say, 'C'mon in!'" I can still say I am 100% certain in the mercy and the promises of Christ. I can say that...

FKF ...that if I am a faithful servant, I will receive the mercy and promises of Christ...

DRG: ...if I am a faithful servant. That doesn't mean I'm <u>working</u> my way to heaven, does it?

FKF: No, it doesn't mean that you can earn your way into heaven. But it does mean that in response to Christ—as He said, "You are My friend, if you do as I have commanded you"—that Christ gave us clear cut commandments that we need to <u>do</u> and to <u>show</u> that we truly are his friend.

DRG: One more question. Catholics of my mother's generation make lots of jokes about guilt —Catholic guilt. And non-Catholics look at this and say, "Hey, hey! I've got to get out of a church that makes me feel guilty. I've got to get out of a church where I can't say I know the peace and love of Jesus Christ and where I'm looking over my shoulder every four seconds going, 'Did I commit a serious sin? Am I no longer in God's fellowship?" Respond to that.

EVANGELICALS
A group of Christian fellowships that emphasize Bible study, evangelism, and spiritual holiness.

FUNDAMENTALISTS
A sub-group of Evangelicals that emphasize separation from non-Christians and even other Christians who do not share the same views and practices.

FKF: First of all, I think that there <u>are</u> times when we priests did make people feel guilty in an unnecessary fashion. But guilt is also a great blessing. There are some times we should feel remorse for what we are thinking about doing. Even in our <u>thoughts</u>, Christ tells us that He upped the ante. He says, "You know if you look at someone angrily, you're breaking the commandment, 'Thou shalt not kill.'" There's a commandment, "Thou shall not commit adultery." Jesus said, "Even if you look at someone lustfully, you're breaking the commandment."

There's a need to look at ourselves and not be content with how we're acting, the choices we're making, or the thoughts we're having and that's a blessing. That's God's way of letting us know we're alive in the Spirit. We can know what's wrong, and we can regret participating in it, and we can be free from it if we accept the sanctifying grace of our Lord, Jesus.

DRG: So the Church would say that with God's grace, if we cooperate and persevere in our faithfulness, that the Lord will be faithful to His promises, and call us Home.

FKF: Right.

DRG: And it is not a matter of thinking that we have to always walk on this theological edge, afraid we are going to fall into the abyss every six seconds for fear that we'll just do something where the Church will go (Ray smacks his own hand), "There! You're off the edge! You're done!"

FKF: Again, if you go back to the celebration of Mass, when the cup is taken, it's the cup of the "new and everlasting covenant." And you have to understand the nature of covenant. A covenant is an agreement as it was found in the Old Testament.

St. Peter's
Albany, NY

DRG: We'd better understand the nature of covenant in one more minute, because that's all we have left.

FKF: In one minute? It's easy. A covenant was between a greater and a lesser. The greater promised his protection and the guarantee of life if the lesser pledged devotion and service to the greater. The covenant Christ made, the covenant Christ keeps.

DRG: The Catholic Church says, "Jesus Christ is Lord and Savior. He is the Son of God. He is the Redeemer of the human race. The Catholic Church teaches that we can have the security of salvation if we persevere and believe in Christ's mercy and promises. The Catholic Church has Christ on the cross because it reminds us of what He did for us. And, the Catholic Church essentially says, "We can help and guide you to find our Lord and Savior through the Scriptures, which is what we are going to be talking about next time...

FKF: "...The Tradition of the Church."

DRG: That's right, along with the Bible. What are the differences between the way Catholics approach Scripture and non-Catholics do?

FKF: And we'll get to that the next time.

DRG: (to audience) I am Ray Guarendi. I am a psychologist. And, this is "What Catholics Really Believe." Join us next time. With me and, if I haven't intellectually, cognitively battered him too much, Pastor Kevin Fete, who will be — (to Fr. Fete) since we'll be taping this in about six minutes — you'll probably be here next time.

FKF: I'll stick around. And that would answer why you have the same shirt on in each show.

DRG: (laughing — to the audience) God Bless and keep you. May our Lord watch over you. Thank you very much for joining us.

When Eternity Enters The Finite

Gloucester Cathedral
Gloucester, England

Episode 1 Study Questions

These study questions can be used for quizzes, or the starting place for additional research, and discussion. The questions are listed numerically under the Objections to Catholicism (A, B, C…) discussed in the episode. Students can write their answers on a separate sheet of paper. Where appropriate, students can review the episode in this book, on the DVD, look up answers in the *Catechism of the Catholic Church* (CCC), or research possible answers on the Internet, especially in the on-line writings of the Early Church Fathers. Answers can be found in the Answer Guide available at the back of this book.

Some non-Catholics will say:

A - Catholics do not give Jesus the titles he deserves.

    1.   How does Fr. Kevin describe who Jesus is?

    2.   What titles does Catholic teaching give to Jesus? (CCC 430-455)

    3.   Who do Catholics confess that Jesus is? (CCC 184 Nicene Creed, 422-429)

B - The Catholic Church does not teach that to be "saved" a person has to be "born again" and have a "personal relationship" with Jesus Christ.

    4.   Why do Catholics typically not refer to themselves as being "born again" or to Jesus as their "personal" savior?

    5.   If we are going to call Jesus our friend, what does Jesus require of us? (John 15:14-15, CCC 2347)

C - There are no "altar calls" during a Catholic Church service for people to accept Jesus as their Lord and Savior.

    6.   What is an "altar call" in an Evangelical Protestant service? (Research)

    7.   Do Catholics have altar calls? (CCC 1182, 1383)

D - "I was raised in the Catholic Church and went to 12 years of Catholic School and never heard the name of Jesus once."

    8.   How many times in a recent Mass did Dr. Ray count the name of Jesus as mentioned as Savior, Son of God, Lord, Redeemer, and Savior of the World? (CCC 790, 1345-1355. Study the Liturgy of the Eucharist, which can be found in every issue of *The Magnificat*.)

E - Catholics don't believe that Jesus rose from the dead because, in their churches, Jesus is still on the cross.

9. Why do Catholics use crucifixes, and not empty crosses, in their churches; don't they believe that Jesus rose from the dead? (1 Corinthians 1:23, CCC 272, 617, 638-658, 769, 1505, 1741)

F - Catholics do not know with absolute certainty that they will go to heaven when they die. The Bible teaches us that we can know for sure.

10. In each Bible passage that follows, what is the promise of salvation and what is the condition of that eternal salvation? Do any of these verses guarantee the absolute assurance of a person's entry into heaven? (Matthew 25:31-46, Luke 21:17, 19, John 1:12, John 5:24, John 10:27-29, John 20:31, Acts 1:25, Hebrews 6:4-19, 2 Peter 2:21, 1 John 5:11-12)

11. What do Catholics really believe about their assurance of salvation? (CCC 107, 112, 134, 679, 682, 1033, 2443-2449)

12. What can the Catholic say about his relationship with Christ if he or she wants assurance, joy, and peace? (CCC 2012-2029)

G - I've got to get out of the church that makes me feel guilty; I can't go on living wondering every four seconds if I've committed a serious sin or not, and wondering if I'm saved or not.

13. What is good about guilt? (Research, CCC 1776-1802)

14. What is a covenant? (Research)

The Church has always venerated the Scripures as she venerates the Lord's Body.

Catechism of the Catholic Church 103
Bethel United Church
Louisville KY

2. The Bible

DRG: Today, Pastor Kevin, we are going to talk about, probably, the number one issue that separates Catholic Christians from Protestant Christians, the issue of authority—the Bible. There are many differences between the way that Catholics approach Scripture and the way the Catholic Church teaches versus non-Catholic Christians about this issue. So, I'm going to start with a couple provocations for you.

FKF: Provocate away.

DRG: Thank you. Why can't Catholics read the Bible for themselves?

FKF: First of all, the perception is that Catholics don't read the Bible, and that is not true. That's a falsehood. Catholics, first of all, come to Church, and they hear the passages of the Scripture—Old Testament, New Testament, and the Gospel—at every Mass. They are preached the Gospel message in the homilies that are prepared for them by the priest and delivered during the Mass. There are Bible study groups in many, many of the parishes and many of the homes and amongst the families of the Catholic believing community.

What we have concern with isn't that people read or do not read the Scriptures, but <u>do become their own authority with regard to how the Bible is interpreted</u>. And there's where we have the concern, wanting people to stay within the context of the Scriptures themselves and within the Tradition of the Church.

DRG: Oh, that word "<u>tradition</u>," Reverend. You and I go round and round about tradition.

FKF: That's correct. A lot of people don't like that word. And when we are talking about the authority of the Bible, as you spoke about it, we make it clear that Catholics do not question the authority of the Bible.

DRG: This is the inspired, inerrant, infallible Word of God.

FKF: Of God. Absolutely. The Catholic Church clings to that.

DRG: Is the Church above <u>this</u>? [Ray holds up his Bible.]

FKF: The Church is not above the Bible.

DRG: Well, that's what you hear all the time.

FKF: The Church could not even teach ANYTHING that would be contrary to what is in the Sacred Scriptures. So the…

DRG: OOoooohhhh, you're going to get some argument on that.

FKF: The authority of the Scriptures is not something we would question. The question is, are we a *Sola Scriptura* community, which means *Scripture only* is the way God reveals things to us, and there is no other authority to speak about anything. But the reality is, everybody who takes Scripture and interprets it, is appealing to all sorts of authorities. The concern that the Church has is that people, when they are going to appeal to all sorts of authorities, appeal only to the authorities that Scripture says we should appeal to.

DRG: Because Christ said so.

FKF: Because Christ said so.

DRG: So, if I turn to John, Chapter 6…

> *Jesus said to them, "Amen, amen, I say to you, unless you eat the flesh of the Son of Man, and drink His blood, you do not have life within you. Whoever eats my flesh and drinks my blood has eternal life, and I will raise him on the last day. For my flesh is true food, and my blood is true drink. Whoever eats my flesh and drinks my blood remains in me and I in him. (John 6:53-56)*

SOLA SCRIPTURA

Latin for *Only Scripture*. Refers to the Protestant concept that for a Christian belief to be accepted as true, it must be found in the Bible. Strangely, Sola Scriptura cannot be found in the Bible.

Now what a Protestant might say is this:

What seems very clear is that the Catholic Church is wrong on this, that, indeed, our Lord did not mean that the Eucharist was His Body and Blood. That, indeed, he was only speaking symbolically.

So, Fr. Fete, are you saying the Catholic Church would say, "Individual believers do not have the authority given them by Christ to go to the Bible and figure out Christianity."

FKF: They have a strong possibility of misinterpreting what Christ is saying, what the Scriptures are saying, what the message is. There's a reason why there are over 25,000 denominations…

DRG: **Wait a minute. What?**

FKF: In the United States, over 25,000 different Christian denominations are currently in existence. And, it's all because people interpret….

DRG: **Wait, wait, wait. Where'd you get that figure?**

FKF: From your class.

DRG: **(Laughing) Okay. It comes from the *Oxford Encyclopedia of Christian Denominations* by the way. Just in case you didn't know that.**

FKF: We should have quoted that source before.

DRG: **Now these folks of these 25,000 …**

FKF: Denominations…

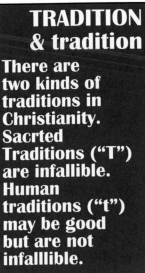

TRADITION & tradition

There are two kinds of traditions in Christianity. Sacrted Traditions ("T") are infallible. Human traditions ("t") may be good but are not infalllible.

DRG: **Are you saying essentially that through a person's understanding of the Word of God— the Scriptures—he or she can come to certain Christian conclusions that are different from that church over there or that church over there or that church over there? (Ray points in many directions.)**

FKF: Right! And if you would ask them, "How did you come to this different conclusion," they would say, "The Holy Spirit directed us." But the problem that you run into is either, one is telling the truth and 24,999 are mistaken, or the Holy Spirit is schizophrenic, and running around, telling each group its own different thing and just sitting back, laughing and saying, "This is pretty cool, look at them. We've got them all going different ways." Which certainly would not be something that we would ever hold to as a Church, saying, "Well, the Holy Spirit is deceiving a bunch of groups. The Holy Spirit is trying to mislead people." We do <u>not</u> want to take that approach.

DRG: **So, there is a problem of a genuine kind of misunderstanding?**

FKF: And with sincerity. These are people of good heart.

DRG: **Who love the Lord.**

FKF: These are people of good heart with all of the most sincere intentions, but the reality is that each, while they might <u>say</u> they are *sola scriptura*, cling to an authority figure that is not the scripture alone. And they're coming up with different interpretations. We don't want that in the Church. There are a lot of passages that can mean different things to us at different times.

DRG: **A Protestant might say:**

> That is what the Catholic Church has done, Father, recently to protect its position of power. But back in the early days of Christianity...

FKF: The early days...

> ...the first, the second, the third century the people relied only upon the Bible.

That's what you'll hear, message-wise. But here's a problem with that particular approach.

Faith Presbyterian Horseshoe Bend, AR

DRG: **What?**

FKF: Well, when we take this Bible, when we take this book, and say, "Okay, here it is. We got it all, lock, stock, and barrel." There's almost this mythical sense that somehow God sent angels down and in the first century right after Jesus rose from the dead, they said, "Here, we have the Bible!" But the reality is, the part of the Bible that we call the New Testament, at the time of Christ isn't written yet. Jesus, the Word made Flesh, is the Living Word. And He teaches. And the tradition of His teaching is what people orally start repeating. It's not until later that people actually start recording what Jesus did and said.

What's even more important is we have <u>this</u> Bible, the one with Matthew, Mark, Luke and John. There were other people making records of what Jesus did, too. There were other Gospel accounts that we do <u>not</u> have in the Bible.

DRG: **Do you know how many, by the way?**

FKF: Not exactly.

DRG: There were <u>over 50 Gospel accounts</u> written. There were <u>22 Acts</u>, as well as many other kinds of instructional letters for the faithful. Most of which claimed to be Scripture. And, indeed, in many of the local churches these letters were used as Scripture.

FKF: Were used, yes, as Scripture.

DRG: The Didache of the Apostles, the letters of Clement, the letters of Ignatius—the Christians alive at the time of these letters viewed those as Scripture.

FKF: Correct.

DRG: Not that these are just good, helpful things to read, but that these had the status as the Word of God. Correct?

FKF: They said the Gospel of Thomas would have had the same weight as the Gospel of Matthew. But we don't have the Gospel of Thomas now.

DIDACHE
Early catechism of the Catholic Church dating from 70-100 AD... literally means "the teaching of the 12 Apostles."

DRG: Why not?

FKF: Well, if you're a *sola scriptura* person, you'd have to say, "They looked up the table of contents, and they found out it wasn't in there. So, we had to drop it." But, there was no book with the table of contents. So the Church, through the passage of time, finally has to <u>choose</u> a *canon*. The *Biblical Canon* is the collection of books that are divinely inspired and should be kept as Sacred Scripture. The other books, even though they may have some insightful anecdotes about Christ or about His followers, weren't considered Sacred Scripture. They weren't considered the Word of God. But, the discernment of which books go into the Canon of Scriptures…

DRG: Who made that decision?

FKF: The discernment was left to the Church.

DRG: What Church?

FKF: The Church that we now historically understand to be the Catholic Church. If you look at the issue of the canon, and also when we talked last show about the identity of Christ, even those <u>Christological controversies</u> —

DRG: You're getting into big words.

FKF: Christological controversies occurred when people would argue about who Jesus was or wasn't.

DRG: Christological – who Jesus was. Okay.

FKF: Even those controversies – sooner or later the Church said, "What do we do to resolve these problems?" And they would form councils. Councils are not something new to people who are Bible believing Christians. Right in the Acts of the Apostles, you hear testimony that when there was a controversy over whether or not people coming into the Church who were Gentiles, needed to follow all the Jewish laws, most particularly the controversy over circumcision…

CHRISTOLOGICAL
Adjective form of Christology, or the study of Jesus Christ.

DRG: That's a rough one.

FKF: And that <u>was</u> a tough one…

DRG: You don't get a whole lot of converts…

FKF: …especially if you're forty years old, wanting to show up at the Church, and you're a guy that's not an easy one to go along with. Well, you've got to remember that originally Peter says, "Hey, you want in, you follow the rules." Paul starts to say, "Hey, let's look at this." Now all of a sudden, they've got to take and look at the Scriptures, which is interesting, because the Scriptures prescribed circumcision, if you look at the Old Testament, which was all they had at that time.

DRG: Genesis Chapter 12 calls circumcision an <u>everlasting</u> covenant.

FKF: That's correct.

DRG: So, if you used <u>Scripture alone</u> at the time of the First Jerusalem Council in the 15th Chapter of Acts, <u>you would have to stand up</u> and say,

> On the basis of Scripture, we have to say you must be circumcised because Scripture says it's an **everlasting** covenant.

So who decided, then, how to interpret the Scriptures—the Old Testament at that time? Who decided in the unfolding revelation of God that this is, or is not, what our Lord would have us do?

FKF: And that is why in 49, according to the Acts of the Apostles…

DRG: 49 A.D., not the Chapter 49 in Acts?

FKF: A.D.

DRG: Got it.

FKF: In the 49th year of our Lord, we had the Church being called together, which was basically what we'd call the bishops today. So, the Apostles and Paul got together to discern prayerfully and to be guided by the Holy Spirit to reveal what's going to go on. What happens? What should we do? Do we hold to the teaching that circumcision is required, or do we relinquish that? And they didn't just look at the Scriptures. Like you said, they actually had to have a prayerful discernment.

And it wasn't just anybody who could come up and say, "Well, I'll discern with you, I'll pray too." There was a select group of people, called by Christ, who also had successors, that are always called together in a Council, and they're given the responsibility of prayerfully discerning and being guided by God as to what is the right thing to do. <u>And Scripture attests to that</u>.

First Lutheran
East Grand Forks, MN

DRG: Let me see if I can paraphrase what you are saying... I am a shrink type so I can say those kinds of things... So, you're saying—that you can't say that because you are not licensed to say that—I mean, those are dangerous phrases in the hand of a layman.

FKF: You <u>are</u> the shrink. I <u>need</u> a shrink!

DRG: I am specifically trained.

FKF: That's right.

DRG: So, you're telling me that indeed our Lord gave the teaching authority <u>to</u> somebody.

FKF: Yes, somebody specifically set apart.

DRG: Look, here in Luke, Chapter 10:

> *Whoever listens to you listens to me. Whoever rejects you rejects me. And whoever rejects me rejects the one who sent me. (Luke 10:16)*

He was speaking to the Apostles, so he gave the authority to the Apostles. He said, "You're in charge now. What you bind, is bound. What you loose, is loosed." They had their first Council in 49 AD. and, said, "We got a problem here, boys, and we've got to figure out how to handle it." After they met, the Apostles and presbyters wrote a letter to Christians outside of Jerusalem that said:

It is the decision of the Holy Spirit and of us not to place on you any burden beyond these necessities. (Acts 15:28)

FKF: Correct.

DRG: So, the Apostles acting in a teaching role said, "We're going to interpret Scripture, and the Revelation of God, through Christ to you."

FKF: It's a very important passage, too, because later in another show together we'll be looking at the whole issue of the Pope and his authority, which Peter shows us in this Scripture. But if you remember, when we started talking about this, Peter wasn't in favor of revoking the call to circumcision. He, in prayer, finally changes and goes along with Paul and the others. But it's interesting, they would not do it until Peter was on board with them. That was a requirement they somehow understood that Christ called them to say, "Whatever we do, Peter's got to be with us on this."

DRG: We do this in unity.

FKF: We do it in unity. And Peter, open to the Holy Spirit, <u>changes</u> and says, "Okay, we'll relinquish this now. The Spirit's calling us to this."

DRG: You've touched on one of the main differences in the approach to the Bible between Catholics and non-Catholics. The Catholic view is that the Church, through the commission of Christ, has been given the authority to pass on the <u>traditional understanding</u> (from the Apostles) of Scripture. That is, the Church has been charged by Christ to answer, "What does this book, the Bible, mean? How is it to be interpreted?"

Okay, that's one difference.

Now, the second difference is that ugly word: <u>TRADITION</u>.

FKF: Right.

DRG: When I was on my journey to try to understand what Christ wanted of me and my wife in terms of where we would serve Him, I routinely heard, and this was in churches other than the Catholic Church:

The Catholic Church has added an awful lot of traditions that are not in the Bible. The Catholic Church has done things over centuries and centuries and centuries like barnacles attaching themselves to the hull of a ship. And those barnacles have not been scraped off. We need to scrape them off, get back to the pure Gospel message, and this tradition of yours is condemned by Our Lord, several times in Scripture.

Jesus tells the Scribes and Pharisees, however, and I just happen to have the verse here.

FKF: Indeed!

DRG: Yeah. That surprises you, doesn't it—Catholics referencing Scripture? Well, get used to it.

> *Then the Pharisees and the scribes asked Him, "Why do your disciples not walk according to the tradition of the elders, but eat bread with unwashed hands?" He answered, "Well did Isaiah prophecy of you hypocrites. As it is written, "This people honors me with their lips, but their heart is far from me and in vain they worship me, teaching as doctrines, the traditions of men." (Mark 7:5-7 paraphrased)*

Come on, Father, that's pretty clear.

FKF: Actually, as a Catholic, I embrace the teaching of Christ there, and I welcome it in our Sacred Scriptures, because Christ makes it very clear there is tradition that is led by mere human beings…

FIRST JERUSALEM COUNCIL

The first time that the combined bishops of the Church gathered together to make a determination about doctrine that was not evident clearly in Christ's teachings, but later revealed by the Holy Spirit. (See John 16:13)

DRG: **And the Catholic Church would condemn that type of tradition.**

FKF: Well, it would…sometimes…

DRG: **You mean if the tradition were against the Word of God.**

FKF: Yes, if the tradition were against the Word of God. But there are times, for instance, when we practice certain (human) traditions that are not against the Word of God.

DRG: **Everybody does.**

FKF: And they're appropriate for a certain age; and there comes a time when they're not as appropriate for another age. For example, a <u>human</u> tradition that was good for spiritual development among Catholics was when on Fridays we wouldn't eat meat.

DRG: That's exactly right. That's when we got extra credit.

FKF: Those were the old days—peanut butter and jelly every Friday. Remember how the bread got soaked in with all that jelly? Personally, I loved it. But there are some people who didn't. They wanted meat. But what happened is our culture changed. It used to be giving up meat was a sacrifice. Well, all of a sudden you had people… (both laugh heartily)

DRG: They just go to the seafood buffet now!

FKF: "Give me six lobster tails, please!"

DRG: "I'm Catholic and I can't eat meat on Friday!"

FKF: Your little crab's saying, "No, no. Got to get me out of here. The fat priest is coming. Got to get out of the tank."

DRG: "It's been rough for us crabs ever since the Catholics said you can't eat meat."

FKF: That's right. "Now they can fly us in from Maine. Oh no!"

Well, now, there's no big sacrifice. People are going to their seafood restaurant. They're chowing down better than they normally would on a Friday night. So the Church looks at some of those things and says, "You know, the tradition we had of giving up meat on Friday, noble when it was set up, hasn't got the same sense of sacrifice as it did." So the Church told its people, "We still want you to make a Friday sacrifice, and going without meat may be the sacrifice you still make, but there may be other ways that are a more true sacrifice for you."

EUCHARIST
Literally means "thanksgiving." Refers to the Mass in general, and particularly to the second half of the Mass where bread and wine are transformed into the body and blood of Jesus and partaken by members of the Church in Holy Communion.

DRG: And that's a Church discipline. That's not equal to the Truth of the faith, which would be a doctrine.

FKF: Not eating meat on Fridays is a specific practice of the Church to comply with the discipline of making a sacrifice every Friday. We would not say that that's a doctrine.

DRG: Because people will say, "Well, you Catholics got all kinds of traditions, you know." But, the Church in 2000 years has had to make decisions regarding how the faithful are to conduct themselves as a culture in a society of change, <u>but those are different from the apostolic "deposit of faith" that the Church is to protect.</u>

FKF: That's absolutely correct. And one of the things we have to protect…

DRG: And can't change…

FKF: One of the things we have to be fair about is that sometimes the idea of tradition that the Spirit calls us to — which we would say is tradition with a capital "T" — is <u>locked in</u>.

DRG: That is, <u>Sacred</u> Tradition.

FKF: It's sacred, it's unchangeable, it's immutable Truth — that God gives to us.

DRG: Okay, let me understand that. That means this <u>Sacred Tradition</u> is the <u>Truth of the faith</u>, handed on from the Apostles to their successors. For example, the proper understanding/interpretation of Scripture.

FKF: Correct.

DRG: Another Tradition would be the Truths of the faith that might not have been recorded in Scripture. They're implied there, but they're not written down word for word.

First Presbyterian
Mason City, IA

FKF: Correct.

DRG: And interesting, Father, if I could continue to ramble here. Don't all denominations accept a certain amount of tradition, no matter what they say?

FKF: Oh, certainly!

DRG: For example, give me one.

FKF: For example: just the basic books of the Scripture that we have. Even if you don't agree on the number of books in the Bible, it's through tradition that the four Gospels get chosen.

DRG: Matthew, Mark, Luke, and John.

FKF: If you have a Bible with those four books, you've accepted the Tradition that picked them, to some extent.

DRG: So, you're saying then, with Matthew, Mark, Luke, and John, somebody said, "Yes, I attest that Matthew was written by Matthew, Luke was written by Luke, Mark was written by Mark?

FKF: Well, the authorship of the particular Gospel record isn't the key focus. The fact that <u>that</u> particular record over other records was kept, and other records were dismissed, is the point.

DRG: In other words the Church said, "We will accept these four Gospels because the <u>Tradition</u> has said they were written by these men who were intimately close to Christ."

FKF: Yes, these Gospels are in keeping with what has been revealed to us by the Spirit.

DRG: The other many, many books that were not accepted as part of the Canon of Sacred Gospel Scriptures—and by the way, you can get those books, there are 1300 pages of them....

FKF: They are available different ways…

DRG: As helpful as some of them might be, these other books were not accepted as the divine Word of God, because Tradition said they were not written by people close enough to the Apostles.

FKF: That's correct.

*Holy Cross Church
Onamia, MN*

DRG: Okay, so that's another Sacred Tradition. There are some other big ones, and I think <u>all</u> Christians accept these Traditions. But they don't label it as Tradition—like, the Tradition that no other books are to be included in this Bible after the death of the last Apostle.

FKF: Yes, all Christians agree with that. The Canon is closed.

DRG: There is a verse in John's Revelation that says, "Anybody who adds to this book will have the plagues added to him."

FKF: Right.

DRG: But the problem with that is he was talking about Revelation.

FKF: <u>His</u> book only—not the entire book of Scriptures.

DRG: However, Deuteronomy has the same line. So if I go back into the Old Testament…

FKF: …and use that verse for the entire book of Scriptures, you couldn't add the New Testament, because you'd be breaking the Scriptures.

DRG: **You'd be breaking the Scriptures, as in <u>breaking the law</u>, to add the New Testament.**

FKF: If you interpret it that way. But all Christians accept the <u>Tradition</u> of not adding any books to the Canon of Scriptures.

DRG: **Another Tradition, for example, is the Sabbath moving from Saturday to Sunday.**

FKF: Big change.

DRG: **They talked about worshiping on the first day of the week, but they didn't come out and say, "Okay, we have a new Sabbath, let's move it."**

FKF: Even in our own day, the celebration of Christmas on December 25th. Some Christian faith communities celebrate Christmas in January, but by and large December 25th is the tradition that's evolved. There's no record that Jesus was born on this day. But traditionally, we celebrate it that day.

Now, do we say, "God revealed December 25th to us?" No, we wouldn't make that claim. But that is one of those areas where you have a human tradition that a lot of people ascribe to, and a lot of people go along with, and say, "This is fine, <u>this is not against the Sacred Scriptures</u>. We can live this way." And, we do that in our lives all the time.

DRG: **Does the Bible talk about the importance of tradition? Does the Bible itself say that it isn't just the written Word of God that counts, but also the <u>oral</u> Word of God that is protected by His Church?**

FKF: Well, certainly. Scripture itself makes clear proclamation of it.

DRG: **Second Thessalonians 2, verse 15, Paul says,**

> *Therefore, brothers, stand firm and hold fast to the traditions that you were taught, either by an oral statement or by a letter of ours.*
> *(2 Thessalonians 2:15)*

Cleveland Ave. Methodist
St. Paul, MN

So he wasn't saying, "Okay, once you get the Bible, you're done. You don't need my stuff anymore." He's basically saying, whether I <u>tell</u> you this or whether I <u>write</u> it to you, you have to hold on to this.

There's a verse at the end of John, the Gospel of John, where he says -- remember about the books? Can you paraphrase it?

FKF: Basically, not everything is in here. (He points to his Bible.)

> *If we were to write everything Christ did, we'd fill volumes that would cover the earth. (John 21:25, paraphrased)*

DRG: So essentially the Church's view on that is, much is handed on to us: the deposits...

FKF: The essence of the faith.

DRG: ....were given by Christ to the Apostles, and He commissioned these Apostles and said, "Go and teach whatsoever I have <u>commanded you.</u>"—NOT whatsoever is <u>written down</u> but "whatsoever I have commanded you." It is their obligation, and the Church views this as their <u>divine ordained obligation</u>, to protect that faith.

FKF: Yes. To embrace it. To protect it.

DRG: Can you change it?

FKF: You cannot change what's there. But that doesn't mean that there's not more knowledge about it to come in the future.

DRG: To understand it better.

FKF: To understand it more fully, and to be led in that understanding by the Spirit. Otherwise, what's the function of Pentecost? If one by a mere cognitive use of literacy could come and know the fullness of truth that saves them and say, "I've read it, I know it, I believe it," well, why then do you need the Holy Spirit to come into our lives? Why do we need to be guided as we prayerfully <u>discern</u> what to do with our lives?

Because, while the Scriptures indeed give us the essence of the faith, each day offers us particular challenges that you wouldn't find an explicit reference in the Scripture for. And a lot of people try to impose it. You'll see people really try to stretch a Scripture quote and say, "Oh, it applies exactly to that!" At that point they almost start using Scripture like the *Psychic Friends Hotline*.

DRG: You've got to be careful. This is why we have two shows on <u>Scripture, Tradition, and the Church's teaching</u> here on, "What Catholics Really Believe".

If you will stay with me, Fr. Fete, I'll double your salary.

FKF: I'm up to two donuts?

DRG: Not in one sitting.

Father, now, don't go anywhere. Stay right there.

(to audience) Until next show, when we'll talk some more about Tradition and Scripture.

I'm Ray Guarendi. God keep you, God watch over you and guide you, and God willing, we'll see you next time.

St. Mary's Church
Little Falls,` MN

Episode 2 Study Questions

Some non-Catholics will claim:

A - The Catholic Church does not let Catholics read the Bible for themselves.

1. What does Scripture say about itself? (2 Timothy 3:16-17)

2. What does the Catholic Church teach about reading and studying the Bible? (CCC 133)

3. While the Church encourages Christians to read the Bible and study it, what does the Church caution? (CCC 119, 2653)

4. What evidence do Fr. Kevin and Dr. Ray provide that indicates that the Bible can be misinterpreted without the single infallible authority?

B - The Catholic Church thinks it is above the authority of the Bible.

5. Can the Church teach anything that is contrary to Scripture? (CCC 86, 101-141)

C - The Catholic Church doesn't let its members interpret the Bible.

6. What Scriptures imply that the Church and its councils, and not individuals, should be the final arbiters of how Scripture should be interpreted? (Matthew 16:19, John 16:12-13, Acts 15, 2 Peter 1:19-21)

7. What does the Catholic Church teach about the interpretation of Scripture? (CCC 106-119)

8. How does Jesus give explicit authority to the Apostles to teach?   (Luke 10:16, Matthew 16:18-19)

D - Throughout Church history Christians relied only on the Bible for doctrine, not on the Church.

9. When and by whom was the Canon of Sacred Scripture first determined and affirmed? (Research)

10. What is the model for how a Church council should operate? (Acts 15)

11. Explain how Acts 15 and the story of what happened in the Jerusalem Council demonstrates that Church teaching does not come from the Bible alone.

12. Explain how Genesis 17:1-14 and the result of the Jerusalem Council (Acts 15) demonstrate that doctrine does not come from the Bible alone.

E - The Catholics have added a lot of traditions that are not in the Bible. They have added things to Christianity like barnacles on the hull of a ship that need to be scraped off.

13. In Mark 7:5-7 Jesus draws a distinction between the traditions of men and what else? What is it that Jesus is most concerned with?

14. What is the difference between the traditions of men and Sacred Traditions of God? (CCC 74-100)

15. List several traditions that all Christians accept that are not in the Bible.

16. How does the Bible explicitly state that we should accept Sacred Traditions in addition to written traditions? (John 21:25, 2 Thessalonians 2:15)

F - Catholicism has changed what the Bible teaches.

17. Does the Catholic Church teach anything that is contrary to Scripture? (CCC 78-87)

18. The Church claims that it has not declared any doctrine that was not believed as true during the time of the Apostles; but how does the Church keep Christianity relevant to the modern day? (CCC 53, 66-67, 69, 73, 76)

What Did Moses And Noah Have In Common With Mary?

Ss Peter & Paul Church
Mankato, MN

3. Scripture & Tradition

DRG: This time around, Fr. Fete, we are dealing with Scripture, Tradition, and the Church's role in protecting Scripture and guiding us to correct interpretation of Scripture. Last time we visited, we began the topic, Father.

FKF: Indeed we did, Ray.

DRG: I'll summarize. We talked about the different approach to Scripture between Catholic Christians and non-Catholic Christians.

Essentially it revolves around a view of the Bible. Non-Catholic Christians, predominantly of the Protestant denominations, would say that the Bible alone, *Sola Scriptura*, is our only source of God's revelation. It is binding and authoritative, and nothing outside the Bible could be viewed as a source of Divine revelation. The Bible is the sole and sufficient source in morals and doctrine.

The Catholic Church would say, "Absolutely, Scripture is infallible. It is God's Word. It is utmost, at the top of God's revelation. However, it is properly understood, taught, and protected, through the <u>Traditional understanding</u> of Scripture, which has been handed on orally, and through a God-ordained, Christ-commissioned body to hold and protect and teach the faith."

Given that, we talked a little bit about the misperception that Catholics don't read the Bible -- and by the way, I don't want to call it trivia because it's very important -- Father, if I were to attend daily Mass, how long would it take me as a Catholic to hear virtually all of the Bible read at the Mass?

FKF: Well, you get the core of the Scriptures, both the Old Testament and New Testament cycled in the Church's readings at Mass. And it is important to understand that the weekend liturgy, the liturgy of Sunday, is on a three-year cycle. You'd have the readings going through on that three-year cycle.

DRG: So I would hear...

FKF: The essence, not the whole of Scripture...

DRG: Not word-for-word-for-word, but major parts of the New Testament and Old Testament, if I were attending Sunday Mass for three years as a Catholic.

FKF: For three years, you would pick that up.

DRG: So as Catholics who say, "I never heard the Bible in church..."

FKF: That's because, see, if you're like this in church (Father tips head back and snores)...

DRG: You don't hear. You're not there.

FKF: And that crosses denominational lines. That's one of the great places, where ecumenically we can have dialogue. Because I've been in all kinds of churches, and every one of them has someone back there like that (Ray laughs. Father Fete tips head back sleeping.) So that's one place a lot of people can find some common ground.

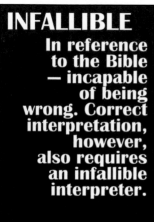

INFALLIBLE
In reference to the Bible — incapable of being wrong. Correct interpretation, however, also requires an infallible interpreter.

DRG: I don't like your implication. I was tired last Sunday. The kids kept me up.

FKF: I understand.

DRG: If I know someone, for example, who says that he has never heard the Bible in the Catholic Church, and I ask, "How long have you been a Catholic?" and he says, "I'm 37 years old," is it safe to say that since the time he has been able to read—some 30 years ago—that he, in fact, has been through the Bible—a majority of it—approximately ten times during his attendance of the Sunday Mass?

FKF: That's correct. One of the other things as a Catholic community is that we have a rich tradition of celebrating Mass <u>every day</u>. The weekday readings are on a two-year cycle. And we have large numbers of people who come each day. I can remember when I was invited to come to an ecumenical prayer service, and I asked if I could have the opening spot at 7:00 A.M., because I needed to be back to my church for morning Mass. A lot of the other ministers were in shock because they said, "Well you know, we have service Wednesday night and Sunday." As a Catholic community we gather together <u>every</u> day and proclaim the Scriptures and celebrate the Lord's Supper.

DRG: So this idea that Catholics don't read the Bible, or that Catholics are not familiar with the Bible -- it is probably more accurate to say that many faithful Catholics, I'm using the word faithful now, because anybody can call themselves anything...

FKF: Right.

DRG: ...many faithful Catholics are simply not aware of how much Scripture they're soaking in by attending daily or weekly Mass.

Maybe they don't hear it, maybe they don't take it in, maybe it has to be phrased another way after they leave the [Catholic] Church and go to another denomination.

FKF: I think that when something's around you SO much, you become less aware of it. Perhaps that's some of the effect that we get in Catholicism, because the Sacred Scriptures are there every day, proclaimed every day, sometimes people become so used to it being there that they don't notice it there.

You see people in their homes that way. The decorations and stuff are there, and all of a sudden the wife moves the coffee table over four feet and you walk through and whack into that thing, and say, "When did we get a coffee table?" Well, it's because it got moved four feet.

DRG: I do that with my wife. I go in there and say, "When did I get this wife?"

FKF: That's the problem with getting married. You get married, and the next thing you know you've got a wife. Happens all the time.

DRG: (Ray laughs heartily, addresses the camera) Honey, I just want you to know, this is not uh,... I didn't script this.

(back to Fr. Fete) Here's the next question. The Bible that Protestants and Catholics alike both accept as the inspired and infallible Word of God...

Guest House Chapel
Rochester, MN

FKF: Irrefutably.

DRG: When indeed, historically now—I want dates—when did this Bible actually get declared as the Word of God? When did that happen?

FKF: You're actually taking almost three centuries to get to the point where what we have now is the Sacred Scripture. And of course, there are brothers and sisters who are of other denominations, unfortunately, who waited until the time of Luther to change it again.

DRG: Now let me make sure I understand this. You're telling me, that for approximately three to four hundred years, the early Christians did not have a defined—officially defined—

book that IS the Bible, the Word of God that 21ˢᵗ Century Americans can look at and say, "Yes, this is the Word of God."

FKF: This collection of books.

DRG: **They did not have that?**

FKF: That's right.

DRG: **What did they have?**

FKF: They had all kinds of written and oral <u>traditions</u> that were floating around amongst the communities. Some of Paul's Epistles/letters to the churches were in writing, preserved by the communities. You know, the Epistles were actually the first things written that are in our New Testament. The Gospel accounts were being spread <u>orally</u> by the Apostles. It was only as the Apostles approached the end of their lives and realized the second coming may not be in their lifetime that they started writing this Word down. And a lot of others (that we talked about in the previous show on the Bible) wrote different stories about the Christ event. Not all of these were kept as part of the New Testament.

So what you have is this collection now of epistles and gospels, and finally the Church saying, "We need a solid core of books."

INSPIRED
Without affecting the free will of the authors, the presence of God in the lives of the Biblical authors so powerfully that they freely wrote down, in the Biblical books, truth without error, that could only be attributed to God himself, through the Holy Spirit.

DRG: **Well then, you've got a problem, Father. Because the Protestant Bible is different from the Catholic Bible.**

FKF: It is.

DRG: **The Protestant Bible has seven less books in the Old Testament as well as parts of Daniel and Esther that are in the Catholic Bible.**

FKF: We call those the *Deuterocanonical Books.*

DRG: **The Protestants would say, that the Catholics added those books in the 1500's at the Council of Trent.**

FKF: They would say that.

DRG: **The Catholics would say, "Those books were part and parcel of that forming tradition early on. From the get-go."**

FKF: Correct. I don't want to get too technical here with the Septuagint, but there's a whole group of books that the Jewish community at a certain point didn't accept. And so a lot of the early Christian people took that and said, "Well then we can't accept those into Scripture either, if that group of books is not accepted in the Jewish community." But at the same time what we have are verses from Jesus (in the New Testament) quoting from the Septuagint, and being used by Christ. Seventy percent of the quotes by Christ...

DRG: ... of the 350 allusions and quotations found in the New Testament, 70% were from the Septuagint that Protestants rejected.

FKF: But now in all fairness to our Protestant brothers and sisters, what they would say is there were some books Jesus did not quote from. When the Jewish community got rid of the Septuagint books, some said, "Okay, we should get rid of these unquoted-from books, too." Jesus didn't quote from them, but...

DRG: Jesus didn't quote from ten other books in the Old Testament either.

FKF: That's right. There are <u>ten</u> other books that are <u>still included</u> <u>that Jesus didn't quote from</u>, so that's a tough argument to work with.

> **DEUTEROCANONICAL**
> Literally "the second canon." In the Old Testament (OT), refers to those books the Catholic Church accepts as the inspired Word of God because of their presence in the Greek version of the OT used during Jesus' time in Galilee: Tobit, Judith, Wisdom, Sirach (Ecclesiasticus), Baruch, 1 & 2 Maccabees, and parts of Esther and Daniel.

DRG: In the early Church around the late 300's, there were some Councils, local Church Councils, and there were some <u>proclamations</u> made at those Councils that said, "Our Canon is these Old Testament books and these New Testament books." And when they made that declaration, those seven books that the Catholics accept now as Old Testament were in it. They were included.

FKF: Correct.

DRG: Those Councils were in 393 and in 397. In 405, the <u>Pope ratified</u> those Councils. He said, "Absolutely, those councils are legitimate. In fact, that is the traditional Church's teaching that <u>these are the books of Scripture</u>." Then the Church did it again several more times: in 419 A.D., in 787 A.D. at the Second Council of Nicea, and then at the Council of Florence in the 1400's, they again said, "YES! These are our books!"

At the time of the Reformation, Martin Luther basically said, "No. Those seven books don't belong there."

FKF: But there were more than seven he wanted removed, including James (in the New Testament). He did not like James. He called it the "Epistle of Straw." He said, "I will not have it in my Bible. It has nothing of the character of the Gospel in it."

DRG: He also didn't want Revelation and Hebrews and, I believe, Jude. That's when the Church at the Council of Trent said, "Absolutely not!"

FKF: "This is it! This is the Bible!" ...in response to Luther.

Tobias
Sacred Heart Church
Faribault MN

DRG: So you're saying that the misunderstanding then among the non-Catholics is that when the Church did that, when the Church said, "This is our Bible," they weren't adding, they were reaffirming what had always been.

FKF: That's correct. And most of the time people don't understand that. When the Church has a proclamation, either through a Papal statement or through a Council gathering, usually it is to affirm what the Church already held as true.

DRG: From the beginning...

FKF: The Church held it true from the beginning. A Council is not formed to make up new things, but to reaffirm something that has always been held from the beginning.

DRG: So, when they had the Council of Nicea in 325, it wasn't to say, "Hey, we're going to make this up that Christ was God."

FKF: "We got a new teaching about Jesus now." (in jest.)

DRG: "We've got a new teaching, He is God." (in jest)

No. They're basically saying, (pounds his fist with emphasis) "HE IS GOD. He has always been viewed as God, and this is a heresy that says He is not God."

FKF: The problem is that you don't need to define it until people challenge it. And that's when the necessity of definition finds itself.

DRG: If I ask you, "How old are you Father?" And you answer, "I'm 42." But I say, "No you're not, you're 49."

FKF: Good example. Then I've got to <u>prove</u> I'm 42.

DRG: You bring out your birth certificate and say, "I <u>am</u> 42! Look, here's the proof. Here's my birthdate on my birth certificate." And then would I say, "Aww, <u>you made that up</u> on your birth certificate"?

FKF: And I don't walk around all day saying, "I'm 42, I'm 42, I'm 42." And keep saying that until somebody challenges it. It's only <u>when</u> somebody challenges it that I have to come out with the proof of I.D.

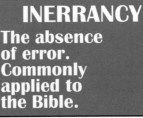

DRG: Then here's a logic problem -- something I struggled with. If indeed, the whole Christian world—Protestants, Catholics, Orthodox—accept the books of the New Testament, those 27 books as <u>infallibly given to us</u> by the Holy Spirit through the Church—when the Canon of Scriptures was decided in the Councils back in the 4th–5th century—are they saying <u>the Holy Spirit was wrong about the Old Testament</u>? Because He gave us the 27 new ones at the same time that He affirmed to us the old ones.

FKF: That's a good question. You've got these 27 new books that we finally, after looking at things, said, "No, no, they all go in there." And Protestant, Catholic, Orthodox, we all agree. And then what you're saying is, "Well, what about the Old Testament?"

DRG: Then the Holy Spirit missed it on that?

FKF: You almost have to say:

> Well, the Holy Spirit got only half of it right!

DRG: ...and, waited until 1500 to correct it.

FKF: Or you're going to say:

> Well, the Church was corrupt; therefore they only got part of it right, and they missed the other half. Probably what happened was that half of men at the council, the corrupt ones, must have spoken up during the discussion about what to include in the Old Testament. But when the discussion turned to the New Testament the corrupt guys shut up and only the ones led infallibly got to speak.

Or something like that. But at that point, you're starting to get into preposterous ideas about how did this get shifted and changed. And that starts to question the boundaries of logic, and also of the Church and the way God works.

DRG: I will tell you, Father, on a personal basis, that was one of the issues that brought me back to the Catholic Church. When I started to say, "Let me see if I understand this reasoning. You accept the 27 New Testament books because the Holy Spirit guided the Church." And even if you say that the Church is corrupt, the Holy Spirit can still work through corruption, the Holy Spirit guided the Church to these 27 but these other ones, you say:

> The Holy Spirit got it wrong because the Church misunderstood and added them in and then they waited 1100 years to correct it with Martin Luther who said these books should not be in here.

FKF: Or, you have to say that the Holy Spirit wasn't a part of anything and the Church just got lucky and kept 27.

DRG: If the Holy Spirit was not part of the Canon process, then I don't even know if this is the Bible. I don't know what it is. Just a bunch of guys decided those books are the ones.

FKF: Then you really have a problem.

DRG: Yes. You have to say that the Holy Spirit gave this to us, in order to believe it. To say that I stand on the Word of God, I have to...

FKF: ...say it's Divinely inspired.

DRG: It has to be.

FKF: Not only the writings, but the <u>choice</u> of the writings. These are writings you'd say, "We were told God wrote these. These were from God, presented to man from God." <u>You have to cling to that.</u>

DRG: Let me read you, Father, some of the writings of the early Church Fathers...

St. Francis de Sales'
St. Paul, MN

FKF: (in jest) The scripture passages about *Sola Scriptura*...

DRG: **Well...(Ray laughs)**

FKF: ...where the Bible says, the Bible itself is the only Bible that there is, and there's nothing else?

DRG: **See, that's a problem, because there is no verse in the Bible that says that.**

FKF: The argument for using the Bible alone/*Sola Scriptura* is <u>not in the Bible</u>, because that's <u>part</u> of the <u>tradition</u> accepted by non-Catholic Christians. Indeed, *Sola Scriptura* <u>is a tradition of non-Catholics</u>.

DRG: **That's right! This is one of the early Church Fathers. This is Irenaeus, and Irenaeus was a disciple of Polycarp, who was a disciple of the apostle John, so we're looking at one generation removed. He wrote in the middle of the second century, and he said,**

> This preaching and this faith the Church diligently observes, the meaning of the Traditions is one and the same. (Irenaeus, *Against Heresies*, I.10.2)

In 315 A.D., St. Epiphanius says,

> It is needful also to make use of Tradition for not everything can be gathered from Sacred Scripture. The Holy Apostles handed down some things in the Scriptures, other things in Tradition. (St. Epiphanius of Salamis, *Medicine Chest Against All Heresies* 61:6)

This is Augustine:

> I believe this practice comes from Apostolic Tradition just as so many other practices not found in their writings, but which because they are kept by the whole Church everywhere, we believe to have been commended and handed down by the Apostles themselves. (St. Augustine, *On Baptism*, 1.12.20)

DRG: **Is there anything in Scripture that says that indeed tradition is important? I gave you one verse last time when I quoted from 2nd Thessalonians 2:15. You remember it?**

FKF: Sure.

DRG: **You do?**

FKF: (Laughing) It was such a long time ago.

DRG: **Okay, 2nd Thessalonians:**

> *Therefore, Brothers, stand firm and hold fast to the traditions that you were taught, either by an oral statement or by a letter of ours.*
> *(2 Thessalonians 2:15)*

Paul tells that to the Thessalonians. I have some more from Scripture. You figured I would, didn't you?

FKF: I counted on you, Ray.

DRG: **I wrote them down. I wanted to have a little brighter light here so I could read them. You know at my age, I have to print bigger. It's been a problem. (Chuckling.) This is 1 Corinthians, Chapter 10, verse 4. Paul says,**

> *...and all drank the same spiritual drink, for they drank from a spiritual rock that followed them, and the rock was the Christ.*
> *(1 Corinthians 10:4)*

That alludes to an Old Testament passage, Numbers chapter 11 and Exodus 17. Now you know the interesting thing about that supernatural rock which follows them?

FKF: It's not mentioned in the Old Testament. But it's part of the tradition.

St. Augustine of Hippo
Newman Center U of MN
Minneapolis, MN

DRG: **It's part of the <u>Oral Rabbinic Tradition</u>.**

FKF: <u>Yes. But, it's not a part of the Scripture</u>.

DRG: **You want another one?**

FKF: Sure.

DRG: **Here's one from Jude:**

> *Enoch, of the seventh generation from Adam, prophesied also about them when he said, "Behold, the Lord has come with his countless holy ones to execute judgment on all and to convict everyone for all the godless deeds that they committed and for all the harsh words godless sinners have uttered against him." (Jude 1:14, 15)*

You know what Old Testament book that was referring to?

FKF: (Fr. Fete shakes his head, no.)

DRG: None. It's from the apocryphal book of Enoch that was never accepted in Scripture.

FKF: It's not from an Old Testament book, because the passage Jude refers to didn't make it into the Old Testament.

DRG: One more?

FKF: Certainly.

DRG: We'll get into this when we talk more about Church authority, but this is Matthew, chapter 23, verses 1-3.

> *Then Jesus spoke to the crowds and to his disciples, saying, "The scribes and the Pharisees have taken their seat on the chair of Moses. Therefore, do and observe all things whatsoever they tell you, but do not follow their example." (Matthew 23: 1-3)*

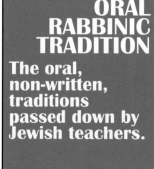

ORAL RABBINIC TRADITION

The oral, non-written, traditions passed down by Jewish teachers.

APOSTOLIC TRADITION

A teaching of the Church that can be traced back to teachings of the apostles.

FKF: This talk of the Seat or the Chair of Moses.

DRG: Where is that?

FKF: It's not in the Scriptures.

DRG: Well, it's in Matthew. (Ray smiles.)

FKF: Okay, but not in the Scriptures they had at that time. They're talking again about the Tradition of the "chair" or "seat" or "authority" of Moses and that whole approach to tradition.

DRG: Father, I've got to be honest. That idea of tradition, that idea of -- you've heard this: If you walk into a classroom, and you tell a story to the first person that by the time it gets to the thirtieth person it's so warped and so different from what it was originally, you can't recognize it. So the argument would be:

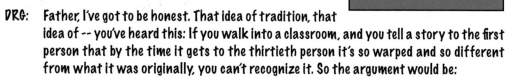

You can't keep oral tradition. Oral tradition would simply become mangled. It would be abused. You're now talking about passing orally something over centuries.

What's your response?

FKF: First of all, where is the trust in the Holy Spirit to protect the teachings of God? And do you believe in that protection?

Secondly, if you trust, especially in the Old Testament Scriptures, it's well documented that they come from a strong oral tradition. That was the nature of story telling back then. Take, for example, the Exodus story. Do you imagine that when Moses was looking for water that he was taking time each day to write stuff down? Moses, when he's got the Ten Commandments on those stone tablets? Just carrying those babies around, that's some work right there.

DRG: **That's a workman's comp charge! (Chuckling)**

FKF: You know, if he has to write all of Exodus on stone tablets, and take the book of Exodus and walk it around, that's a tough gig. You can understand why there was complaining in the desert at that point, carrying these tablets around.

We know, however, from our study of things that the tradition was carried on <u>orally</u>. Even the tradition of Christ is carried on orally. Only when the Apostles start getting older do they start realizing a need to write these things down.

DRG: **But once we have them written down, then we don't need the oral tradition anymore. Right?**

FKF: If Scripture itself said it contained everything, if it (Scripture) really did contain everything, that would be fine.

Priory Church
Christchurch, England

Or, if everything explicitly pertains to every situation that transpires through the passage of time, that would be fine. How do you take the essence, this truth, this Scripture? How does it work in our life now? What's God calling to us as a people of God in this age, and how does the Scripture enlighten us? Who interprets this? How does it get interpreted?

That's where we fall into a need of 1) trusting the Holy Spirit, and 2) trusting the Scriptures. The Scriptures, as we talked about last time, support the idea and give us the certainty that the interpretation will be protected by the Holy Spirit.

DRG: God protects His Church. So, in other words, you don't just interpret Scripture yourself, because that leads to chaos.

FKF: Sure, it's not a free-for-all. Sadly, that's one of the great sins of Christianity…

DRG: …is the division.

FKF: …is the amount of division that comes from everyone just <u>assuming</u> that they in themselves are the great prophet that has been endowed by the Spirit with the possession of all truth.

DRG: You gave us a shocking number last time, a number of denominations that have predominantly evolved from the idea that every person, with the guidance of the Holy Spirit, can interpret Scripture. What was that number?

St. Gregory's
Marysville, MO

FKF: We were over 25,000.

DRG: And growing?

FKF: And growing.

DRG: All people who love the Lord.

FKF: Good-hearted, sincere people.

DRG: No implications about their motive of loving the Lord.

FKF: That's right.

DRG: They're just simply the real result…

FKF: …of each having their own differences, and each saying and clinging to the idea that, "The Holy Spirit told <u>me</u> this is the way."

DRG: Do you baptize infants or don't you? Is this the [sacramentally real] Body and Blood or is it not? Can you lose your salvation or can you not lose your salvation? Do you pray to saints or don't you pray to saints? Is baptism a sign or is it actually something that regenerates? All of those theological issues have divided Christians.

FKF: And Christ Himself told us that <u>wouldn't happen</u> to the "Church." Christ gave us some assurances that the jaws of hell would not prevail against His Church. And that the Holy Spirit would lead us into all Truth, that there wouldn't be this mega-division amongst us as a people of God, that we're called to this sense of unity and <u>to be unified in the Truth</u>.

DRG: When people say:

> But the Catholic Church has changed just as much as everybody else in their teaching.

How do you respond?

FKF: That's not true. The response is, <u>that's not true</u>.

DRG: So you're saying morally and doctrinally, everything that the Church has taught, it has taught for 2000 years. The only changes have been in certain disciplines and practices.

FKF: That's right.

DRG: Disciplines and practices such as: Can priests get married, can they not get married, do you eat meat on Friday, don't you eat meat on Friday? That kind of thing.

FKF: That's right. The church has changed its <u>clothes</u>, but not its <u>body</u>.

St. Pius X Church
Lourdes, France

DRG: Well put! That's a good sound bite. So then, it is a great <u>myth</u> to say that in the deposit of faith—that the Church is commissioned to protect—it has changed. Great myth.

FKF: That's the great myth.

DRG: A couple of questions from our studio audience, they've been here with us many times. All right?

FKF: Rrriigght!

DRG: I have seen <u>timelines</u> showing the Catholic Church in existence from the time of Christ to the present, with the Orthodox and Protestant churches branching off. I have also seen an Orthodox and Baptist timeline, showing each of these churches as the trunk of the timeline <u>with</u> the Catholic Church. How do you know which timeline is correct?

FKF: Well, one of the things I would tell people to do is just to call on someone to be objective in studying history. If you are to take someone who has no investment personally in their own faith community -- you can take someone from even the atheist community -- and say, "Study this. Study it historically. No other way." And, you're going to find out the Tradition of the Catholic Church flows out of the Apostolic Tradition.

DRG: <u>That's what brought me back to the Church</u>. When I read the original, early writers themselves, what we would view as the theologians and the commentators of the first and second century, when I read them for myself, I, at the time, was in the non-Catholic world, and I looked and said:

> Wait a minute! That's Catholic!

FKF: When you look at the early Church teachers, especially on the teaching of the Holy Eucharist, the Mass, the Body of Christ there are too many traditions that have unfortunately thrown the baby out with the bath water.

DRG: Do you think the Church will ever succumb to changing the Scriptures to keep morally relative movements, faddish kinds of trends, happy?

FKF: No.

DRG: It has no power to do that.

FKF: It doesn't have the power to do that. It would <u>never</u> change the essence of Scripture.

DRG: If the Pope stood up tomorrow, and said, "I declare that the Gospel of John does not belong in scriptures." Could he?

FKF: No! He could not.

DRG: He does <u>not</u> have the power?

FKF: He doesn't have the authority to do that. He could never go against what the Sacred Scriptures are. Now, do we translate them in a way that speaks to people in the current age? Certainly, or else it wouldn't even be here in English.

Now, there are people who quote the scripture and say, "Well, I'm quoting it." Well, you're quoting a <u>translation</u>. We don't have the original passages here.

DRG: These are good questions. But we're going to save them for a future show.

FKF: Another time?

DRG: Yes, because we are out of time.

FKF: We're going to wrap it up?

DRG: We've got to wrap it up.

Next time around, you and I are going to talk about that issue which among Catholic practices is very much misunderstood, and among hard core folks who hate the Catholic Church, is blasphemous, which is the Holy Eucharist. In fact, is that the Body and Blood of Christ? In fact, is that what our Lord taught? In fact, is that what the early Church believed? Or is it indeed a memorial meal, and where in Scripture do you come off with this idea that it is much more? And furthermore, how do you re-sacrifice Christ every day at the Mass? So, that's what's facing you, come next time.

FKF: Those myths will be addressed.

DRG: You'd better be prepared.

(to audience) I'm Ray Guarendi. Thank you very much for joining us. We appreciate your company. May God walk with you, guide you, and God willing, see you next time around.

Ignorance of the Scriptures is ignorance of Christ

Catechism of the Catholic Church 133
Pilgrim Lutheran
St. Paul MN

Episode 3 Study Questions

Some non-Catholics will claim:

A - Catholicism is not based on the Bible because many Catholics who have attended Mass for most of their lives are not familiar with Scripture.

1.   If Catholics attended only Sunday Mass, how long would it take them to hear the core or the essence of the whole Bible?

2.   If Catholics attended Sunday Mass AND daily Mass, how long before they would hear the core or the essence of the whole Bible?

3.   What could some of the reasons be that Catholics are unaware of the Scripture that they are exposed to in the Mass throughout their lives?

B - Catholics have changed the Bible and, in fact, have added seven books to the Old Testament, along with other non-inspired sections known as the Apocrypha.

4.   How long after the beginning the Church (at Pentecost) were the first New Testament Scriptures written, and what were they?

5.   When was the New Testament canon of Scripture first collected together and declared inspired and inerrant?

6.   When did the Catholic Church proclaim the canon of Scripture to be closed?

7.   How many books are in the Catholic Bible vs. the Protestant Bible?

8.   The books included in the Catholic Old Testament that are not in the Protestant Old Testament are called the *Apocrypha* by many Protestants. What do Catholics call these books?

9.   According to Dr. Ray, in what years did various councils and popes authenticate the canon of Scripture that included these seven books?

10. When does the Church find it necessary to define a teaching as doctrine?

11. When the Holy Spirit guided the Church to declare what books were in the Bible, did the Holy Spirit get the canon of the New Testament right and the Old Testament wrong? Why or why not?

C - The only traditions that should be part of Christian doctrine are those explained in the Bible. Catholics have doctrines that are based on traditions that are not in the Bible.

12. There are two kinds of traditions in Catholic understanding. What are they, and in regards to the Holy Spirit's involvement, how are they different?

13. What traditions not explained in the Bible do Protestants believe?

14. Quote three writings from the Early Church Fathers who write about the importance of Sacred Tradition in order to understand Christianity.

15. What New Testament Bible passages support the importance traditions played in passing down a correct understanding of Christianity?

16. What New Testament Bible passages refer to Old Testament traditions that are not found in the Old Testament?

17. Who protects the truth and authenticity of the Church's teachings and the Bible's interpretation?

D - The Catholic Church has changed many of its teachings and beliefs just like Protestants from one denomination to another have changed beliefs.

18. Why has Catholic doctrine, law, practice or devotions changed over the centuries?

19. What are some ways for anyone to discover if distinctly Catholic or distinctly Protestant doctrine was taught in the first century of the Church?

20. Since the Pope is infallible in certain situations, does he have the authority to change a doctrine that has been taught by the Church in previous years?

It's Not What It Appears

St. Cecilia's School
Hastings, NE

4. The Eucharist I
Logical & Early Church Evidence

DRG: Hello. I'm Ray Guarendi, and welcome to "What Catholics Really Believe." Today we are going to talk about what Catholics really believe regarding the Eucharist. In this series, Father Fete and I have been the dialoguers. I have a special guest today, Dr. Bernie Richards. Bernie is a physicist from Kent State University where he teaches. He has a Ph.D. and is also a Roman Catholic. He has had an interesting journey. Bernie, is it safe to say that you drifted into agnosticism for awhile?

PBR: (Professor Bernie Richards, Ph.D.) Yes, definitely.

DRG: Briefly, could you tell us how you started to re-think certain things about the faith?

PBR: Well, when I started to consider the things that I teach in physics, I began to wonder if what the Church teaches wasn't even more <u>reasonable</u> than had I thought before. I thought originally that, speaking about the world that we live in, what we see is what we'd find. But I find that everything in the physical world is not what it appears to be. And so many things that were taught in the Church end up being very reasonable compared to some of the things that we teach in physics.

DRG: Give me an example.

PBR: In my lectures, I would say "the world began with an infinitely small dot that exploded and created everything we see—the universe, the stars, the plants, the trees, the people, the amoebas, the cows, everything we see." And everyone would say, "Ahhhh! Wow! That's science!"

DRG: But if you said there was a God at the beginning of all this, their reaction was..

PBR: They'd say, "Ah, there we go—superstition!"

DRG: The reason you're here, Dr. Richards, will allow us to begin this episode on the Eucharist with probably the most basic argument against the Eucharist. Catholics of course believe... Father, why don't you speak for Catholics? What do Catholics believe about the Eucharist?

FKF: The bottom line belief, Ray, is that in the Eucharist, Jesus Christ has given to us the gift of Himself. The Body and Blood of Christ is truly present in the celebration of the Eucharist. It is the gift that feeds us and nourishes our faith, and enables us to continue the journey, the pilgrimage to salvation and eternal life with our Lord.

DRG: In some miraculous way our Lord left us His Body, Blood, Soul, and Divinity, under the presence of bread and wine, given to us to nourish our body, soul, and spirit.

FKF: Correct.

DRG: When I was out of the Catholic world, one of the common arguments I got was,

> You Catholics can't really believe that. Clearly, look at that wafer. It is a white little piece of flour. You can't actually think, belying the senses, that that is somehow Jesus! I mean (whistles)... You guys are getting a little loopy on us here!

FKF: The "seeing is believing" approach to life.

DRG: Dr. Richards...you are a physicist?

PBR: That's correct.

DRG: A Ph.D?

PBR: That's correct.

DRG: (Ray has a pen in his hand.) I look at this pen, (tapping pen in his hand). Now, my senses tell me clearly, Father, that this pen is made of solid material. Would you check this pen out? (hands pen to Father Fete).

FKF: It's beautiful, Ray.

DRG: Beautiful pen.

FKF: It's a nice pen.

DRG: Solid.

PBR: Solid.

DRG: Is this solid, Doctor?

PBR: Definitely solid --a well, it LOOKS solid.

DRG: Wait, wait, wait. What do you mean, "It looks solid?" It IS solid. What do you mean, "It looks solid?"

PBR: Well, when you look at the atoms of which it's composed, they're not nearly as solid as things appear.

DRG: Excuse me? My senses tell me this pen is solid, now you're saying this pen is NOT solid?

PBR: That's correct.

DRG: Is that what physics says?

PBR: Yes.

DRG: Is this bizarro physics, or is this basic, elementary physics?

PBR: It's bizarro, and it is elementary physics. (chuckles)

DRG: It's both. (Chuckling). The two are not mutually exclusive?

PBR: That's right.

> **PHYSICAL OBJECTS**
>
> They look and feel solid but in reality their substance is 99.9999999% empty space.

DRG: All right. Then you're telling me, and I remember learning this when I was at Case Technical University, that this thing is basically 99.99999999 percent space.

PBR: If not more.

DRG: If not more!

PBR: (chuckling) That's right.

DRG: Let me see if I understand you. I'm looking at this pen. My senses tell me this is a pen that is absolutely solid, and you're telling me that the laws of physics say, "No. That is the illusion of solid, because in fact the amount of matter in this pen is very, very, very, very little?"

PBR: In terms of the actual elements, that's correct. Yes.

DRG: Now the next weird thing you're going to tell me is that I can hold this pen like this, and my senses tell me this pen is still—it is not moving. Would you at least agree that this pen is not moving?

PBR: Well, all of the parts of it are moving, right now....

DRG: Whoa, whoa, whoa...

PBR: All the atoms are vibrating and moving...

DRG: What do you mean all parts of it are moving?

PBR: That pen is composed of atoms, and all of the atoms are vibrating right now.

DRG: The next bizarre thing you'll tell me, Dr. Richards, is that these atoms are moving fast.

PBR: Very fast, yes.

DRG: What do you mean very fast? Thirty miles an hour? Fifty miles an hour?

PBR: You're talking speeds that can approach a significant portion of the speed of light in some cases.

DRG: Wait a minute. You're messing with my head here. You're telling me that this thing is not only <u>not solid</u>, but that it is in fact, <u>in motion</u>?

PBR: Yeah, the electrons within the structure there are moving very, very quickly, and the atoms themselves are vibrating.

DRG: What is this speed of light you're talking about? How fast is that?

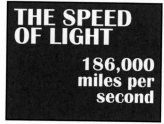

PBR: 186,000 miles a second.

DRG: A hundred...in a school zone? They let light go that fast in a school zone? 186,000 miles per second...the atoms....the small little particles that we can't see of this pen are moving that fast?

PBR: Well, some significant portion of it, yes.

DRG: Okay, so, let's just say they're putzing along at 100,000 miles a second. Clearly the things you're telling me are totally contrary to anything I can see or understand regarding this pen.

PBR: That's correct.

DRG: Father, as a priest, do you have any trouble understanding that this pen is what Dr. Richards says it is, which is mostly space and moving at upwards of 100,000 plus miles per second internally, as opposed to looking at the Eucharist and saying, "Well, clearly that's a wafer. That isn't any way, shape, or form a miraculous presence of the Body and Blood of our Lord."

FKF: I think the idea of the pen perhaps appeals to the logic more. You know, if you put out your hand and you wave it real quick (Father waves his hand in front of his face), instead of looking like a singular hand it can look like it's moving back and forth so that sense of speed gives a sense of something appearing to be there that's not there.

DRG: In other words, things are not what they seem.

FKF: By the sense's appearance, no. But you could break it down and logically look at it and say, "Well, I can understand why the pen looks solid even though it's in constant motion, because of its quick movement, that gives it its sense of being one solid entity. That wouldn't make us understand the Eucharist in and of itself. One of the problems is that when we deal with physics, we're dealing with the properties and laws of nature, or natural law. Dealing with God is dealing with the nature of God, which is <u>super</u>natural.

So when we're talking about the bread and the wine being transformed into the Body and Blood of Christ, one of the things that you've pointed out is that you <u>can't trust your senses</u> to determine that transformation. Nor could you logically figure out <u>how it is</u> that this bread and this wine is transformed into the Body and Blood of Christ. That's because it's not reducing nature to logic. It's a matter of embracing what is <u>super</u>natural. That's why St. Paul says, "We walk by faith, not by sight" (2 Cor. 5:7). <u>That means you can't always trust your senses in assessing things.</u> And even if you could trust the senses or reduce things to scientific knowledge, there comes a point where you're either a <u>people of faith</u>, or you're <u>not a people of faith</u>.

DRG: But you can at least say that the argument — that my senses tell me that that wafer is clearly <u>just</u> a wafer can be wrong — because our senses don't tell us really anything about the <u>essence</u> of that wafer; we don't even understand the very substance of what I'm looking at in this pen, for example. So, what the Church said nearly 2,000 years ago — which was that the substance of the bread and wine <u>is</u> our Lord and Savior — would be pretty much understandable, at least not deniable by physics. <u>And the Church, back then, knew little, if anything, about modern day physics.</u>

PBR: That's correct. What we know in physics today is that virtually nothing that we see is the way that it actually is. So it leads us to think routinely in physics today of a mathematical world, a world that exists outside the one that we live in; yet, it describes the world that we're in. It reminds me of theology that way, that you're looking at something outside this world. That is, these laws which we cannot directly perceive, actually govern the world that we do see.

DRG: Next point. When did the second person of the Blessed Trinity become human? At what point?

FKF: I would say at the moment of conception.

DRG: Moment of conception. So, at that time there was one cell.

FKF: One cell.

DRG: If we could take that cell out of the womb of Mary, place it under a microscope, look at it...

FKF: ...and see God waving?

DRG: <u>What would we see?</u> Would we see a cell with its nucleus and its membrane, and if we could see the cytoplasm, would we see God?

FKF: No. Even people who saw Jesus, and saw Him throughout the course of His public ministry, still had problems recognizing God. They could see Jesus, but they just couldn't recognize God. That was the difference between believers and non-believers. The non-believer says, "I'm just going to diagnose who this person is based on my senses."

DRG: And they said,

> There's no way this guy (squeezing Father's arm) can be God.

FKF: "He's a man."

*Parish Church
Egletons, France*

> He's some guy, look. God can't be human, and
> therefore, since this is a human, this can't be God.

DRG: **So is it any more difficult to believe from a Christian perspective, that if God can be in a human body, He can be under the appearance of bread and wine?**

FKF: (chuckling) That's right. One of the things you have to recognize is that God is God.

DRG: **That's very profound.**

FKF: And, why do we think that we ought to <u>limit</u> what God can do on the basis of <u>human understanding</u>? When I used to teach school, one of the kids had the old philosophical question, "Can God make a rock so heavy He couldn't lift it?" And my answer was, "Yes." And he'd say, "Well, that can't be, because if it was so heavy He couldn't lift it then there's something He couldn't do." And I just said, "Your little human mind just can't comprehend how that can be. You can't reduce God to the inabilities of your human expectations."

And that's the problem. We have people wanting to limit God. Can you take water, from a scientific point of view, and make water into wine? Well, if you're a human being, no, you can't do that. If you're God, what's natural to God is what's supernatural to us, and if Jesus wants to say, "Okay, water, you're wine now," He can make it wine.

DRG: **And bread, you're my Body and Blood...**

FKF: Bread. This is my Body; this is my Blood. He can do it. <u>It's amazing that people would believe that Jesus could turn water into wine, but He can't turn wine into His Blood.</u>

DRG: **All right. Then the question is, as we move further — if He <u>can</u> do it, DID He do it? The accusation against the Catholic Church is:**

> This is one of those really loosey-goosey, flaky theological
> things that you Catholic people made up over the centuries.
> You just kind of <u>decided</u> that, "Well, this is a nice thing.
> Why don't we just sort of develop this idea that this bread
> that we're eating—which our Lord intended to be a memorial
> meal, now, and nothing more (in jest)—Why don't we sort
> of develop this concoction that, in fact, Jesus is present?"

Now, when did the Catholic Church actually <u>make this up</u>, or actually come up with this idea?

FKF: Well, if you go back to the early Church Fathers, one of the things you'll see is that sense of the presence of <u>Christ in the Eucharist there from the beginning</u>.

DRG: What's the beginning?

FKF: Well, if you had to go back to THE beginning, you'd have to take the Gospel account of the Last Supper.

DRG: Which is what we're going to do...

FKF: Which is where Jesus says, "This is my Body; this is my Blood." The Apostle John, in John, chapter 6, elaborates on that more by quoting Jesus:

> *Amen, amen, I say to you, unless you eat the flesh of the Son of Man and drink his Blood, you do not have life within you. (John 6:53)*

St. Paul, who actually is one of the first writers of New Testament Scriptures, affirms what Christ did in the Last Supper and shows that <u>this pattern</u> of celebration of Christ [in the Eucharist] is done <u>from the very beginning</u> in the Church.

Epiphany Church
Coon Rapids MN

A lot of people think that the worship service, first and foremost, is the celebration of the Word of God, but the reality is, first and foremost, that <u>the first century Christians celebrated the Eucharist</u>. Paul had to write letters, and that's where the Word or New Testament Scriptures started to develop. When Paul is writing letters to the people who are celebrating the Eucharist, about the <u>way</u> they're celebrating it—most specifically how upset he is with the way the Corinthians (in First Corinthians) are dealing with their social norms…

DRG: (Chuckling) They had kind of like a wild buffet, here.

FKF: And Corinth was a wild town. So you know that Paul knew he was dealing with some characters that hadn't always been raised in the most moral of ways.

DRG: So you're telling me, and this is really the claim the Catholic Church makes, that <u>from the very beginning of Christianity</u>, as far back as we can go—and for the moment let's leave out the Gospels for the non-Catholic's sake who might look at us and say we're misinterpreting the Gospels, especially John, chapter 6 — let's just look at the writings of the time, of what people believed, from the bishops, and the theologians, and the

defenders of the faith in the first centuries. <u>They believed that the Eucharist was the Body and Blood of Jesus Christ.</u>

FKF: Sure.

DRG: Do you have evidence for that?

St Quentin's Church
St-Quentin, France

FKF: First of all, if people would look at us and say, "Well, you're misinterpreting the Gospels," we'd also have to say, "Well then so, too, did the first century Christians misinterpret the Gospels." John Chrysostom would be one of those fourth century, early Church Fathers. When he talks about receiving Holy Communion, <u>he speaks of not even losing a single speck of the host you receive</u>, for the Body of Christ is more precious than gold. And, just as one would not want to lose even the smallest piece of gold dust, so too, all the more reason to embrace the Lord, and not lose any part of the Lord, that he's offered us in His sacrifice.

DRG: I have quotes from some of these Early Fathers that you're talking about.

FKF: Ignatius, I hope…

DRG: Oh yeah, he's one of my favorites.

FKF: Good! Tell them a little bit about Ignatius!

DRG: Ignatius was a disciple of the apostle John. He was bishop of -- was it Antioch?

FKF: Ignatius of Antioch…

DRG: Bishop of Antioch. He died approximately 107-110 A.D., somewhere in there. History and Tradition tell us that for many, many years, he was personally under the tutelage of John the Apostle. So for him to misunderstand John the Apostle regarding the Eucharist, means, oh my, he could basically misunderstand just about anything John told him.

FKF: (Chuckles) Yup.

DRG: And here's what Ignatius said -- by the way, I like Ignatius, he's quite a guy:

The heretics confess not the Eucharist to be the flesh of our Savior Jesus Christ, which suffered for our sins, and which the Father in His goodness raised up again. Take heed then to have but one

Eucharist, for there is one flesh of our Lord Jesus Christ. (St. Ignatius of Antioch, *Smyrnaeans*, 7)

Irenaeus was another bishop, Bishop of Lyons, Second century. Irenaeus says this:

How can they say that the flesh, which is nourished with the Body of the Lord and with his Blood, passes into corruption? (Irenaeus, *Against Heresies*, V.2.3)

Now some might say:

Oh, that's symbolic.

Well, let me read you Justin Martyr, early Second Century, probably the greatest defender of the faith at that time:

We call this food Eucharist, and no one else is permitted to partake of it except the one who believes our teaching to be true and who has been washed in the remission of sins. Since Jesus Christ, our Savior, was made incarnate by the Word of God, and had both Flesh and Blood, so too we have been taught, (is) the food which has been made into the Eucharist by the Eucharistic prayer. And set down by Him and by the change of which our blood and flesh is nourished, *is both the Flesh and the Blood of the incarnate Jesus*. (Justin Martyr, *First Apology*, 66)

Melchizedek
Crosier Community
Anoka, MN

DRG: Let me give you an intellectual now, St. Augustine.

FKF: Before you move on to Augustine, real quick, with Justin Martyr some great insights there. First, if you go back and read some of the Eucharistic prayers Justin Martyr used, you would find very little difference between that and what they celebrate in a Catholic Church Mass on Sunday now. Very close in terms of the words…

DRG: In other words you're talking 1900 years ago, those prayers…

FKF: Almost the exact same prayers are used today in the Catholic Church.

Second, Justin Martyr talks about the faithful. And one of the things we can eventually get into, is the whole sense of becoming a member of the Christian Church, and the whole catechumen process. The fact is that catechumens were not allowed to stay for the celebration of the Eucharist until they were fully received into the Church. The reason was the great controversy over receiving the Body and Blood of Christ.

Sacred Heart Church
Springfield IL

One of the documented claims by pagans against the early Church was that the Christians were cannibalistic. And therefore, until someone truly, fully, embraced the faith, they were not permitted to stay for the Liturgy of the Eucharist. Only after they had proven that they were sincere to the teachings of Jesus Christ were they permitted to stay for that part of the celebration.

DRG: I've got a couple of things I want to get straightened out here. People said about the early Church, one of the accusations against them was, they were <u>cannibals?</u>

FKF: That's correct.

DRG: This whole idea of eating the Flesh and drinking the Blood --

FKF: -- was so clear… "This <u>is</u> my Body; this <u>is</u> my Blood,"…that non-Christians believed Christians were practicing cannibalism.

DRG: **Many, many of the cultures of that time, including the Jews, had memorial meals. Nobody accused them of being cannibals. If this were just a <u>memorial</u> meal, they would <u>not</u> have called Christians <u>cannibals</u>.**

FKF: That's right. And that's one of the things that gives us a great insight into the fact that this is NOT a memorial meal that's celebrated by other religions in the culture at the time of Christ. The sense of Justin Martyr's writings is that this is over and above anything we've ever seen before. There's a sense of the reality of Christ's presence in the celebration that was never before promoted by any denomination or religion at that time.

DRG: **It lends new meaning to Christ's words, "<u>I will be with you always</u> even until the end of time," doesn't it?**

FKF: It does. When you talk about how Christ tells us He's going to send His Spirit, some people say, "Well, that's how He means He's going to be with us." But that's a different person in the Trinity. Christ in the Eucharist, fulfills His promise to be with us until the end of time. And is present to us, literally present to us, <u>literally enters into us</u>. We are what we eat. The proclamation by Ludwig Feuerback (Bavarian philosopher , 1804-1872) to reduce our humanity to nothing more than <u>a biological process</u>, really confirms the Christian teaching that it is in receiving the Body of Christ that we <u>become</u> the Body of Christ.

St. Thomas More's
Munster IN

DRG: **Let me quote Augustine here, because I promised I would, but then I want to ask you a follow-up question on this. This is Augustine:**

> That which has been on the Table of the Lord is bread and wine. But this bread and wine, when the Word is added, <u>becomes the Body and Blood</u> of Christ's Body. (St. Augustine, *Sermons* 234:2)

That's pretty clear.

FKF: Not only pretty clear, but if you give consideration to the Word made flesh, that's what John starts his Gospel with. One of the great things in the celebration of the Mass for us Catholics -- two things happen in the celebration of the Mass: *One* is the <u>proclamation of the Word</u>; *Secondly* is the celebration of the Eucharist, <u>the Word made flesh</u>.

The Word's proclamation takes its depth of meaning from it becoming flesh. That was the very nature of the Incarnation. So the mystery of the Incarnation, the Crucifixion through sacrifice, and the Resurrection (in the flesh), is celebrated by Catholic-Christians in the celebration of the Mass. We have the Word, the Word made flesh celebrated at the altar of sacrifice that gives new life and nourishes that new life that we have in us.

THE WORD MADE FLESH

"Logos" is the Greek form of "the Word" which John uses to reference Jesus Christ in John 1. "Logos" also is the root for our concept of logic, rational thought, and reason—the attributes that sets humanity above the rest of creation.

DRG: We're going to talk more about the Mass in the second part of this series, and we're also going to talk about the Scripture quotes that lend overwhelming evidence to the Eucharist.

First, back to my question just before Augustine. One comeback I hear often is:

> You Catholics always cite the early Church Fathers. First of all, they're not infallible. Second of all, you're just picking and choosing. There are other early Church Fathers that would say, 'Oh, no, no, no, no! This is a memorial meal.' You just picked the Fathers that would say it's the Eucharist.

FKF: "Show me." The only response is, "Show me the Fathers that say, 'It's only a memorial meal.'" I haven't read <u>any</u> Fathers that make that claim.

DRG: In fact, there are none, Father. There is not a single writing that we have, and <u>this is what brought me back to the Catholic Church</u> in a very strong way. Throughout the first 1,000 years of the Church's history, the writings of the Christians of that time, the bishops, the theologians, the people that we would revere now as giants in the faith for our centuries, were giants in the faith for their centuries. They all said, "This is miraculously the Body and Blood of our Lord, Jesus Christ, He left to His Church." <u>There's not a single one of them that says, "You people are wrong; it's a memorial meal."</u>

FKF: Right.

DRG: Now there are a few who say that Christ is present in a spiritual way. But what about the catacombs?

FKF: Catacombs are <u>filled</u> with images about the celebration of the Eucharist, and the sense of the importance of the Eucharist, and the presence of Christ in the Eucharist. Very much filled with it.

And going back to what you said about the first 1000 years, one of the things that's really interesting is that even if you go all the way up to the Reformation, if you think anybody would challenge the idea of Christ being present in the Eucharist, it would be Luther when he's moving into this Reformation. <u>Luther himself doesn't even challenge it</u>.

DRG: No, he doesn't.

FKF: He gets into semantics about consubstantiation versus transubstantiation, but the reality is he still has a sense that there's one thing you don't mess with, and that is this idea that Jesus Christ is present in Body and in Blood in the celebration of the Eucharist.

DRG: I want to give you this classic quote from Martin Luther. You jogged my memory on this. Martin Luther says he was tempted to deny the real presence of Christ in the Eucharist. He writes:

> I could thus have given a great smack in the face of the popery. But I am caught. I cannot escape. The text is too forcible....I wrestled and struggled and would gladly have escaped." (Martin Luther, Letter to the Christians of Stassburg, Dec. 14, 1524)

One of my favorite images in the catacombs is the picture of a loaf of bread, with the fish above it. And the fish, of course, was the sign for Jesus Christ...

PBR: Ichthys...

DRG: Ichthys, which means what? The first letters of: <u>J</u>esus <u>C</u>hrist, <u>S</u>on of <u>G</u>od, <u>S</u>avior.

PBR: Yes.

DRG: And the bread with Christ over top of it, pictured in the catacombs...

ICHTHYS

English version for the capital Greek letters, capitalized $\mathrm{IX\Theta Y\Sigma}$, **which has come to mean "the sign of the fish" and consequently the secret symbol used by persecuted Christians in the Early Church to identify themselves as Christians. The symbol looks like this:**

It was a symbol for Christianity because the letters stand for the name and titles of Jesus; I= Iesous [Jesus]; CH=Christos [Christ]; TH=Y=Theou Yious [Son of God]; S=Soter [Savior].

PBR: Pretty dynamic...

DRG: So even if people would argue and say, "Well, okay, the early Church Fathers were wrong," you still have all this in stone in the catacombs.

PBR: Right. Sure.

FKF: One of the things I had a great advantage of doing was going to the Holy Land this past year. And one of the churches by the Sea of Galilee has that image in a mosaic, of the loaves and the fish. But what's interesting is that instead of five loaves in the mosaic, there are four loaves. And the reason for the four loaves is because the one loaf would be on the altar in that church. And so, this ancient church understood that there's this link -- this image of <u>fish and loaves</u> is not just about the multiplication of fish and loaves, it's about the presence of Christ in the Eucharist, that this bread is made flesh through the grace of God.

CONSUBSTANTIATION

The Lutheran belief, contrary to Catholic teaching of transubstantiation, is that in the Eucharist the Body of Christ and the bread co-exist.

TRANSUBSTANTIATION

The Catholic belief that in the Eucharist the substance of the bread and wine are completely changed into the substance of Christ's Body, Soul, and Divinity. Only the "accidents" or "outward appearances" remain.

DRG: Thank you, Father. Thank you, Dr. Richards.

PBR: Thank you.

DRG: (to audience) Well, we have attempted briefly to present a logical case on the strength of the Church's teaching of the Eucharist. We've also looked at history. When we get together next time, we will talk about the overwhelming Scriptural evidence that indicates that indeed our Lord intended to leave this most precious gift, His Body and Blood, for all time, with His Church.

I'm Doctor Ray Guarendi. For Pastor Kevin Fete and Doctor Bernie Richards, thanks for joining us. God be with you. God keep you. Walk with God.

Episode 4 Study Questions

Some non-Catholics claim:

A - Catholics cannot really believe that the bread and wine taken in communion are truly the Body and Blood of Jesus Christ; our physical senses tell us that it's flour and wine.

1. Physical objects that appear solid are mostly composed of what?

2. Describe the motion of physical objects that appear to be still?

3. How fast are parts of the atoms in a still object actually moving?

4. Do our physical senses give us an accurate or an inaccurate understanding of an object's actual nature? Why?

5. How does Dr. Guarendi and Dr. Richard's explanation of the laws of physics and our observations of a physical object apply to our understanding of the nature of The Eucharist?

6. If our physical senses are incapable of accurately describing a natural object, by what can we accurately describe a <u>super</u>natural object?

7. The elementary, fundamental substance of physical objects are atoms and their particles; what does the Church claim is the elementary, fundamental substance of the Eucharist?

B - Jesus was not God because he didn't look like God, but like man.

8. If we could have looked through a microscope at the embryo of Jesus Christ in Mary's womb, would our senses have perceived God or just a human cell reproducing? Why?

9. When Jesus was a man did people generally see a man, or did they recognize God? Why?

10. What prevents humans from recognizing God in any form, such as Jesus the Man, or Jesus in the Eucharist?

11. If we cannot use our senses to determine if something is God or not, what can we use? Why?

12. What is wrong with using natural law to explain the "super" natural?

C - The Eucharist is just a memorial or symbolic meal. That it is the real Body and Blood of Christ, is something made up by the Catholic Church over the centuries.

13. Explain how John 6 refutes this objection?

14. How do the writings of the Early Church Fathers refute this objection? (Research the writings of St. John Chrysostom, Ignatius of Antioch, Irenaeus, Justin Martyr, and St. Augustine.)

15. When Christ says "I will be with you always, even until the end of the world," why do Catholics believe this promise to be the literal physical presence of Jesus and <u>not</u> the Holy Spirit?

16. One of the objections against the early Christians was that during their worship services they were practicing cannibalism. How does this historical fact reinforce the Early Church belief in the True Presence of Christ in the Eucharist?

17. Explain how John 1:1 ("In the beginning was the Word...") and John 1:14 ("And The Word was made flesh, and dwelt among us...") reflect the Catholic Mass and the Real Presence of Christ in the Eucharist.

D - Catholics just pick and choose the writings of the Early Church Fathers in an attempt to prove that the early Christians believed in the Real Presence of Christ in the Eucharist. There were other writers who said it was only symbolic.

18. What is the best way to refute this objection?

19. What did Luther say about the True Presence of the Eucharist?

20. What symbol in the catacombs and ancient churches reinforced the early Church's belief in the True Presence of Christ in the Eucharist?

We Adore You, O Christ...

*Tabernacle at St. Cyprian's
Riverview MI*

5. The Eucharist II
Scriptural Evidence

DRG: Hello. Welcome to "What Catholics Really Believe"—a historical, Biblical, logical study of the truth of the Catholic faith. I'm Ray Guarendi, a psychologist and lay member of the Catholic Church. With me is Pastor Kevin Fete, Pastor of Little Flower Parish in Canton, Ohio.

Father, you're here to help me. (Father nods). Thank you. We're talking about the Eucharist. This is the second part of our Eucharistic approach to what the Church really teaches about Holy Communion. Let's summarize a little bit about what we talked about last time.

FKF: Okay.

DRG: I had a physicist with us, and I held up a pen, and he basically said, "Ray, that pen is not what you see. That pen is in incredible motion. The atomic particles are moving nearly the speed of light, 186,000 miles a second. The majority of this very solid looking pen is nothing but space, 99.99999999 % space. And the point, of course, was that our senses <u>can</u> totally fool us. So that when we look at that little white wafer, and we say, "Well, clearly, it's just a wafer. It's not anything but. I mean, my senses <u>can't</u> be fooled!" He essentially said as a physicist, the truth is, everything you see is not what it appears.

FKF: Right.

DRG: My question for you is, back in the very beginning, historically, very quickly, summarize the evidence that the early Church believed that the Eucharist indeed was a precious gift our Lord left us.

FKF: Well, we talked a little bit about the early Fathers, and we had a number of quotes from them about how they viewed the Eucharist to be the Body and Blood of Christ, how precious it had to be treated, how it wasn't just a symbol...

DRG: How early were these Fathers?

FKF: We go all the way back as early as Ignatius of Antioch, Ignatius being a direct disciple of the Apostle John, so you're talking <u>first generation</u>.

And now we're going to move a little further back, back into John, and back into the writings of Paul, and even back into the <u>other</u> Gospel writers and look at the nature of the Eucharist as explained in Scripture.

We know that the early Church Fathers had this understanding of the Eucharist that was the same as what exists in the Gospels—not just our interpretation of it, but as the early Church community celebrated it.

DRG: **They interpreted it and celebrated it as the Body and Blood.**

FKF: That's right.

DRG: **They didn't look at it and say, "Well, gee, it's a memorial meal," and then over the centuries the Catholic Church kind of got loopy and said, "Oh, no, we're going to make it into this big wild theology of a Mass, (Father Fete laughs), and we're going to re-crucify Christ!" or some mistaken notion like that.**

FKF: As if we're going to <u>create</u> this idea — like some bizarre kind of cult that we're making up.

St. Ignatius of Antioch
St. Pius X Church
La Crosse, WI

In fact, one of the things we talked about before the show is the Old Testament, how everything is looking forward to the Christ event, and how the Word of God points toward what's going to be happening in terms of the Eucharist. So, why don't you share with the people some of those Scriptures?

DRG: **Okay, I will do that, Father. I've got to clear something up. And this was so important on my journey back to the Catholic Church. When I read the early Church Fathers, I saw that <u>without exception</u> that we have no writings by anyone, anywhere, during the first thousand years of the Church, who said that this thing that the Church calls Communion was a memorial meal and nothing more. They <u>all</u> believed that Holy Communion was the Body and Blood of our Lord, Jesus Christ.**

I remember looking at a Protestant pastor and saying—and this is back when I was agonizing about the truth of the Eucharist—"You don't understand. For me, the Eucharist

is a lynch pin, because if the Catholic Church is wrong about the Eucharist, what else are they wrong about?"

Who would ever make up such a crazy idea, that you're holding bread, and through consecrated prayers of an appointed Apostolic Priest, that this somehow miraculously becomes Christ's Body and Blood? I mean that's pretty flaky, if it's <u>not</u> true.

FKF: But if it IS true...

DRG: If it IS true, then it is a most incredible, precious gift that sadly many of our non-Catholic brothers and sisters in Christ have left behind and rejected.

FKF: And if it is true, its ability to persevere throughout the course of 2,000 years could only be attributed to the Grace of God, not to the logic or initiative of man. Because, by man's standards, the Eucharist doesn't look like something that's logical, or something that's reasonable.

DRG: It's interesting, Father, I remember reading in a Church history text that up until the time of Martin Luther everybody—with the exception of a very few—believed the interpretation that our Lord meant this to be <u>literal</u> that this <u>was</u> really his Body and Blood to be left for us. Seventy-five years after Luther there were 200 different interpretations of what "this is my Body" means.

FKF: Once you remove or get out from under the authority of the Church, the problem with the Reformation becomes evident. It opened the <u>floodgates of subjectivism</u>. It was:

> We'll all be our own interpreters of the Word, and we'll all claim the primacy of the Spirit in what we do, even though the Spirit leads all of us in a different direction.

St. Joseph's Church
Baraboo, WI

One of the magnificent things about the Church's teachings, specifically in the Eucharist and other areas, is the amazing <u>consistency</u> throughout the ages that it adheres to.

DRG: <u>So this is not an add-on.</u> This isn't something that...

FKF: No, this is not an add-on.

DRG: (in jest) You know, in the Twelfth Century, the idea of transubstantiation happened when one of the Councils decided to make up this idea that the Eucharist was the Body and Blood of Christ.

FKF: That's often times the claim that people counter the Catholic Church's teachings with. But the reality is that definitions of things only occur when those things are challenged. So, the teaching of the Church about the presence of Christ in the Eucharist had always been the teaching of the Church. To articulate it into specific terms, to explain it only has to come up when somebody didn't understand it anymore and didn't want to experience it anymore. There's no need for those terms in the early Church, because all of the people in the early Church adhered to the primacy of the teaching that this is the Body and Blood of Christ.

Prince of Glory Lutheran Minneapolis, MN

In fact, when you said there were no dissenters among the early Church Fathers, that's true. And any time there were dissenters, they were branded heretics immediately. They were proclaimed to be unfaithful to the point of being thrown out of the community of believers—so central was the belief that this is truly the Body and Blood of Christ. And if one did not believe that, to not believe that was to reject all of the truths of the Church. Because at that point you were rejecting the guidance of the Spirit. You were rejecting Christ's promise to be with us until the end of the ages.

DRG: You said something very powerful after I quoted just a very few of the early Church Fathers, and their POWERFUL witness that indeed they believe this, throughout the whole Christian world, not just one little place.

FKF: Right!

DRG: And I said to you, a common objection is, "Well, you're simply reading <u>Catholic history.</u> You are simply reading and selecting certain people, because there are others who would say it's just a memorial meal." And you said--I loved your response--it was two words:

FKF: Show me.

DRG: (nodding) Show me.

FKF: Show me the "others" of the early Church who would say it's just a memorial meal. And one of the things we talked about in the last show was the fact that even <u>Luther</u>, the first of the Reformers, doesn't reject the Eucharist. You had a magnificent quote from Luther where he wanted to reject the Eucharistic teachings of the Church, because it was his way to put down the papacy and his way to say, "Well see, they're making stuff up." But even he, himself, in all of his zeal, didn't have the ability to reject the presence of Christ in the Eucharist. He <u>could not reject it</u>, if he wanted to at all maintain any level of integrity.

DRG: Awesome.

Let's move into more Scripture then.

FKF: Sure.

DRG: The area where most non-Catholic Christians will accept any kind of evidence for a position, a theological position, would be the Scriptures. I have many, (fanning pages) as you see, Scripture verses. Obviously—we have twenty-eight minutes—we don't have time...

FKF: We'll never get to them all.

DRG: Let me just give you two from the Old Testament. The priest Melchizedek appeared twice in the Old Testament. One time he appeared offering bread and wine. Was our Lord called anything related to Melchizedek?

FKF: Melchizedek has to be understood because of the role Melchizedek plays in the Scriptures. He is the <u>High Priest</u>. And it's the priesthood of Melchizedek <u>that's forever</u>. That's listed as the one, eternal ministry bestowed by God. Christ Jesus is seen as being in the line of Melchizedek.

DRG: In Psalm 110 it says that:

> The LORD has sworn and will not waver: "Like Melchizedek you are a priest forever." (Psalm 110:4)

FKF: So when Christ is seen as being a priest we see that the function of the priest was to offer the sacrifice in atonement for the sins of the

MELCHIZEDEK

The king of Salem (peace) and priest of God is first mentioned in Genesis 14:18-20, and in Hebrews 7:1-10 we learn why Melchizedek was important to understanding who Christ is. As a prototype of Christ, Melchizedek was a king of peace and a priest. He was without father, mother, or ancestry, without beginning of days or end of life, and Abraham gives 10% of all he has to Melchizedek out of honor for the priesthood's office. Also see Psalm 110:4.

people, and to offer thanksgiving in the name of the people for the blessings God's bestowed. And what you see at the Last Supper is this: Jesus takes the bread, and He also takes the wine, parallel to Melchizedek; and the first thing Christ does, Scripture says, is that He gave thanks. The second thing is that He breaks the bread, and then He offers it as a sacrifice.

Melchizedek
Sacred Heart Church
Fillmore, IA

DRG: Blessed it and offered it.

FKF: Blessed and broken, and then offered this as a sacrifice. But Christ doesn't tell you the sacrifice is the bread. He takes the bread and then says, "This is my Body...."

DRG: Three of the synoptic Gospels say that, right, in the Last Supper account? "This is my Body..."

FKF: All of the synoptic Gospels...

DRG: I'll interrupt you for a second, because this quote from Augustine applies.

> At the Last Supper our Lord held Himself in His own hands. (St. Augustine, *Enarr. in Ps. 33 Sermo 1, 10*)

FKF: That's a beautiful quote, and it does illustrate what's happening with the bread in the Last Supper Gospel accounts.

And then Christ does the same thing with the wine. But links it again to this giving thanks, this blessing,

> *...for this is my Blood of the covenant, which will be shed on behalf of many for the forgiveness of sins. (Matthew 26:28)*

Parallel to that would have been the celebration of the Passover Feast for the Jewish people; that meal would have been for Christ Jesus. But Jesus takes us a notch higher now, because there's no blood of a lamb. It's Himself that becomes the Lamb ...of God. It's a reminder now that this is the cup of "MY Blood. I'm the Lamb of God, the Eternal Sacrifice."

He makes it new, by linking it also to the old. It's everlasting, linking it to this Priesthood that is forever, and this Covenant, this relationship between God and His people, sealed in the Blood of Christ.

DRG: Wouldn't many scholars say that Jesus was indeed—and this would be Catholic <u>and</u> non-Catholic Scholars who would say this—that Jesus was indeed <u>transforming</u> the Passover meal into the new Eucharist, the new sacrifice?

FKF: Oh, sure.

DRG: At the Passover meal, to make it complete, what did they have to do to the lamb?

FKF: The lamb had to be slaughtered and consumed…

DRG: Consumed. Eaten…

FKF: …completely…

DRG: …eaten.

FKF: Yes, eaten.

DRG: Fascinating.

FKF: And that's going to take you into some terminology that we'll get into in John 6, but we'll get there in a little bit, because I know there's more Old Testament you wanted to look at.

*Holy Trinity Greek Orthodox
Phoenix, AZ*

DRG: Let me hit you with Malachi. I love this verse in Malachi. And the thing that's fascinating is that when you read the early Church Fathers, what you find is they took these verses from Malachi, and interpreted them a certain way. This verse is found in the Didache. <u>The Didache</u>, which means <u>the Teaching of the Twelve Apostles</u>, is estimated to have been written around 70 A.D..

FKF: Very early.

DRG: As a matter of fact, it was read as Scripture in some places, in those days.

FKF: Yes, and it's written contemporary to Scripture writings.

DRG: And to many of the Apostles, right?

FKF: Right.

DRG: This is the verse. Malachi 1, verse 11.

> *For from the rising of the sun, even to its setting, my name is great among the nations; and everywhere they bring sacrifice to my name, and a pure offering; For great is my name among the nations, says the LORD of hosts. (Malachi 1:11)*

The early Church Fathers interpreted that as the Eucharist. They **said that the pure offering had to be the Eucharist.** No offering is pure other than Christ Himself.

FKF: And specifically what links that, too, to the Eucharist is not just the purity of Christ — that links it to Christ — but <u>amongst the Gentiles</u>. What that does is take the Eucharistic sacrifice out beyond the Jewish community.

DRG: There were no sacrifices in the Gentile community at that time.

FKF: The Gentiles weren't making the sacrifices that would parallel the Passover, because they weren't part of the Passover experience. They weren't the Chosen People at the time of the Passover. Now, through the Christ event, they join with the Chosen People. So, this Good News of Jesus branches out now to the whole world — to all the Gentiles.

DRG: And I remember in my readings, finding the early Church Fathers looking at that verse and thinking (shakes head) "DUH! Of course, that's what it means! You know it's everywhere. It's from the rising to the setting of the sun." All over the world!

I read an interesting statistic the other day. Do you know how many Masses are offered worldwide in the Catholic Church? Take a guess.

FKF: On a daily basis?

DRG: On a daily basis.

FKF: On a daily — I wouldn't have a clue, but it's got to be a lot because they're everywhere all over the globe.

DRG: 300,000.

FKF: Per day?

DRG: Yeah.

FKF: Wow!

DRG: That's a lot from the rising to the setting...

FKF: And that's one of the things I love about being Catholic. We don't just gather on certain nights of the week or on Sunday alone to worship the Lord.

Sacred Heart Church
Seattle, WA

No! We have the celebration at Little Flower Parish, where I'm from, <u>every day</u>. Every day we celebrate the Liturgy of the Word, the Liturgy of the Eucharist and the celebration of the Mass. We are called to be Christians every day. Certainly celebrating every day is what we need to be about as a people of God.

DRG: Okay, let's move to John, Chapter 6, Father.

FKF: Huge! Huge!

DRG: This comes right after Jesus multiplied the loaves and fishes.

> *The Jews quarreled among themselves, saying, "How can this man give us (his) flesh to eat?" Jesus said to them, "Amen, amen, I say to you, unless you eat the flesh of the Son of Man and drink his Blood, you do not have life within you. Whoever eats my flesh and drinks my Blood has eternal life, and I will raise him on the last day. (John 6:52-54)*

> *"For my flesh is true food and my Blood is true drink. Whoever eats my flesh and drinks my Blood remains in me and I in him…Unlike your ancestors who ate and still died, whoever eats this bread will live forever"…Then many of his disciples who were listening said, "This saying is hard, who can accept it?" …As a result of this, <u>many of his disciples</u> returned to their former way of life and <u>no longer accompanied him</u>. (John 6: 55, 58, 60, 66)*

Let's comment on that, Father.

FKF: Well, there's a lot to comment on. The first thing is that, "Many of His disciples no longer accompanied or 'followed' Him." This is the only time that I can recall in the Gospel accounts when we have people walking away as a group from Jesus Christ.

DRG: You're absolutely right. It <u>is</u> the only time.

FKF: Now there is the story about the rich man who doesn't want to separate himself from his <u>things</u>, and he walks away sadly.

DRG: But he <u>wasn't a follower</u>.

FKF: He wasn't a follower, and that was a change of lifestyle. <u>These are followers</u> who now have reached a point where they are not going to accept Jesus' teachings.

DRG: We're outta here...

FKF: Yes. Because these teachings are too hard, as it says, "This saying is (too) hard."

DRG: And didn't Jesus say, a few verses down, "Wait a minute you guys, you misunderstood me! I was only speaking symbolically. Get back here!" Didn't He do that?

FKF: NO! The amazing thing is that <u>Jesus reiterates what He just said</u>. And when He reiterates it, John specifically chooses verbs in the language that He uses—Greek—to not refer to just <u>eaten</u> bread. They had different words. We have different words, too. We have chewing, or we have gnawing something. If you're going to gnaw something, it's kind of...

DRG: ...kind of like grinding.

FKF: My mom's here today. My mother hates to take me out to eat, because one of the things I like—this is a sad thing, but—I like a T-bone steak, and I like to pick up the bone at the end. I know it's not proper etiquette...

DRG: Grind...

FKF: Like, rip that flesh off that puppy. That's something that I just love to do.

DRG: I'm glad you did that before you got on camera. And you got a little bit right there (wiping his own chin).

FKF: Juice is still dripping down my chin. (Both laughing)

But one of the words is "gnawing." <u>Gnawing</u>, as used in the Greek language meant specifically, for the <u>eating of meat</u>, flesh. Flesh is a word that applies to meat, not skin, but meat. And so that <u>verb</u> is chosen with great precision. And one of the things you've got to remember is He wants to distance Himself from the sense of <u>bread</u>.

If you go back to the story that you've got in John 6, it follows the fish and the loaves. And, one of the things that John is critical of, in the way Christ is critical of, is that these people are just coming for food. Jesus looks at them and says,

> *Amen, amen, I say to you, you are looking for me not because you saw signs but because you ate the loaves and were filled... (John 6:26)*

This idea that you're just in this for the bread. This isn't about the bread. The other thing that's interesting is you've got to take John in the context of all the Gospels. John's is the last account written. John must understand that people are

*Blue Cloud Abbey
Marvin SD*

having a hard time with what was written in the other three Gospel accounts where Jesus is saying, "This is my Body; this is my Blood." So John…

DRG: Like, did Jesus really mean that??

FKF: Did He really mean that, or is this just symbolic? So John, being the last one writing, recalling what Christ has said, is recalling it specifically with this task of reminding everyone that what Matthew, Mark, and Luke had put down is trustworthy.

DRG: "This IS my body," not, "This represents my body."

FKF: That's right.

DRG: …not, "This symbolizes my body." He didn't say, "Do this in memory of me," because He means it's a "memorial" meal.

John is saying, "No, no, no, no, no. Anybody who's got doubts about this, let me rehammer this home."

FKF: That's correct.

DRG: He says six times—I just noticed this in my notes—Jesus says we must eat His flesh six times. Four times the word is the exact word you say: "gnaw."

We've got a bunch of verses, but we're running short on time. Let's hit a couple more. Verse 63. This is the verse people often will complain about. Jesus says,

> It is the spirit that gives life, while the flesh is of no avail. The words I have spoken to you are spirit and life. (John 6:63)

So some say, "See, He wasn't speaking literally, He was speaking symbolically."

FKF: Well, if He were speaking symbolically, He would have spoken symbolically a lot quicker, before He starts to get people leaving Him…. unless He's just really stupid.

DRG: Or He just wants to get them all to leave.

FKF: (in jest) Maybe He didn't have a church big enough to hold them all, so He decides, well, let's get some of them mad, and we'll shrink it down…

EAT IN GREEK

In John 6:54-58 John uses the Greek word "trogo" four times which can be translated as a more aggressive chewing, gnawing, as an animal would eat meat. Interspersed with the use of "trogo" John uses the more normal words for eating which are "esthio" or "phago."

DRG: "Spirit" never means <u>symbol</u> in Scripture, does it? When you say, "The words are spirit," there's no place in Scripture where "spirit" is ever translated as "symbol." Spirit is real.

FKF: Yes, there's a reality to that, too.

DRG: I heard the "spirit" of it explained to me this way: Our Lord was saying, "Look, you're not going to chew on my raw flesh, I'm going to give it to you in a way you don't understand."

*St. Mary's Cathedral
Winnipeg, Manitoba*

FKF: Right!

DRG: But the other interesting thing is He says, "The words I speak to you are spirit." Indeed, He just basically hammered home this whole point: It's real, it's real, it's real, it's real. So if He says, "<u>The words I tell you are spirit and life</u>," you have to understand them in that way. It doesn't negate everything that He said up to that point.

FKF: That's right. Now, let me just pick up one thing more before we go on. In the celebration of the Eucharistic prayer, the words of institution are very important—what we call the *CONSECRATION*—the time for the <u>transformation</u> of the bread and wine to become Body and Blood. But also, what is important is the *EPIKLESIS*, which is a fancy word for <u>the calling down of the Holy Spirit</u> to make the transformation.

There is this sense in the Catholic celebration of the Eucharist—and it has been this way all the way back to the early Church—of it being <u>in the Spirit</u>— that the life-giving bread is transformed into the Body and Blood of Christ. So that sense of Spirit is not something completely foreign to the celebration of the Mass.

DRG: I see. So the Eucharist is also Spirit, too?

FKF: Certainly. <u>The Spirit is used in this transformation</u>. It's the grace of God, the supernatural power of God that enables this natural thing to be transformed into this presence of Christ.

DRG: Luke (22:19) and Paul (1 Cor. 11:24-25) quote Jesus the same, "Do this in memory of me." *Anamnesis* is the Greek word. In the New Testament and the Old Testament, *anamnesis* is always used in the context of the sacrifice, and it doesn't mean <u>to remember</u>, it means <u>to make alive again</u>, to bring into reality.

FKF: To make real. Yes, to make alive. It's not an intellectual, cognitive recalling of past events. When we talk about <u>memory</u>, we're just talking about thinking about something that used to be. Their idea is that in doing this, <u>it becomes what it was</u>. It enters into this timeless realm.

DRG: **Let me read this:**

> *For I received from the Lord what I also handed on to you, that the Lord Jesus, on the night he was handed over, took bread, and after he had given thanks, broke it and said, "This is my Body that is for you." (1 Corinthians 11:23-24a)*

Skip down a couple verses:

> *Whoever, therefore, eats the bread and drinks the cup of the Lord without <u>discerning the Body and Blood</u> will be guilty and eat and drink <u>condemnation</u> upon himself… That is why many of you are ill and some have died. (1 Corinthians 11:27-30 paraphrased)*

Now wait a minute. If this is a memorial meal, how can you be condemned? His words are "anyone who eats and drinks without discerning the Body, eats and drinks condemnation upon himself." That's STRONG!

FKF: Very strong language. Some people would take this passage, and they'd say, "Well, what they're saying is 'without discerning the <u>Body</u>' is the <u>body of believers</u>, the people around you." One of the things that's going on in 1 Corinthians, of course, is that Jesus is upset. Paul's saying there's a reason to be upset, because we're not treating people as Jesus would say we should. The brothers and

St. Edward's Church
Seattle WA

sisters of the community are dividing themselves according to their worldly means. And so that's why sometimes people take this application of "the body of believers" meaning here.

But, we're <u>not</u> just talking about a <u>social meal</u>. The reason why the social meal takes on any <u>importance</u> is because of the importance of this <u>sacrificial meal</u>, this Body and Blood of Christ. If you say it is the discernment of the body of believers that becomes the focus, then what you are saying is the social meal is the great importance, and that's just kind of why they got together for this memorial of Jesus. But that doesn't make sense logically.

DRG: Because at that point...

FKF: <u>The social gathering of the community becomes the focus, not the sacrifice of Christ</u>. It's only when you look at the sacrifice of Christ being the focus, and realize the body being spoken about is the Body of Christ, that the social issue starts to take on grave importance, because then social body becomes <u>offensive to the Body of Christ</u>. Then the social gathering becomes <u>a sacrilege to the Body of Christ</u>. Then the social body proclaims, "We are NOT the Body of Christ, and therefore we did not become what we eat. We did not receive the body of Christ, because if we had, we would have been the body of Christ."

DRG: You are theologically deep, but you are, in the media, somewhat a rookie. We've got two minutes left, and we didn't get to about eight quotes.

FKF: And I didn't use any pithy quotes myself.

DRG: No. No pithy quotes yourself. Nothing that we can just take as a sound bite for a promo...

FKF: I'm sorry.

DRG: You have forty-five seconds. Road to Emmaus, Gospel of Luke. The disciples after the Resurrection. Jesus comes up behind them. He asks them what they're so sad about. They say, "Don't you know what has happened?" And then He goes on to explain to them all the prophecies regarding Him. They don't recognize Him! When did they recognize Him?

FKF: In the breaking of the bread.

DRG: In that very same context.

FKF: Right. And again, you've got to go pretty far if you want to change this. Somebody is going to tell you, "Oh, is this like the peek-a-boo?" Like Jesus broke the bread and then peeked through. Oh look! It's Jesus!

EMMAUS ROAD

After His Resurrection Jesus appears to a couple of disciples on the road out of Jerusalem to the city of Emmaus. But they do not recognize him. As they walk, he explains to them the prophecies in the Old Testament and how they were fulfilled in the His life, death, and resurrection. He stays with them for dinner, and after he takes the bread, blesses it, breaks it, gives it to them – and just as they recognize who He is... He disappears. The juxtaposition of the consecrated bread, becoming Christ, is palatable, visible, and physical.

DRG: It's Jesus! I've heard some say the Emmaus disciples saw the nail marks on his hands for the first time as he picked up the bread.

FKF: The wounds on His hands. It's important for us, because as Catholic Christians — we talked about that last show — the order and sequence of the Word and the Body of Christ, <u>it's in the breaking of the bread that the Word makes sense</u>.

DRG: AHH!!

FKF: That's the celebration of the Mass; that's the celebration of the early Christian community; that's the celebration of the Church throughout history, that the Word is proclaimed — both from the Old Testament and from the Gospels — and then <u>the understanding of that Word comes when you break the bread</u>. That's when you <u>recognize</u> the Word made flesh. That is what John proclaims to be Jesus Christ.

DRG: You have tried to pour the ocean through a funnel. Even with two shows, we cannot touch upon the depth of the Catholic teaching regarding the Eucharist. Historically, logically, Scripturally, the evidence is profound.

(to audience) I'm Dr. Ray Guarendi, psychologist. My friend, my spiritual mentor, Pastor Kevin Fete of Little Flower Parish. Thank you for joining us. God be with you, God walk with you. Hold onto God's hand real tight.

St. Michael's Church
Sneem, Ireland

The Church has always venerated the divine Scriptures as she venerated the Body of the Lord

Catechism of the Catholic Church 141
Our Lady of Perpetual Help
Ord, NE

Episode 5 Study Questions

REVIEW of EPISODE 4 - EUCHARIST I

Some non-Catholics will claim:

A - The Catholic Church invented this crazy idea that Jesus' Body and Blood are really present in the Eucharist. It's really nuts to think that a priest can pray over a wafer and turn it miraculously into Jesus Christ.

1. If the Catholic claim that Jesus is truly present in the Eucharist is true, who is the only person that could be responsible for the miracle of it?

2. Explain why the nearly 2,000-year duration of the claim actually lends credibility to it.

3. For approximately how many years after Christ was on Earth was there a universal acceptance that the consecrated host and wine were the true Body and Blood of Christ?

4. According to Dr. Ray, 75 years after Luther died, how many different interpretations of Christ's words "this is my Body" existed? (Matthew 26:26, Mark 14:21-23, Luke 22:18-20)

5. How early in the writings of the early Church Fathers, and in what context, can you find the concept of transubstantiation? (Research: Justin Martyr's *First Apology*, Section 66:5. The answer to this question is implied but not given in Dr. Ray and Fr. Kevin's dialogue.)

6. According to Fr. Fete, to reject the true presence of Christ in the Eucharist in the early Church, was to reject what else? (Luke 10:16)

7. When someone claims that there were early Church Fathers who claimed that communion was simply symbolic or just a memorial meal, what two-word defense is effective?

8. Did Luther reject or defend the real presence of Christ in the Eucharist?

NEW MATERIAL - EPISODE 5 - EUCHARIST II

B - The concept of the true presence of Christ in the Eucharist is not in the Bible.

9. While non-Catholic Christians will reject evidence from explicit Catholic sources, what kind of evidence do they say they accept?

10. With respect to the consecration of the Eucharist, what is the significance of Melchizedek? (Genesis 14:18, Psalm 110:4, Hebrews 7)

11. What was the function of the Old Testament priest?

12. How did Christ's actions and words at the Last Supper parallel the Old Testament priestly sacrifice for people's sins?

13. Although Christ lifts up the bread at the Last Supper what does He say the bread is? (Matthew 26:26, Mark 14:22-23, Luke 22:19-20, 1 Corinthians 11:23-25)

14. When Christ prays over the bread and wine at the Last Supper, what words does he use that can be implied to mean that the bread and wine are only symbolic of his Body and Blood?

15. What did St. Augustine say Jesus held in his hands at the Last Supper?

16. At the Last Supper to what everlasting Old Testament concept did Jesus relate the cup of wine? (Matthew 26:28, Mark 14:24)

17. What Old Testament object of sacrifice did the Blood of Christ represent? (2 Chronicles 29:22, Revelation 7:14, Revelation 12:11)

18. Jesus' words and actions at the Last Supper revisited the Jewish Passover meal. What were those that celebrated the Passover meal required to eat — completely?

19. Explain the significance of the following Scripture in terms of the real presence of Christ in the Eucharist and the Jewish community?

    My name will be great among the gentiles, from the rising to the setting of the sun. In every place, incense and pure offerings will be brought to my name. (Malachi 1:11, paraphrase)

20. According to Dr. Ray, on a daily basis how many Catholic Masses are offered from the rising to the setting of the sun, in every place, around the world?

21. In John 6:52-66, how many times does Jesus say or allude to His Body or Blood as being <u>true food</u>?

22. In John 6:52-66, how many times does Jesus say or allude to His Body or Blood as being <u>symbolic</u>?

23. Fr. Kevin makes the point that John 6:66 is the only place in the Gospels where a group of believers walked away from Jesus and did not follow Him again. What was Jesus teaching that was too hard for them to believe?

24. In terms of what Matthew, Mark, and Luke wrote about the bread and wine being the Body and Blood of Christ (Matthew 26:26, Mark 14:22-23, Luke 22:19-20) what is significant about <u>when</u> John wrote his Gospel and <u>why</u>?

25. Non-Catholics might quote John 6:63 as "evidence" that Christ was speaking symbolically and not literally about the bread and wine being his true Body and Blood. Why is this not likely a good interpretation, and how does this verse reinforce Catholic understanding of the Eucharist's reality?

    It is the spirit that gives life, while the flesh is of no avail. The words I have spoken to you are spirit and life. (John 6:63)

26. In the Eucharistic consecration what does the *"EPIKLESIS"* prayer do, and why is it significant in relation to John 6:63?

27. In Luke 22:19 Christ says during the Last Supper, "Do this in remembrance of me." Non-Catholics believe that the word "remembrance" here means to remember *symbolically*. But what does "remembrance", or *"ANAMNESIS"* in Greek, really mean? Why does this mean the opposite of "symbolic?" (1 Corinthians 11:23-24, 25)

28. Some non-Catholics interpret 1 Corinthians 11:27-30—which includes Paul's admonition about not discerning the *Body* of Christ—as referencing the *body* of *believers* and not the real flesh of Christ. Why does Fr. Kevin say this makes no sense? (1 Corinthians 11:27-30)

29. In Luke 24 Jesus appears to Cleopas and another disciple on the road to Emmaus. During their walk Jesus explains the Old Testament prophecies about the Messiah. But the disciples do not recognize Jesus until when? What does Jesus do that suddenly opens their eyes with understanding? (Luke 24:13-35) How does this event parallel the Mass?

30. Explain how John 1:1, 14, 18 and Luke 24:30-31 can be related and apply to the true presence of Christ in the Eucharist.

Baptize In The Name Of...

St. Patrick's Cathedral
Thunder Bay, Ontario

6. Baptism

DRG: Today, Father, we are going to talk about what the Church really teaches, about Baptism. Big argument — to use a word nobody likes to use, but that is the word regarding Baptism. The argument goes that Baptism is not necessary for salvation. Non-Catholics will say:

> Our salvation comes from faith in Jesus Christ. And therefore, to say, like the Catholic Church does, that in normal circumstances, where it is possible, we are to be baptized in order to fulfill the conditions of our salvation laid down by Christ, is a misunderstanding of Scripture.

Now, before I let you talk, because once I start letting you talk I don't get a word in edgewise, I have with me answers to the question, "How are we saved?" according to Scripture. Can I recite these?

FKF: Run down the list.

DRG: This is how Scripture says we are saved.

By Believing in Christ (John 3:16)
By Repentance (Acts 2:38)
By Baptism (John 3:5)
By the Work of the Holy Spirit (2 Corinthians 3:6)
By Declaring with Our Mouths (Romans 10:9)
By Coming to a Knowledge of Faith (1 Timothy 2:4)
By Works (James 2:24)
By Grace (Acts 15:11)
By His Blood (Romans 5:9)
By His Righteousness (2 Peter 1:1)
By His Cross (Ephesians 2:16)

In other words, Scripture says, as the Catholic Church says, we are saved by the <u>whole package</u>, not just simply saying:

> I believe in Jesus Christ, therefore, I don't need to be baptized.

So, given that lengthy introduction, it's your turn. What does the Church teach about Baptism?

FKF: Baptism is one of the Seven Sacraments we as Catholics would teach, and as a Sacrament, it has both the symbolic nature and an *efficacious* nature.

DRG: Big word.

FKF: Big word. Huge word. *Efficacious* just means something, like Baptism, <u>has real effects</u>.

> **EFFICACIOUS**
> The action referred to has "real" effect.

DRG: Not a symbol.

FKF: Not <u>just</u> a symbol. Therein lies the difference. Would somebody—again we go back to that image of marriage—would someone say that their wedding was just symbolic? They didn't really mean anything life changing there? There was no real commitment made that day? It was just some rings, and it was just a little candle, and we blew out some other little candles? It was all symbolic?

DRG: I tried that on my wife, and it didn't work. No, she called me on it.

FKF: So that's the nature of any of the Sacraments. But here we're talking specifically about Baptism, about the sense that <u>the gift of faith is a gift from God</u>. That gift of faith comes to us in the celebration of the Sacrament of Baptism. It comes to us as the child is immersed, or as the water is poured over the child or the adult, and the words, "I baptize you in the name of the Father, and of the Son, and of the Holy Spirit," are said.

DRG: Matthew 28, verse 18. We'll get to that.

FKF: It's a great thing for us as Catholics to remember our Baptism.

A lot of people wonder, "Why do we make the sign of the cross? In the name of the Father, and of the Son, and of the Holy Spirit. Amen." That was the command that Christ gave us. How do you welcome people into the Church; how do they begin their life of faith in the Church? They're baptized in the name of the Father, and of the Son, and of the Holy Spirit.

DRG: Just a digression for a second. How old is that prayer, by the way? When do we have first indications through writings that "In the name of the Father, and of the Son, and of the Holy Spirit," began?

FKF: Oh, we had it way back. It's in Scripture — Matthew 28.

DRG: Well, okay, but outside of Scripture. Historically. Second Century.

FKF: Is that right?

DRG: Second Century.

FKF: The sign of the Cross?

DRG: Yes, as a formal prayer. "Mark yourself with the sign of the cross."

In the name of the Father, and of the Son, and of the Holy Spirit, Amen.

So now, getting back to Baptism, for the Catholic then, Baptism forgives sins, and it brings us to new life in Christ, makes us a member of His Church.

FKF: True.

DRG: We enter into our Lord's body, the Church.

In the non-Catholic world the view of Baptism is varied. Some say that you **must** baptize infants. Some say Baptism does forgive sins. Some say it's not necessary for salvation. Some say you **don't** baptize infants. Some say that it's just a symbol. The evangelical fundamentalist groups tend to view it more as a public sign that you have accepted Jesus Christ, so you are now making this commitment public. The theological understanding of Baptism, on the basis of Scripture alone, is wide open.

St. Raphael's
Crystal, MN

FKF: In fact, some baptize just in the name of Jesus, while we as Catholics would say it has to be in the name of the Father and the Son and the Holy Spirit.

DRG: Because Christ said so.

FKF: Right. Jesus Himself puts this down so that it's not just a matter of a personal relationship with Jesus Christ, <u>there's a relationship being established with Father, Son, and Holy Spirit in the celebration of this Baptism</u>.

DRG: Friends who are non-Catholic, ask,

> Why do you Catholics say
> that it forgives sins? Why
> do you baptize babies?

...and we'll get to that in a little bit. But I have to cite Scripture verses for them. They will not accept anything on the authority of this 2000-year old Church that our Lord established as to why we believe as we do. They'll say,

> If indeed Baptism is part and
> parcel of a Christian's accepting
> of salvation, where in the Bible
> does it say that Baptism is
> necessary and that it saves you?

FKF: Sure, and that's an area where I know you've spent a lot of time researching. I'm just going to kick it right back over to you, Ray. I know you're ready for this one.

DRG: What I'll do... Let me recite these verses to you, and you comment. In John 3:5, probably one of the strongest verses for the linking of Baptism with salvation, Jesus says to Nicodemus — and by the way, do you know what the name "Nicodemus," means literally? I know you don't, but I looked it up: People Crusher!

FKF: People Crusher?

St. Edward's
Bloomington, MN

DRG: Nicodemus was a Pharisee, crushing the people. Jesus says to him:

> *Amen, amen, I say to you, no one can enter the kingdom of God*
> *without being born of water and Spirit. (John 3:5)*

Now, it says "water" there. When I show that verse to non-Catholic friends, they say,

> Well that doesn't mean "water." It means amniotic
> fluid, or It means the Word of God.

I look at it, and I say to them: "It says water. There's nothing anywhere in the preceding verses or the verses after it that would say, "You know, it does mean the 'Word of God'!"

Do you remember the context, Father, when Jesus was talking to Nicodemus? Nicodemus came at night, but the whole context of the preceding chapters and the chapter right after that was a context of...

FKF: Nicodemus was called to the faith...

DRG: Yes. Nicodemus was called to the faith in the context of Baptism. In other words, Jesus, immediately after talking to Nicodemus, went out and baptized. Well, He didn't baptize, but His Apostles did. Right? The whole context is Baptism. So when He says water, He means water.

FKF: So your sense is that because they go do this immediately they took it as water. They wouldn't be taking it as amniotic fluid.

DRG: Exactly! So, I ask people just to look at that verse in the context and take it at face value. I always used to hear this when I was in the non-Catholic world, "What does Scripture say?" It says water. It says water and Spirit.

FKF: Gotcha!

DRG: Comment for me, Father, about Jesus' Baptism. If Baptism washes away sin, and Jesus is sinless, why did He have to be baptized?

FKF: In the context of Jesus' own Baptism, what you're seeing again is this relationship between the symbolic and *efficacious*, this sense of a real effect. The coming and the outpouring of the Holy Spirit, that's not just symbolic. People see this symbol, this dove, but they would not say,

> Well, there was a symbol of a dove there, but the real Holy
> Spirit never came into Christ. There was no sending of the

Spirit, and the voice heard from the sky really wasn't heard.
That was just sound effects somewhere off on a sound stage.

DRG: **Non-Catholics would say,**

Jesus was just making a public commitment of His acceptance
of Himself and the mission God the Father had sent him to do.

FKF: But that's not the nature of Baptism. <u>The nature of Baptism is really an</u>
<u>outpouring of the Spirit</u> and a washing away of our sins.

*St. Anthony's
Fargo, ND*

Now in Christ's case, does Christ have to have His sins
washed away? Certainly not, because He was born
without sin. But remember in His Baptism is this sense
of the water flowing. Now, parallel that to the crucifixion,
and when His side is pierced and the water and blood
flows out. There is this sense that with the flowing of
water, the sinfulness of man is going to be washed away,
through His death and His resurrection.

**DRG: John even talks about that parallel of the two events in
Scripture.**

FKF: Yes, foreshadowed in the Baptism. But that doesn't
mean that what we see and hear there is all symbol and
no substance. There's real substance there.

**DRG: In the passage that you and I were talking about, John
3:5, born again of water and Spirit...here's John 3:22, fifteen
verses later:**

*After this, Jesus and his disciples went into
the region of Judea, where he spent some time
with them baptizing. (John 3:22)*

So it's immediate, the context of the Nicodemus story is immediate to Baptism.

A couple more verses for you. This is Romans 6:

*Or are you unaware that we who were baptized into Christ Jesus were
baptized into his death? We were indeed buried with him through
Baptism into death, so that, just as Christ was raised from the dead by
the glory of the Father, we too might live in newness of life. (Romans
6:3-4)*

Does that support the parallel that the Church teaches?

FKF: Certainly. In fact one of the magnificent ceremonies of the Church is actually the celebration of the funeral rite. The very first thing done is that the casket is brought into the Church and is blessed with the Holy Water taken from the Baptismal font, with the words that say, "You were promised that those who were baptized into the death of Christ would rise with Him into the newness of life." Being baptized into the death of Christ and rising to new life is something that we begin with at the celebration of Baptism, but also we do this looking forward to the resurrection at the moment of death.

DRG: **It's amazing how those Catholic [Sacraments] are all so Scripturally soaked.**

FKF: Very much so. Sadly often overlooked.

DRG: **This is a very strong verse for Baptism. It is one of the verses I usually cite to friends who want proof, Scriptural texts, that say you must be Baptized in a normal course of events. This is Mark 16:15-16. Jesus says to the disciples:**

> *Go into the whole world and proclaim the gospel to every creature. Whoever believes and is baptized will be saved; whoever does not believe will be condemned. (Mark 16:15-16)*

It speaks for itself.

St. John Episcopal Minneapolis, MN

FKF: It's not an "OR." It's not, "He who believes <u>OR</u> is baptized." And there is a necessity here to understand that we as Catholics believe that one must <u>believe</u>. Being baptized in and of itself is the gift presented from God. The person does reach a point where they have a personal responsibility to accept the gift.

So that does need to be clarified. We don't view Baptism as some magical thing, where you go, "woooo"…

DRG: **…sprinkle a baby, and the kid is automatically a Christian now, and he can live the next seventy-two years and can do whatever he wants. I hear that all the time.**

FKF: That's <u>not</u> the teaching of the Church. The teaching of the Church <u>is</u> we give this gift to this child who is entrusted into the care of the family. But when this gift is given, there comes a point where every person has a responsibility to the best of their ability to accept the gift and to live the faith.

DRG: **So the idea that many people think about the Church:**

> You Catholics just think that all because when you were two months old you got water poured on you that you're now Christians. And at age 11, 15, 35, 62, you can do whatever you want, and you're still a Christian.

The Church does not teach that, correct?

FKF: The Church does NOT teach that. You have a responsibility to follow the call of the Gospel, to live the life of faith and to profess that faith in the way you live.

DRG: **Interestingly enough Father, there are other denominations among mainline Protestantism who also baptize infants. So theologically, not all non-Catholics look at the Catholic Church and say, "We totally disagree with you." It depends upon the view you have as a non-Catholic.**

FKF: Sure.

DRG: **A couple more verses here. I've got a whole bunch but I don't have time to go through all of them. This is Acts 22:**

> A certain Ananias, a devout observer of the law, and highly spoken of by all the Jews who lived there, came to me and stood there and said, "Saul, my brother, regain your sight." And at that very moment I regained my sight and saw him... "Now, why delay? Get up and have yourself baptized and your sins washed away, calling upon his name." (Acts 22:12-13, 16)

THE GREAT SCHISM

The formal split between Roman Catholicism and Eastern Orthodoxy in 1054.

Again, it's real clear.

FKF: Yes, it's clear. But if someone wants to take that passage and interpret it symbolically, they're going to do that, and that's where we run into problems. We talked about that in our show on Scripture. Who's doing the interpreting and how? One of the things that we have to our credit—Catholics and the Orthodox Tradition—is the historical understanding of Baptism, as held by the two earliest traditions of Christianity. It's amazing that both of them adhere to the exact same position on Baptism, and the celebration of Baptism, on the nature of Baptism, and on infant Baptism.

DRG: So, in other words, this idea that the Roman Catholic Church went KAFLOOEY! in the Third, Fourth, and Fifth Century and just incorporated all of these pagan practices and became non-Gospel-like, well, that didn't happen to the Eastern Churches because they weren't under the direct influence of Rome and its political situation. And they still believe the same things.

*Parkway United Church
Minneapolis, MN*

FKF: Some would say, well, at that time they were the exact same Church. They were the same community. They hadn't had the Great Schism yet, so they'd say the Orthodox were corrupted by the Western people, and then when they got away from Rome, they just didn't straighten themselves out. But then, after you start to get cycles and epicycles, it starts to get real complex about why the early Church community did what they did. The reality is <u>the early Church community did what they did because they did it from the very beginning</u>.

DRG: I have quotes on that, too...

FKF: Scripturally, we have evidence of that from the early Church Fathers.

DRG: In other words, the accusation against the Catholic Church is:

> You're not practicing Baptism as the Apostles did and as the early Church did. This is something you guys have developed over time.

FKF: Like we've come up with our own system. But, Scripture bears out support for what we as Catholics have done in the unfolding of our tradition.

DRG: I don't want to keep hammering this, but let me read you a few more examples from scripture. This is 1 Peter 3:18-22.

> *For Christ also suffered for sins once, the righteous for the sake of the unrighteous, that he might lead you to God. Put to death in the flesh, he was brought to life in the spirit. In it he also went to preach to the spirits in prison, who had once been disobedient while God patiently waited in the days of Noah during the building of the ark, in which a few persons, eight in all, were saved through water. This*

prefigured baptism, <u>which saves you now</u>. It is not a removal of dirt from the body but an appeal to God for a clear conscience, through the resurrection of Jesus Christ. (1 Peter 3:18-21)

DRG: **Comment.**

FKF: Well, again you have strong statements here that this sacrament is a great <u>gift</u> from God. That it is a <u>necessary</u> celebration, and it is a celebration that bestows God's <u>grace</u> in it. The Scriptures make it very clear. That's the key and the heart of what we're talking about here.

DRG: **This is one of my favorites, and of course we talked a little bit about Matthew 28:18 where Jesus says, "Go make disciples of all nations, baptizing them." So if nothing else, it was <u>a command of Christ</u>.**

FKF: Right.

DRG: **And that's what I don't understand. There are those non-denominational churches who don't baptize. They will simply say, "we don't want any part of it," and I often wonder how can they ignore a direct command of Christ?**

But I'll read you this last one and we'll move into a topic area that is really misunderstood.

*St. Boniface Church
Minneapolis, MN*

FKF: Okay.

DRG: **This is Acts 2:37-41. It's after Pentecost, Peter is out preaching and he's saying, "You killed the Messiah!"**

Now when they heard this, they were cut to the heart, and they asked Peter and the other apostles, "What are we to do, my brothers?" Peter (said) to them, "Repent and <u>be baptized</u>, every one of you, in the name of Jesus Christ for the forgiveness of your sins; and you will *receive the gift of the holy Spirit. For the promise is made to you and to your children and to all those far off, whomever the Lord our God will call." (Acts 2:37-39)*

Now wait a minute, Father. What's Peter saying here? Is he saying that if you repent and accept our Lord Jesus and become baptized, that your children, when they are old like you, can repent and be baptized, or is he saying this is a promise for you and your children <u>now</u>? What's he saying?

FKF: There's a clear indication that people of faith in the early Church would have been so profoundly moved by the grace of God that they would want for their children the same life in Christ they themselves have found. And we as a people of God would never look at God and say:

> Well, no, God's going to limit this. God is just taking it to the older, rational person who has the cognitive ability to understand God's wisdom and fully comprehend it, but to others it doesn't go.

Christ Himself talks about what God has hidden from the learned has been revealed to the merest of children.

DRG: **Let the children come unto me, and they were bringing infants to Him, "for of such is the kingdom of heaven."**

FKF: His own Apostles, His own followers were saying, "No, no, not the kids, not the kids, don't get them over here."

DRG: **Now I can understand that. I've got ten kids. "Now leave Jesus alone, you guys. Just stay back here. Don't sneeze on Him, and if you do sneeze, cover your mouth (for God's sake) and say, "Excuse me.' This is God, say, "Excuse me.'"**

FKF: (chuckling) That's right. But you can't say, "God bless you" because…

DRG: **(chuckling) That's true, what do you say to Jesus?**

FKF: (chuckling) Blow the whole scheme, "Bless yourself!" It'd be a whole different gig.

But, that's the reality, that Christ loved the kids. Christ welcomed the kid. And there are no parents experiencing God's love that are not going to want their children to share in that same love. I mean that's the very nature of being parents.

DRG: **All right. Given that logic. In the Old Testament, what was circumcision?**

FKF: That was the formation of the Covenant with the child on the eighth day. That the child had to be brought in as an infant and the child then, through the circumcision, enters into this relationship with God and with the Jewish community.

DRG: So an eight-day-old child was eligible...

FKF: Eight days old. Yes.

DRG: ...to enter into the community of God, the family of God.

FKF: Right. And there are parallels in Scripture between circumcision and Baptism.

DRG: Paul says that.

FKF: Paul picks up on the sense of that parallel.

DRG: Paul basically says, "We are circumcised with a circumcision made without hands."

> *In him you were also circumcised with a circumcision not administered by hand, (but) by stripping off the carnal body, with the circumcision of Christ. You were buried with him <u>in baptism</u>, in which you were also raised with him through faith in the power of God, who raised him from the dead. (Colossians 2:11-12)*

Here he shows that Baptism corresponds to circumcision, where infant boys were circumcisecd on the eighth day. And is the New Covenant broader than the Old Covenant?

FKF: What do you mean by broader? In what sense, Ray?

*Sacred Heart Church
Seattle, WA*

DRG: Is it open to more people?

FKF: Oh, certainly!

DRG: The New Covenant is offered to the whole world.

FKF: It's open to all.

DRG: **So, for the early Jewish Christians to understand that this New Covenant, given through Christ, was only open to those who are the age of reason and older, would almost be a big step backwards from the Old Covenant.**

FKF: It'd be huge. It'd be a huge step backwards.

DRG: **So they couldn't have <u>fathomed</u> that:**

> *Oh, all of a sudden now what you're saying with this "new covenant" is that we <u>can't have our children</u> be a part of it.*

FKF: I agree. The big problem you get into here, Ray, is this: The very people that say that "faith is a gift from God, we can't earn it," are the very same people who say,

> *Well, you can't baptize children. They don't understand what's going on; they haven't made a personal commitment to Jesus Christ. They haven't professed Jesus as their Lord with their lips.*

All of that depends on <u>my</u> ability, <u>my</u> actions—the way I think, the way I speak, the way I talk; that's what gives me the ability to be baptized now. All of a sudden you're getting pretty close to saying it's my abilities that "earn" my ability to be baptized. *If faith is a real gift, who are we as people to say God has limitations on who He can bestow that gift to?*

> **J.N.D. KELLY**
> John Normal Davidson Kelly (1909-1997) was an Oxford professor and principal, an Anglican, a fellow of the British Academy, and presided over an Anglican commission on Roman Catholic relations. He was a respected expert on the early Church Fathers in both Roman and Protestant organizations.

DRG: **This is an early Church historian, a Protestant early Church historian, a man named J.N.D. Kelly. He's kind of viewed as the grandfather of historians. He said this:**

> From the beginning, Baptism was the universally accepted rite of admission into the Church. As regards its significance, it was always held to convey the remission of sins, the Spirit of God Himself dwelling in the believer. Prior to Baptism, our heart was the abode of demons. (J.N.D. Kelly, Protestant Scholar, *Early Christian Doctrines*, 193–4)

So, he admits that in the early Church, flat out, no question about it: Baptism was the way to be birthed into the Church, and its significance to the recipient was the removal of sin. Let me read a few more quotes. This is Origen. In 248 A.D., he said:

> In the Church, Baptism is given for the remission of sins, and according to the usage of the Church, Baptism is given even to infants. If there [were] nothing in infants that required the remission of sins, the grace of Baptism would be superfluous. (Origen 248 A.D., *Homilies on Leviticus* 8:3)

DRG: I got others...

FKF: Well, you find it in Acts of the Apostles. You find it in Paul's writing to Corinthians…

DRG: ...and Saint Iranaeus. He was probably the greatest theologian of the Second Century He was a disciple of Polycarp, who was a direct disciple of John. He says:

> For Jesus came to save all through Himself. All I say who through Him are born again to God; infants and children and boys and youths and old men. (Iranaeus *Against Heresies* 2:22:4)

R.C. Sproul, a well-known, still living, Protestant theologian says:

> The first direct mention of infant Baptism is around the middle of the second century. What is notable about this reference is that it assumes infant Baptism to be the universal practice of the Church. If infant Baptism was not the practice of the first century Church, how and why did this departure from orthodoxy happen so fast and so pervasively? (R.C. Sproul, *Essential Truths of the Christian Faith*, [Wheaton, IL: Tyndale House, 1992], 228)

This is a Protestant-Evangelical theologian. In other words, he's saying, "Hey, nobody argued against this in the early Church!"

FKF: Right. It was there already.

DRG: It was there. Nobody came and said, "Whoa, whoa, whoa! What are you doing baptizing infants? The Apostles never told us to baptize infants." St. Augustine says the same thing. He says that this practice is nothing but Apostolic.

FKF: That's right.

DRG: So the Church, regarding Baptism, is saying we are only preaching what Christ gave to the Apostles and then gave to us.

FKF: And, we cannot be the ones who are going to say that we're going to limit the grace of God. We do not have the ability to do that.

DRG: So for us Catholics, Baptism is Scriptural. It's historical. It's logical. It is the teaching of the Church for two thousand years. It has not been changed.

FKF: It is consistent with the Tradition of the Church <u>and</u> the Scriptural Tradition.

DRG: (to audience) Thank you for joining us. Again, I'm Ray Guarendi, psychologist, lay member of the Catholic Church, with Father Kevin Fete, pastor of Little Flower Parish in Canton, Ohio. We are attempting to uncover, dispel, and answer common misunderstandings and misperceptions about the Church. God bless, God keep you, God walk with you. Stay faithful. Bye for now.

Sacred Heart Church
Indianapolis, IN

Episode 6 Study Questions

Some non-Catholics will claim:

A - Baptism is not necessary for salvation. Catholics misunderstand Scripture. We are saved entirely by faith in Jesus Christ.

1. List the 11 different ways by which the Bible says we are saved, as described in the following Bible passages:

John 3:16	Romans 10:9	Romans 5:9
Acts 2:38	1 Timothy 2:4	2 Peter 1:1
John 3:52	James 2:24	Ephesians 2:16-18
Corinthians 3:6	Acts 15:11	

2. Explain how Baptism and Marriage are similar in terms of the ceremonies being symbolic and/or having a real effect.

3. What words does Jesus use to describe how we are to be baptized? (Matthew 28:19)

4. List four ways non-Catholic Christians might say we can be baptized.

5. Write out the following Bible verses that link Baptism, salvation and sin?

John 3:5	Romans 6:3-4	Acts 22:12-13, 16	1 Peter 3:18-22
John 3:22	Mark 16:15-16	Acts 2:37-39	

6. Many non-Catholic Christians interpret the word "water" in John 3:5 to refer to the water associated with physical birth. But, how does John 3:22 suggest that the water in John 3:5 refers to Baptism?

7. When a casket is brought into a Catholic Church for a funeral, it is sprinkled with Holy Water. What is said at this moment, and what is its significance?

8. What Evangelical Protestant theologian wrote that "Baptism was the universally accepted rite of admission" into the Early Church?

B - There is no Scripture passage that says infants should be baptized.

9. How does Acts 2:37-39 reinforce Catholic teaching that infants should be baptized?

10. How does Matthew 19:13-15: (a) remind us of non-Catholic Christians who do not want children to be baptized, and (b) reinforce the Catholic Church's teaching that Christ wanted children baptized?

11. Explain how the circumcision of Jewish male infants on the 8th day (as explained in the Old Testament) parallels and gives support to the New Testament Church's instruction that infants should be baptized?

12. What does St. Paul say that connects circumcision to Baptism? (Colossians 2:11)

13. Explain the logical inconsistency of people who say that "faith is a gift from God, we can't earn it" and then claim that children cannot be baptized because they have not made a personal commitment to Jesus Christ.

14. Quote the Early Church Father Origen about infant Baptism. When did he write this? (Research)

15. The Early Church Father Irenaeus wrote: "Jesus came to save all...infants and children and boys and youths and old men." How was Irenaeus connected to the Apostle John?

C - Catholics believe that because they had water poured on them when they were two-weeks old that later in life they can do whatever they please and still be a Christian.

16. In Catholic Baptism, what role does faith play in a person's salvation? (Mark 16:15-16).

17. What role does obedience to Christ play in our salvation, after Baptism?

D - Catholics are alone in believing that Baptism is necessary for salvation. No other Christian Church believes that.

18. What other Christian Church with roots to the first century of the Church believe exactly the same as Catholics about Baptism, and how does this prove that the Catholic doctrine of Baptism is the same as what the Apostles taught?

Christ Came To Fulfill The Law

Blue Cloud Abbey
Marvin, SD

7. Morality

DRG: Welcome to What Catholics Really Believe. I'm Ray Guarendi, a psychologist and lay member of the Catholic Church. With me is Father Kevin Fete, pastor of Little Flower Parish in Canton, Ohio.

       Today, Fr. Kevin, in our twenty-eight minutes together, we are going to try to capture a little of the essence of the Church's teachings on morality. Big subject.

FKF: Huge subject.

DRG: So we've got to narrow it down. I'm counting on ya.

FKF: All right.

DRG: First complaint. When I was in the non-Catholic world, and I'm sure you hear this from ex-Catholics all the time, people complained about their former years as a Catholic by saying:

> I was in Church. I was just taught that you had to be good and work your way to heaven. If you did good things, you were going to heaven.

FKF: I think the response to that is simple. There is an imperative in the Gospels that if you are going to <u>say</u> you are a person of faith, you must <u>do</u> the Lord's work. That's the bottom line. Now it's <u>not</u> that you earn your way into heaven, but you are compelled by your faith to do Christ's works. Scripture tells us repeatedly, as you're well aware of, that if you have the proclamation of faith, but you don't do any of the work that the Lord calls you to, then you have an *empty faith*, <u>a faith that doesn't contain life</u>.

DRG: So if somebody says..,

The Catholic Church teaches that you have to be good and work your way to heaven and they don't talk about faith in Jesus Christ,

...are you telling me that that is a big misconception?

The Prodigal Son
Guardian Angels Cathedral
Las Vegas, NV

FKF: Yes, it is a misconception in the sense that the Catholic Church has <u>never</u> held the position that works, in and of themselves, are all that one needs. There are a lot of great humanists who may do wonderful things for people, but they don't have faith, and therein they lose the possibility of salvation. So there is a necessity for faith, and that <u>faith is a gift from God</u>, but <u>we must respond to God's call to do His works</u>.

DRG: So the Catholic Church says faith in Jesus Christ, good works and obedience and love are tied together—inseparable.

FKF: Absolutely inseparable. It would be like taking your wedding vows and then not ever taking care of your spouse. You can't do that.

DRG: Like, if I were to say to my wife, "Honey, I tell you I love you. You mean the whole world to me, but I gotta go play ball. I don't want to spend any time with you."

FKF: (chuckling) That's right, "It's off to the bowling alley. See you later, Babe."

DRG: (chuckling) But, "just know I love ya. I'm thinking of ya..."

FKF: (chuckling) "...and that should be enough for you."

And sadly, people do that with God.

DRG: Well, just to prove that this is not Father Kevin Fete's read on what the Catholic Church teaches, I have with me this quote from the Catechism.

With regard to God, there is no strict right to any merit on the part of man…The merit of good works is to be attributed in the first place to the grace of God…Man's merit, moreover itself, is due to God. (Catholic Catechism, 2007-2008)

I remember an evangelical pastor telling me once, when I said, "Uh, excuse me sir, the Church doesn't teach you're saved by your good works." And he said, "Yes, it does. I

said, "No it doesn't." He said, "Well, that's what you're saying, Ray, but the Church teaches you are saved by good works." I said, "No. You are saved by faith **and** works, **both** of which are possible <u>through the grace of God.</u>"

Here's another question for you. One of the things I hear all the time:

> You Catholics, you divide up sins. You have big sins. You have little sins. But sin is sin. There's no such thing as degrees of sin.

FKF: Before you even get to that step, one of the amazing things is that some people won't even acknowledge the existence of sin at all, once they say:

> I've been saved.

I always find it interesting how we use terminology and how people talk about sin. They don't want to use that word "sin" so they'll say:

> Well, I've been backsliding.

They'll even get to the point where they believe that they can't turn away from God, so they'll say:

> I didn't turn away from God.

...even through they just killed somebody.

DRG: That's pretty bad. That's over the cliff backsliding.

FKF: That's a big backslide. But when you get past that and deal with the possibility <u>to</u> sin after someone in faith has accepted Jesus Christ as their Lord and Savior, the <u>reality</u> is there are <u>different levels</u> of sin.

*St. Peter's Church
Richfield, MN*

DRG: Do <u>you</u> say that, or <u>does the Bible say that?</u>

FKF: There are definite statements in the Holy Scriptures. One of them that you'd be familiar with is Jesus before Pontius Pilate. What is Pilate talking about, and what is Jesus' response to him?

DRG: You want to paraphrase it, and then I'll go to it.

FKF: Well, the basic thing is that Jesus, when talking to Pilate about His power and where His power comes from, lets Pilate know that it was the one who was handing Him over, namely Judas, who had committed, "the greater sin."

DRG: You didn't paraphrase it. You almost actually quoted it.

FKF: Semi-close to it.

DRG: Very close. You want me to read it here? This is John 19:10-11:

> So Pilate said to him, "Do you not speak to me? Do you not know that I have power to release you and I have power to crucify you?" Jesus answered (him), "You would have no power over me if it had not been given to you from above. For this reason the one who handed me over to you has the greater sin." (John 19:10-11)

Our Lord acknowledged that <u>degree</u> of sin as lesser or greater.

St. Peter's Cathedral
Worms, Germany

FKF: Sure, and the gravity of that sin gets reiterated by Christ. I think one of the most powerful lines in sacred Scriptures is when Jesus speaks about Judas:

> The Son of Man indeed goes, as it is written of him, but woe to that man by whom the Son of Man is betrayed. It would be better for that man if he had never been born." (Matthew 26:24)

The whole idea that it would have been better if he'd never been born is a powerful indictment against Judas. But elsewhere in Scripture we read that there are some <u>sins that deprive us of eternal life</u>, and that there are other sins that while leading us to less than a perfect life in faith, still do not deprive us of salvation.

DRG: The Catholic Church sometimes gets attacked for this, and I know this is hugely misunderstood in the non-Catholic world, this idea that there are gravely serious sins that can sever your fellowship with God, and you, in essence, are no longer a practicing Christian.

FKF: That's right.

DRG: And then there are those sins that can hurt your holiness, your soul, your obedience, your walk with our Lord, but they don't sever that relationship. Now that seems to be kind of an artificial sort of demarcation. Would you address this "mortal sin" versus "non-mortal sin" type-of-a-thing?

FKF: We started with the idea that you could <u>take</u> the marriage vows with your spouse and then walk away and not <u>do</u> anything. As you know, a man of your marital relationship with Randi, your wife, sometimes you do things on the negative side...

DRG: **Wait a minute.**

FKF: Or perhaps <u>she</u> might do things...

DRG: **Okay. I think that's a better way to state it.**

FKF: (nodding) Sorry.

DRG: **For me, it was 1981. That was the last time I did something offensive to her, so...**

FKF: So the numerous times that she has perhaps done things...

DRG: **Numerous! This last week.**

FKF: Yes, I'm sure - - where she would be in your eyes not functioning as fully as a spouse should function. But that doesn't mean you divorce her. That doesn't mean you're ready to separate from her and walk out on her. Or vice versa, that she would be leaving the relationship for some of the things that you might have done — back twenty years ago.

St. Gregory's Church
Marysville, MO

DRG: **Exactly.**

FKF: But the <u>reality</u> is there are <u>different levels</u> in all relationships, and marriage is a great example, because Jesus Christ picks that as His description for His relationship with His Church.

DRG: **Bride and groom.**

FKF: He is the groom and the Church is the bride. And so that <u>sense of vow</u>, of commitment, of having to live a certain way in response to that commitment is important. But also understanding that the person in the relationship — mainly the Church, the people of God — is not always going to be perfect in doing everything the way they ought to.

DRG: **Is there Scripture that says there is sin that is serious, that is deadly, that is mortal, and there is sin that is not?**

FKF: Sure. We were talking about that the other day, in the First Letter of John...

DRG: Chapter 5:17. Here's what he says. 1 John 5:17. I'll start with verse 16.

> If anyone sees his brother sinning, if the sin is not deadly, he should
> pray to God and He will give him life. This is only for those whose sin
> is not deadly. There is such a thing as deadly sin about which I do not
> say that you should pray. All wrongdoing is sin, but there is sin that
> is not deadly. (1 John 5:16-17)

Is this something that the Catholic Church has concocted—this idea that, if I happen to maybe yell at my wife, that's a lesser sin — but, if I happen to have an affair, that's a serious sin? Is that a concoction on the Church's part, or, in fact, way back in the First, Second, Third Century, did the Church practice this?

FKF: Well, one of the things you see in the early Church, again First, Second, Third Century, is that there are three things that are considered grievous sins, three things that undoubtedly take one away from the possibility of salvation if the   person doesn't repent from them. And that would have been murder, adultery, and apostasy. Apostasy would be renouncing the truth of Jesus Christ as Lord and Savior, having once possessed it, and then openly renouncing it.

DRG: **So they would <u>not</u> have called me a "backslider? They would have said, "You're out of the Church."**

FKF: You are out. And in the early Church, in fact, it was seen as so serious that one was given

St. Nicolas Church
Blois, France

the opportunity to reconcile with the community and with God, but the opportunity would be offered once. If the sin were done again, the opportunity wouldn't be reissued. The process, too, was very public and very long.

DRG: In other words, I couldn't just say:

> Okay, Dear God, I'm sorry that I had an affair on my wife. I want to be a Christian. Let me back in the Church again.

FKF: Oh, no! Because again you're in this commitment with Christ, but you're also a member of the Church. You're a part of the Body of Christ. And so, if you do something that offends Christ, such as murder, adultery, apostasy - - those three major sins in the early Church - - you're also hurting the reputation of the Church. You're damaging the Body of the Christ and its efficiency in portraying the message of Christ to the world.

DRG: Our Lord says, "He who causes scandal..."

FKF: "...it would be better to have a millstone fastened around your neck and be chucked into the sea." (Matthew 18:6, paraphrased)

DRG: (chuckling) That's pretty, uh...

FKF: "Chucked" is not in the...

DRG: "Chucked" – that is the revised Kevin Fete version.

FKF: (chuckling) That is a loose translation.

DRG: (laughing) Chucked. From the early Greek "chuck-oia."

FKF: So your offense, if it's <u>against God</u>, is <u>against the Body of Christ</u> as well as <u>against the Church</u>. Therefore, we need to reconcile, not only with God, but also with the Church community. Jesus Himself tells us in Scriptures:

> *Before you come and present your gifts at the altar, go first and reconcile with other people that you have differences with. (Matthrew 5:23, paraphrase)*

<u>We have this necessity</u> to realize that our relationship with God is <u>intrinsically related to</u> our relationship with those who are created in God's image.

DRG: You're scaring me. Because, let's say that according to our Lord, according to Scripture, according to the two-thousand year history of His Church, there is such a thing as serious sin. I don't want to walk around nervous that I committed some big, serious sin, and I don't even know about it, and I'm out of the fellowship with Christ, and I may have forfeited my salvation. I mean, what kind of security and joy in the Gospel is THAT?

FKF: That is the problem in our culture, in a culture that tends to be very self-serving, self-satisfying, and selfish. We have this tendency toward saying,

> I will interpret the Scriptures so it fits MY way, because I want to have this self-assurance that I am going to have my salvation, and I want to make sure that it's guaranteed to me, and I know I got it.

It's the (false) idea that we must have this sense of self-esteem, spiritually.

> Don't say what you're doing is wrong, and don't worry about that. Just make sure everyone thinks they're doing all right and everything's fine all the time.

Well, that's not the Gospel, that's not the Gospel message from Jesus Christ, that's not the Tradition of the Church. We are called by God to look at our lives, and we are called by Christ to look at our lives, even more profoundly than the law requires.

You know, you hear a lot from St. Paul that we're past the law, and that the law doesn't hold us captive anymore...

DRG: That's right, you hear:

> We don't have to be bound by the law anymore.

FKF: Right.

> We don't have to follow these things. It's our faith and faith alone. That is all we need to focus on.

But that's not what Jesus Christ said. You know if you go into Matthew, chapter five, it's Jesus who's talking:

CONFITEOR

The Confiteor: (so named from its first word in Latin) is a general confession of sin recited at the beginning of Mass in the Roman Rite and on some other occasions.

"I confess to almighty God, and to you, my brothers and sisters, that I have sinned through my own fault, in my thoughts and in my words, in what I have done, and in what I have failed to do; and I ask blessed Mary, ever virgin, all the angels and saints, and you, my brothers and sisters, to pray for me to the Lord our God."

Do not think that I have come to abolish the law or the prophets. I have come not to abolish but to fulfill. (Matthew 5:17)

Then Christ makes the rules and regulations even tougher. The commandment was, "Thou shall not kill" but Jesus goes on to say, "I tell you, if you're even <u>angry</u> at people, you've already broken the commandment." It says, "Thou shall not commit adultery." Jesus takes them down more levels.

DRG: He toughened it up.

FKF: That's right. If you <u>even look lustfully</u> at another person, you've broken the commandment. So Christ actually calls us to a higher standard. And as Catholic Christians, one of the things we do at the beginning of the Mass is the *Confiteor*, "I confess to Almighty God, to you my brothers and sisters, that I have sinned through my own fault..."

DRG and FKF: "...in my thoughts, in my words, in what I have done, and what I have failed to do."

DRG: That's a lot of stuff.

FKF: That's correct.

*Sacred Heart Church
Seattle, WA*

DRG: Okay, so a <u>mortal sin</u>, is something that would <u>break fellowship</u>, something that would <u>sever your life blood with our Lord</u>. And I remember when I was -- this is going to be hard for you to believe, Father. I was a neurotic little second-grader, not the well-adjusted package you see before you. (Father chuckles) I was nervous. And, of course, at that time we began to learn about how a mortal sin has to be very serious. You have to <u>know</u> it's serious, be <u>fully aware</u>, and you have to <u>deliberately</u> say, "I don't care!" in order to be a mortal sin.

FKF: You have to <u>choose it</u>...

DRG: Yes. Say, "I'm going to do it anyway, I don't care that it is wrong — going after that woman — I know Christ says no, but I want it." The Church would say at that point, on a matter of flagrant disobedience to a serious commandment of our Lord, "You have chosen to remove yourself from fellowship."

But here is what even some Catholics will say:

You know Father, the Church has changed its morality over the centuries. It doesn't teach the same things. For example: abortion, homosexuality, contraception, divorce. The Church changes in its morality; so therefore how can it be speaking for God if it changes?

Could you comment on that attitude?

FKF: This is one of the times when I really give thanks to God for being Catholic and living in the Catholic Tradition and being called by Christ to my faith in this Tradition. When you look at the major issues, one of the things that is magnificent about being Catholic is we <u>haven't</u> changed. <u>The Church hasn't changed</u>. One of the things that you have mentioned so prevalent in our culture is divorce. If you go into Matthew's Gospel, chapter nineteen, Jesus teaches about divorce and remarriage and says, "If you divorce and re-marry, you commit adultery, or if you marry someone who is already divorced, you commit adultery."

> *I say to you, whoever divorces his wife (unless the marriage is unlawful [not valid]) and marries another commits adultery. (Matthew 19:9)*

Plymouth Congregational Minneapolis, MN

His own followers were baffled by that. They didn't understand it, which is proof that this is a <u>teaching from Christ</u>, because why else would they have included it? They clearly didn't like it.

They said, "Hey, Moses used to let us do this. How come we can't go ahead and do this? Moses said if you wanted to divorce a woman, write a decree of divorce and give it to her."

Well, Jesus says, "You know, in the beginning it wasn't that way, and when two get married they're together for life"…

DRG: They're one...

FKF: …and He makes it very clear that what God has joined—not what the civil law has joined, what God has joined — two people who are truly sincere in their faith that make this commitment and understand the presence of God in it. Once they've done that, they cannot be separated by people. People cannot say, "Divorce it! It's over, we're going to cancel this out."

DRG: You're saying that the Catholic Church has not changed in two thousand years on those issues where other Christian denominations tragically have?

FKF: That's exactly correct. Now there are some people who would say, "Well, if you look at the annulment process, Catholics kind of use that as a loophole." And there may be some people who would say, "Well, if you look at the annulment process, Catholics kind of use that as a loophole." And there may be some people who misuse that process. But if you look at the teaching of the Church, the truth of the teaching, it has stayed consistent with the teaching of Jesus Christ. Other denominations change the teaching of Jesus Christ.

In that passage in Matthew, what you have is a little "gloss" that was added later about lewd conduct as a separate case. If you look at the Greek terms in that passage *lewd conduct* is not the same as *adultery*…

DRG: The Greek word for adultery is *moicheia*…

FKF: …as opposed to *porneia* which refers to fornication/lewd conduct, and is…

DRG …a kind-of a broad term…

FKF: Right.

DRG: …a kind of impurity or illicit sort of conduct.

FKF: Bizarre. I mean bizarre behavior, that even today we would look at as "over the top." Like when Paul is writing about in First Corinthians. He has someone in the Corinthian church who's actually married to and sleeping with his dad's wife and this whole sense of an incestuous relationship. That's the kind of thing *porneia* or *lewd conduct* refers to. But yet, what we have in today's world is so many people on their own, interpreting the Scripture for their own benefit and saying,

I don't care about what Jesus taught.
I'll make it fit what I want to live.

HUMANAE VITAE
(Of Human Life)

The relatively short encyclical letter of Paul VI, promulgated July 25, 1968, that reinforced and clarified, in the midst of the Western sexual revolution, that artificial birth control, as it always had been, was contrary to the laws of God and nature and "intrinsically disordered." It was widely rejected by lay Catholics, but has proved to be prophetic, giving credibility to the Church's claim of infallibility in moral teaching.

DRG: One of the things that brought me on my journey back to the Catholic Church was that I found different teaching on morality, in many cases depending upon what non-Catholic church I attended. Some taught that abortion was okay. They said abortion was a matter of a woman's conscience. They didn't used to teach that. If you go back to virtually <u>all</u> major non-Catholic denominations, they taught <u>abortion was a grave, grave evil</u>, but then later changed.

The same with contraception. The same with homosexuality. Its practice was outside of God's law. Many of these denominations have changed how they viewed these issues, and I remember a question I asked "If it was wrong on the basis of Scripture a hundred years ago, why is it okay on the basis of Scripture now?" As far as I'm aware, the Catholic Church is the only one, (along with many Eastern churches) that still adheres to the teaching that <u>these things have always been taught as being wrong</u>, and they <u>always will be taught as being wrong</u>.

St. Michael's
Ashtead, England

FKF: Right.

DRG: You remember 1968?

FKF: Huge! Huge time. The issue of birth control.

DRG: How much pressure was on Pope Paul VI at that time to change the Church's nineteen-hundred year-old teaching on no artificial contraception to prevent births?

FKF: Well, the pressure was certainly a cultural pressure, but one of the things that's interesting with the Pope at that time is, he invited <u>scientists</u> and <u>doctors</u> to give him information regarding whether or not the Church should look at, as some people say, "getting with" the modern times. And the report they gave to him was, "Yes, the Church should go along with this. There's no reason the Church should be against this."

But, after prayerful discernment, he came back and said in *Humanae Vitae, (Of Human Life)*: "God is calling us <u>not</u> to do this." <u>In spite of the advice</u>

I'm getting from doctors, in spite of the advice I'm getting from scientists, somewhere along the line <u>I'm getting a call from the Holy Spirit</u> that says <u>don't</u> permit the use of contraceptives, most particularly the use of the pill.

DRG: And the Church would say that the function of our Lord—as promised in Scripture—is that He will protect His Church <u>from teaching error.</u>

FKF: Correct.

DRG: And of course, if the Church DOESN'T believe that, then we might as well pack this all up and go home. Because then we're just teaching what <u>men</u> teach...

FKF: ...what <u>we</u> want to teach. And there's a great desire, especially in our American culture, to democratize the Church—'whatever the majority wants to do is right.' You hear that argument all the time from people who say:

> Well, the majority of Catholics practice birth control. The majority of Catholics are in favor of divorce. The majority of Catholics...

And yet the Church's teachings are not determined by a democratic process. There's a reason we call Jesus Christ LORD. If <u>He's Lord</u>, He's Lord, and we are His servants. <u>He's not our president</u>, and we didn't elect Him to be serving us. And we as a people of an American culture are still a people of faith and must say, "<u>This is the Word of the Lord.</u>"

> ## THE PILL
> The first contraceptive pill was made available and approved in the United States in 1961. Legal rulings made them available to married couples in all states in 1965, and to unmarried women in 1972. Within a few years medical problems among users began surfacing.

DRG: I submit, I submit.

FKF: And we either submit to the Word of the Lord, or we don't. And don't say:

> <u>I follow the Lord</u>, but I'm <u>not</u> going to do what He calls me to do.

DRG: So, at the time when the Pope said that artificial contraception, for example through the pill, was still intrinsically wrong, as it had always been, <u>the Church/ the Pope did not know, what we now know</u>, which many Catholics and virtually all non-Catholics do not know even now, that the pill is an abortifacient. In other words ...

FKF: It can work that way…

DRG: It can work to kill an already fertilized, conceived human life.

FKF: Right.

DRG: And the pill can wash that life out…

FKF: Right.

DRG: And that would have put the Church in a position of saying,

> On one hand, we believe life begins at conception, so it's a serious evil to abort at any time. On the other hand, we are permitting you the use of a technology, a pill, a chemical, that could do that.

FKF: Right.

DRG: And at the time the decision was made the Church didn't know that the pill could be abortive.

See, when I looked at that decision, I thought that was a <u>classic example</u> of the <u>Holy Spirit protecting His Church</u>. And if there are other churches out there who teach that contraception is okay, at the very least, they have a problem with <u>moral consistency</u>.

*St. Peter's Church
Soest, Germany*

FKF: Right.

DRG: I'll have to close up with some lines I want to share with you. I talked to a large, non-denominational evangelical ministry and told them what we've just been talking about, and they said to me:

> We are aware that the pill can act to kill a developing fetus. But we just don't think that's something we want to get into at this time.

Basically that's what they said. And I said, "But you say that abortion is wrong from the moment of conception."

> Yes, we do. We're totally pro-life.

I said, "Well, how can you say that and not stand against the use of the pill?"

And they just didn't want to mess with it, Father. I was stunned because I had great respect for this non-Catholic organization.

FKF: And the sad part is, as you know, there are some pastors, even in our own faith, who don't call people to <u>the awareness of the abortive effect of the pill</u> as profoundly as they should. There's this fear that we're going to lose membership. There are fears from different denominations that the support will drop. But, our support has to come from God, not just from God's people, and what we stand on <u>has</u> to be the <u>Truth</u>.

DRG: **To summarize what you and I have been talking about, the Catholic Church teaches that we are saved by faith <u>and</u> works working together <u>through God's grace</u>. So, I went through and I wanted to write down all of the Scripture verses that had to do with obedience...**

FKF: There are too many…

DRG: **There are too many of them. I stopped. But let me just share with you a few verses in Matthew.**

> *But I say to you, whoever is angry with his brother will be liable to judgment, and whoever says to his brother, 'Raqa,' will be answerable to the Sanhedrin, and whoever says, 'You fool,' will be liable to fiery Gehenna. (Matthew 5:22)*

> *But if you do not forgive others, neither will your Father forgive your transgressions. (Matthew 6:15)*

> *I tell you, on the day of judgment people will render an account for every careless word they speak. (Matthew 12:36)*

I'm skipping tons of verses now, and I'm just picking out a few from Saint Paul.

Sankt Marie Kirke
Helsingor, Denmark

> *I have competed well; I have finished the race; I have kept the faith. (2 Timothy 4:7)*

> *Labor the more that by good works you could make firm your calling and election. (2 Peter 1:10, paraphrased)*

> *Not everyone who says to me, "Lord, Lord," will enter the kingdom of heaven, but only the one who does the will of my Father in heaven. (Matthew 7:21)*

> *What good is it, my brothers, if someone says he has faith but does not have works? Can that faith save him?...So also faith of itself, if it does not have works, is dead....See how a person is justified by <u>works</u> and <u>not</u> by <u>faith alone</u>. (James 2:14, 17, 24)*

And by the way that's the only place in Scripture that "faith alone" is ever used.

FKF: Ray, there's an important thing for us as Catholics to remember. <u>Morality is not</u> just abstaining from evil. <u>Morality is also</u> the obligation to participate in what's good.

DRG: **Father. Thank you, again. Wish we had a lot more time, because we could just go on and on, we could have filled up the whole show with just the lines from Scripture that talk about the necessity of us being obedient.**

FKF: Indeed.

DRG: **(to audience) Again, thank you very much for joining us. I'm Ray Guarendi, with Pastor Kevin Fete from Little Flower Parish in Canton, Ohio.**

When we get together again, we will continue talking about "What Catholics Really Believe," the Biblical, the historical, the logical truth of our faith. God bless you and keep you.

Lead Us Not Into Temptation

St. Joseph's Church
Hopkins MN

Episode 7 Study Questions

Some non-Catholics claim:

A - The Catholic Church teaches that you can get to heaven by just doing good works, and you don't have to have faith in Jesus Christ.

1. What do the Gospels teach us about salvation and the relationship between faith and works?

2. What does the *Catechism of the Catholic Church* teach about our ability to do good works? (CCC 2007-2008)

B - The Catholic Church teaches that there are different degrees of sin. There is no such thing in the Bible. Sin is sin.

3. In John 19:10-11 who is Jesus speaking about and what does he say that suggests some sins are greater than others?

4. Explain how the different levels of respect that spouses have toward one another is comparable to different levels of sins we commit against God.

5. In 1 John 5:16-17, the Apostle John says there is sin that is deadly, and that there is sin that is not deadly. Study this passage. What does John imply that you should do if you see a Christian committing a deadly sin?

6. According to 1 John 5:16-17 what should you do if you see someone committing a <u>non</u>-deadly sin?

7. What names does the Catholic Church give to (a) deadly sins, and to (b) non-deadly sins? (CCC 1854-1855)

8. In the first three centuries what three sins of the church were understood to be so grievous that any one of them would remove salvation from an individual if the person did not repent?

9. In the first three centuries, if you sinned in one of these ways, (a) how did you find forgiveness for the sin, and (b) why was the process so public?

10. When we sin, describe why our sin is against the Church at large, and not just between God and us, nor just between us and an individual? (CCC 1440)

11. To fool ourselves into thinking that everything is okay and to assure ourselves that we are saved, (a) what do we tend to do with the Gospel and the teachings of Christ and the Church? (b) Why is this dangerous? (Matthew 5:17)

12. How would you compare the Old Testament moral law with the moral law that Christ asked of his followers? Give at least one example. (Matthew 5: 21-22, 27-28)

13. At the beginning of every Mass we ask God to forgive us for our sins in what five different ways?

14. What three conditions must exist together for a sin to be mortal or deadly? (CCC 1857-1860)

C - **The Catholic Church, over the centuries, has changed its teachings about what is sin. For instance, it uses the annulment process as a loophole for divorce, which Christ taught could lead to adultery if one of the parties remarries.**

15. How has Catholic teaching about what is a sin changed over the centuries?

16. Under what circumstances or situations does the Catholic Church recently allow divorce? (CCC 2382-2384)

17. Over the last 200 years have some non-Catholic Christian churches changed their teachings on divorce and abortion? If so, in what ways?

18. In terms of determining right vs. wrong, what is the difference between a democracy or a republic and the Catholic Church?

19. In 1968, when Pope Paul VI issued his encyclical letter *OF HUMAN LIFE (Humanae Vitae)*, what did he not know, and what later did scientists discover, which provided significant evidence that the Holy Spirit has protected the Church in its purpose to teach infallible truth?

20. For each of the following Scriptures, describe in your own words what they tell us about the importance and or consequence of moral obedience:

Matthew 5:22	Matthew 12:36	2 Peter 1:10	James 2:14, 17,
Matthew 6:15	2 Timothy 4:7	Matthew 7:21	24 21

21. Moral obedience has two sides. It means we must abstain from _____, and it means we have the obligation to _____.

Whose Sins You Forgive Are Forgiven Them

John 20:23
St. Edward's
Waterloo, IA

8. Confession
The Sacrament of Reconciliation

DRG: Today, Father, is going to be all about one of the really big misunderstandings, because this goes against what humans want, and me being a shrink type, I could understand how people would struggle against this—Confession. Why should I have to come to you, a man, and confess my sins? I go to God. Only God can forgive sins. Scripture is very clear on that. Why should I come to you? Well, maybe not to you personally, but a priest. You're giggling as if ...

FKF: (in jest) I would prefer you not come to me. I don't have that much time. But the rest of the folks are welcome to come to me.

DRG: (in jest) I get real nervous when they have to have two or three priests when I come to confession.

FKF: "Confession" is sometimes called one of three other titles: The <u>Sacrament of Confession</u>, the <u>Sacrament of Penance,</u> or <u>Sacrament of Reconciliation</u>. Each of those titles is actually an element of the celebration of the Sacrament. But the reason this sacrament is so important is because of the nature of Christ — the nature of Jesus.

Jesus is both divine and human. The imperative for the incarnation is that Jesus has to become man. People say to me all the time:

> I can tell God my sins any time I want.

And I say that's true, anybody can. You can always say to God:

> I'm really sorry I did that. I really messed up there.
> I chose the wrong path, I took the wrong way.

But, the other question has to be, how does God tell you you're forgiven?

DRG: In other words, let me make sure that—you know, being a shrink type I want to paraphrase and make sure I got this right.

FKF: Shrink away.

DRG: The Church would <u>not</u> say that to be forgiven you need to <u>automatically</u> go straight to a priest. You can say to our Lord at the moment of conviction, "Dear Lord, forgive me my sins," and if you are repentant with a contrite heart, He will forgive you, even though Confession is a <u>necessary</u> Sacrament, right? In other words: <u>it's not either/or, it's and/both?</u>

FKF: Correct.

DRG: Okay, that's the first point about Confession.

FKF: And, if someone came to the priest, confessed their sins, and just rambled through them and had no sincerity of heart, no sense of being sorry to the Lord for what they've done, then there is <u>no automatic absolution</u> of their sins either.

DRG: The sacrament becomes a mockery then.

FKF: Yes. It's a mockery at that point. It is not the teaching of the Church that just because you went through this prescription and mumbled these words, you're covered. That's not the nature of the celebration of the Sacrament. The celebration is to <u>enter into what Christ began for us</u>. God knew that we need to be able to experience God's love in a very human, very personal way. And that's why Christ is not only divine, as he has been throughout all of being, but also human, so that God personally can forgive us our sins in our personal relationship with Christ Jesus. Christ also, when He leaves, makes the Church <u>His body</u>, and He gives His Apostles this charge of being the person of Christ to those who come seeking forgiveness for their sins. And that's Scriptural. Jesus goes into that sense with Peter,

> *Whoever's sins you forgive on earth, shall be forgiven; whoever's are held bound, shall be held bound. (John 20:23, Matthew 16:19, paraphrase)*

SACRAMENTS

The seven unique visible, physical or outward signs, instituted by Jesus Christ, by which grace is given to the receiver for their sanctification are:

1. **Baptism**
2. **Confession**
3. **Holy Eucharist**
4. **Confirmation**
5. **Holy Orders**
6. **Matrimony**
7. **Anointing of the Sick.**

The Sacraments are "powers that come forth" from the Body of Christ, which is ever-living and life-giving. They are actions of the Holy Spirit at work..."the masterworks of God." (CCC 1116)

DRG: This is a distinct point that really needs to be emphasized: Confession is not something where we turn around and automatically say:

> Oh, by the way, we've just sort of decided that we're going to have some guy come and say, "Ray, I forgive ya."

Confession is something our Lord gave to us. It is not something the Church made up.

FKF: The Church did not make this up. Jesus gave this to the Church.

DRG: So our Lord knew, because of the nature of humans, we need to experience His forgiveness through a person.

The Seven Sacraments
St. Joseph's
Lincoln, NE

FKF: That's the whole reason for the incarnation.

DRG: Do you know what I find interesting, Father? When non-Catholic Christians get married, do they just say:

> I don't need a man to tell me I'm married. Let's go out in the field, honey, let's hold hands and look up to the sky and say, "We declare we're married"?

No, of course not. They work it through a person. Do they just pour water on their <u>own</u> heads and say, "I baptize me" ?

*St. Thomas More's
Kansas City, MO*

FKF: Right. Baptism and marriage are sacraments, too.

DRG: Do they not work it through a person?

FKF: Yes, they do. An important thing to understand is that part of marriage and part of baptism is not just a relationship with Christ. It's also a relationship with a <u>community</u>, most specifically a faith community, a Church community. And we have to remember as we talked about when we had the session on morality, our sins are not just sins against God, they're sins against the body of Christ, the Church.

The priest has a unique role given to him by Christ to be both the representative of Christ for expressing forgiveness, but also to represent the community who has been injured by the sinfulness of persons who have turned against God — and have brought shame and disgrace to the faith community — and who bring a sense of lost trust to the world that looks to the Church for its sense of hope and integrity. When people come to confess, they need to understand that they've done damage to the world. They've done damage to the Church as well as to their personal relationship with God.

DRG: The priest, then, represents our Lord <u>and</u> the faith community?

FKF: Correct.

DRG: In the early Church, they often times publicly confessed. One of the problems, of course, was as the local fellowship got bigger you started to get, how shall we say, less of a homogenous crowd. You had maybe curiosity seekers. So, I wouldn't want to get up in Church and say, "I confess to all of my brothers and sisters that I have had three affairs and that I beat my children." Why don't I just tell the whole village?

FKF: Right.

DRG: So the Church in its wisdom developed a method to work with that reality.

Now, before we move further into some of the more resistant arguments against Confession, we need to establish that the Sacrament of Confession is authoritative. In other words, it isn't something that the Catholic Church concocted. In the ninth century some Pope didn't just say, "You know what I think is a great idea? Let's have people come to priests and say, 'Hey Father, I did these things.' And they'll say, 'That'll be twelve bucks.' And we'll forgive people."

Matthew, chapter 9 verses 2 to 8. Permit me to read it here, Father. I won't read the whole thing but I'll read the end. Do you remember the context where Jesus was healing a paralytic?

FKF: And the question Jesus asked the scribes, who thought Jesus was blaspheming by telling the man his sins were forgiven:

> *What is easier to say, your sins are forgiven or pick up your mat and "take off"? (Matthrew 9:5 paraphrased)*

DRG: And "take off"?

FKF: Yeah. "Take off!" That's like the last show when I said we "chuck it."

DRG: "Take off!" I think that's the literal Greek, isn't it? Just, take off!

FKF: Another one of those loose translations by K. Fete here.

But, the scribes think it's easier to <u>say</u>, "Your sins are forgiven," because you can't tell if Jesus can actually do that.

DRG: What's He going to do about this one?

FKF: They don't think Jesus can really forgive sins, because only God is going to do that. But then, Jesus says, "Well, I'm going to prove it to you." Then, to the paralytic, "Pick up your mat and go." And the guy does.

DRG: By the way, I will tell you, if you could do that in Confession, if you could cure us of our maladies, you'd probably have a lot more people coming to Confession.

FKF: Unfortunately, they'd be looking at me as their new health insurance company.

DRG: All right, Jesus says:

> *Rise, pick up your stretcher and go home. He rose and went home....*

*Holy Family Cathedral
Czestochowa, Poland*

Here, my notes say, "He rose and took off."

When the crowd saw this, they were struck with awe…

…and here's the verse…

…and glorified God who had given such authority to <u>men</u>.
(Matthew 9:6-8)

FKF: <u>Men</u>.

DRG: Yes, God gave authority to forgive sins to <u>men</u>.

FKF: Now the counter argument's going to be

Well, they didn't know He was God. Jesus was God, but they didn't know <u>He was God</u>. They thought he was just a man.

DRG: The crowds didn't know it.

Holy Rosary Church
Kenosha WI

FKF: The <u>crowds</u> didn't know it. But the problem with that interpretation is this passage was written by its author <u>after</u> it <u>is</u> known. It was written after the Resurrection. So this sense of giving the authority to men was given its justification post Resurrection.

DRG: So Matthew knew that, in fact, Jesus was God, but he still gave that authority to a human. Jesus was human <u>and</u> God.

FKF: That's right. When this account's written, he's already well aware of the divinity of Christ.

DRG: Take the argument a step further. Jesus can forgive sins—we understand that, we recognize that. We give Him that. He's God. So what? What's your point? But, did He give that authority to anybody else?

FKF: In a broad way, He gave it to everybody. If you go earlier in Matthew, when you get into chapter 5, again the teaching of the *Our Father*, always a great conclusion. It says, you know,

And forgive us our sins as we forgive those who sin against us.
(Matthew 6:12 paraphrased)

Then Jesus goes on to make it a moral imperative, "I'm telling you if you do not forgive the sins of those who do you wrong, nor then shall the Father forgive you your sins."

If you forgive others their transgressions, your heavenly Father will
forgive you. But if you do not forgive others, neither will your Father
forgive your transgressions. (Matthew 6:14-15)

So in this sense, everybody's called to forgive sins.

Now, what you have in Matthew's Gospel, chapter 5, is this sense that we forgive the sins of people who have done <u>us</u> wrong. What about the sins against God, specifically against God? Well, there are two things: one, sins against all people <u>are</u> sins against God. Jesus Christ says, whatever you do to the least of your brothers and sisters, you do to me.

He will answer them, "Amen, I say to you, what you did not do for
one of these least ones, you did not do for me." (Matthew 25:45)

So if you've sinned against a person, you've sinned against God. If someone's sinned against me, they've sinned against God. And if I forgive them, I'm forgiving a sin not only committed against me, but also a sin committed against God.

Now, what about those who are sinning against God and not necessarily against specific people, and the forgiveness isn't just for this personal offense that's happened. That's where it gets broadened out to <u>certain people</u> who are going to be <u>the figure of Christ</u> to those who have sinned.

> **INCARNATION**
> **The greatest proof of God's desire to work through the physical world to give us grace, was the Incarnation—God taking on the form of man in Jesus Christ.**

And again, it's because God understands the necessity of the Incarnation, the need to have a person there who, in the name of God can say, "Your sins are forgiven. Go and sin no more."

DRG: Well, let's just see if in fact Scripture says He did give that authority to His Apostles. John chapter 20 verse 21. This is right after the Resurrection. Jesus says,

> *Peace be with you. As the Father has sent me, so I send you.*
> *(John 20:21)*

FKF: So I send you.

DRG: Here's my authority. You now have it.

> *And when he had said this, he breathed on them and said to them,*
> *"Receive the Holy Spirit. Whose sins you forgive are forgiven them,*
> *and whose sins you retain are retained." (John 20:22-23)*

Now, what about ...

FKF: The Spirit breathing part?

DRG: Is that just Christ blowing on the Apostles — or what?

FKF: That's huge, and it shows up one other place. Do you know where it is?

DRG: One other place in Scripture? Genesis?

FKF: Genesis, right — when He breathed on the waters, making them the wellspring of all holiness.

> *The Spirit breathed on the waters, making them the wellspring of all holiness. (Genesis 1:2 paraphrased)*

Holy Family Cathedral
Czestochowa, Poland

DRG: And He breathed the Spirit into man, too, in Genesis. So, creation.

FKF: Yes, the creation. The whole creation—which by God's nature—is deemed good. "It is good."

DRG: He breathed the Holy Spirit on the Apostles and said,

> *Whose sins you forgive, they are forgiven them.*

I've heard many outside the Catholic Church say,

That's not what He meant. What He meant was if you
proclaim the Gospel, and people believe, then their sins
will be forgiven. If you proclaim the Gospel, and they
reject the Gospel, then they won't be forgiven.

First of all, that's not what it says. It's real clear what Christ says.

FKF: You've got to go with some wild interpretation to accept that "Gospel"
        meaning.

DRG: There's no Gospel mentioned in there anywhere.

FKF: Nowhere.

**DRG: But secondly, that's not how it was understood at
        all by the early Church, and we'll get into that in a
        moment. But now I've heard this argument:**

> Well, He gave that authority
> only to the Apostles. There's no
> mention anywhere else there that
> anybody else got that authority.

FKF: I love that argument too. You know, when Christ
        tells us that the Church will be kept safe from the
        poison of sin, did He just mean that for the first
        generation, too? I mean, "Well, Jesus wanted the
        Apostles to forgive, but as soon as they were all
        dead, we were all supposed to just walk around
        not knowing anything." That's just ludicrous. We
        have the sending of the Spirit for the celebration
        of Pentecost, and that's not a first-generation-
        Christians-only covered group. As if, once they
        die, the Spirit ain't coming no more. Nothing else
        happens anymore. It's all over.

*St. Gregory's
Newberry, MI*

DRG: In Matthew 28:19-20, Jesus says:

> Go, therefore, and make disciples of all nations, baptizing them in the
> name of the Father, and of the Son, and of the holy Spirit, teaching
> them to observe <u>all</u> that I have commanded you. (Matthew 28:19-20)

That means everything Jesus commanded.

And behold, I am with you <u>always</u>, until the end of the age.
(Matthew 28:20)

All days, even.

FKF: Yes, until the end of the age.

And there was confusion in the early Church. There were some people who thought the "end of time" was going to be in the next week, you know, like next month. So they thought this was going to be just amongst their generation. But as the end of time <u>didn't</u> come, then you have to say, "Well, either Jesus didn't do time management very well or He was wrong."

DRG: **Let me read you just some of the early Church's understanding. And, by the way, when I read these Early Fathers of the Church, certainly their writings are not Scripture. But they reflect what was universally understood by the people who lived shortly after the time of Christ.**

St. Thomas More's
La Crosse, WI

FKF: They give an understanding of what the faithful held in the Christian faith.

DRG: **Here is *The Didache*, ("The Teachings of the Apostles") was written at the end of the first century, sometime even before some of the Apostles may have passed away.**

Confess your sins in church and do not go up to your prayer with an evil conscience. This is the way of life. On our Lord's Day gather together, breaking bread, giving thanks <u>after confessing your transgressions</u>. (*Didache*)

It doesn't say anything there about "to a priest." But I have some more. This is Ignatius of Antioch, disciple of John the Apostle for thirty to forty years.

> For as many as are of God and of Jesus Christ <u>and are also with the bishop</u>...

Oh, oh! There's that <u>authority thing</u>.

> ...and as many as shall in the exercise of penance return to the unity of the Church... (St. Ignatius of Antioch, *To the Philadelphians*, 3)

In other words, you could sin and lose that unity, that fellowship with the Church.

FKF: That's correct.

DRG: **Clement of Rome, by the way, in 96 A.D.—Linus, Cletus, Clement—the third successor to Peter said:**

> Be subject in obedience <u>to the priests</u> and receive discipline unto penance bending the knees of your heart. (Clement of Rome, 96 A.D., *Epistle to the Corinthians*, 57)

> The Church has the power of forgiving sins. This I acknowledge and accept. (Tertullian, 203 A.D., *On Modesty*, 21.7)

And I want to read Augustine, because Augustine makes it real clear.

> Was it then said to no purpose, "What you should loose on earth shall be loosed in heaven." Was it for nothing that the keys were given to the Church? Let us not listen to those who deny that the Church of God has the power to forgive all sins. (Augustine, *De agon. Christ.*, iii)

This was not a new idea. The Church didn't concoct confession in the ninth century and say, "Guess what people, we got a new way of doing it."

FKF: And the foundation for this authority is Scriptural. One of the things that people say is, "Well, that was the early Church just starting to make stuff up, starting to concoct this theory of how we're going to do this." But, that's not what happened.

First of all, the practice is already there. Secondly, the practice is based on their understanding of the Scriptures and on their relationship with the Apostles. And thirdly, they're carrying on what the Apostles were given the responsibility to do, which we see given to them in Scriptures by Jesus Christ, who shows His own authority by being able to forgive sins. And people are in awe of this.

DRG: So, I come to you, Father, in confession, and I am as the Church teaches, there for reconciliation with the Church, Christ's body. I confess some serious sins:

> Father. I have embezzled my company out of $52,000.
> Father, in my heart I absolutely cannot stand the neighbor lady. I hate her guts. I wish she would roast in hell.

Okay, I come to you and I confess these sins. And you say, "By the power given to me in Jesus Christ, I absolve you..."

What if I faked you out, Father? What if I'm not sorry? Oh, I cried. I said, "You know, the Spirit's moving me, Father." But this is something <u>not</u> in my heart, and <u>I'm not sorry</u>. I have a wrong disposition of heart.

FKF: One of the things that most Catholics don't realize is it is within the responsibility of the priest, if he is aware of the insincerity of a person, to <u>not</u> give absolution at that time. And to call the person to a more profound sense of what they need to be doing in terms of reorienting their life to God.

DRG: That happened to me once.

FKF: Really? (laughing)

DRG: <u>Seriously</u>, the priest did not absolve me. I said to him, Father, I do A, B, C, D and E, and I don't think it's a sin. He said, "Son, it is a sin." And I said, "Well I don't think so." He said, "Well, I can't absolve you then." I was shocked.

METANOIA
From the Greek word "metanoein"—to change one's mind, repent, and be converted — something necessary for spiritual growth.

FKF: That's right. There has to be a <u>sincerity of heart</u>. But not in a sense of judging everyone's heart. There are some people who come to confession, and you don't know—maybe they're sincere, maybe they're not. Again, as a representative of Christ, I say what Christ calls us as priests to say, and I do what Christ calls us to do. But if someone is rejecting the grace of the Sacrament through their insincerity, then even if the grace is offered, it's still rejected by the very ill will of their approach to the Sacrament.

DRG: And that's a worse sin.

FKF: It is. It's a terrible sin.

DRG: What about penance? You confess your sins, and the priest tells you, "I want you to say five prayers to Our Lord. I want you to go back to the neighbor lady and do something nice around her home. I want you to make some effort." What is that? What's that all about?

FKF: Well, there is in the early Church this whole sense of *metanoia*, this sense of a <u>conversion</u>.

DRG: Change of mind.

DISPOSITION OF HEART

For the sacraments to fully "confer the grace they signify," and be efficacious, they must be celebrated by the recipient "worthily in faith." That is "the fruits of the sacraments [in part] depend on the disposition of the one who receives them."
(CCC 1127-1128)

FKF: A change of mind and <u>a change of life</u> — <u>conversion</u>. You can't just say, "Well, I've changed my mind. I'm going to be a better person," and then go out and kill twelve people. Words are not enough. You have to show a sincerity of what you're going to be about and be willing to show that sincerity by what you do.

Remember when we talked about those three words: confession, penance, and reconciliation? <u>Confession</u>, first and foremost, is not just to "say" your sins. It's to confess your *belief* in Jesus Christ as the One Who can bring forgiveness and healing to your sinfulness and then to say what sins you've committed for which you need healing. The <u>penance</u> is to show that you are sincere in your desire to reunite yourself with Christ and with His Church. And then the <u>Reconciliation</u> happens <u>in</u> that rejoining of the person who has sinned to the people and to God.

DRG: Would anybody have occasion, in your opinion, outside the Sacrament of Penance, to actually "scour your conscience"—to look deep within their soul for the way they are—if they didn't regularly go to Confession?

FKF: The problem is that humans have a tendency to kid ourselves, and to justify what we do.

DRG: (in jest) You're kidding.

FKF: To not recognize the painfulness that we inflict on others and God through our actions. And this Sacrament calls us to that honest humility that truly brings us to experience the grace and mercy of God.

DRG: Many, many Catholics will tell you, Father, and I've felt the same way, that I sometimes don't do things because I don't want to have to go to another human being and say, "Let me tell you what I did."

It's so much easier to go into my bedroom, kneel by my bed and say, "Dear God, forgive me,"—He already knew what I did—than to come to you and say, "Father, let me tell you some of the things I do in the deep recesses of my heart."

FKF: And that fear is a motivation. It <u>does</u> keep you from sinning. That's what we'd call, however, an imperfect moral life. <u>The real thing should be desiring to do what God wants</u>, not fearing what the pain of hell will be like, or fearing what people will think. Yet, if the fear of hell, or that fear of what others are going to think keeps you on the straight and narrow, then it's a blessing.

One of the other things I find amazing, Ray, is the number of Protestant ministers who come to me and say:

> I wish we had what you have in the Sacrament of Reconciliation. I wish I had a way for my people to experience that love and to be able to touch their lives so profoundly.

And it's sad that doesn't happen.

DRG: Confession is <u>Scriptural</u>.

FKF: Right.

DRG: It is <u>historical</u>. The Church believes it and has taught it for 2000 years, from the very lips of Christ. It is <u>beneficial</u> to holiness. We scour our conscience. We confess to one another. As James says, we are called by Scripture to confess our sins to one another.

> *Therefore, confess your sins to one another and pray for one another, that you may be healed. (James 5:16)*

Confession is a vehicle, a means for us to make up for what we do wrong—a penance. And those Catholics who take full advantage of the Sacrament of Reconciliation will tell you that in their walk with Our Lord, their relationship with God simply becomes deeper and deeper.

FKF: Yes.

DRG: Thanks, Father. I have to go because I have to get to Confession. You reminded me of some things that I've done that I kind of neglected to mention, you know.

I used to tease my wife. "Honey, I can tell by your penance how bad you were in Confession." She'd say, "Why, what was your penance?" I'd say, "I got a half a sign of the Cross. What was yours?" She'd say, "Well, I had to do the Stations of the Cross..." which I didn't think was too bad. But, then she said, "...for each bead of the Rosary." I'm thinking, "Fr. Fete must have been pretty rough."

FKF: (laughs)

DRG: (to audience) Once again, thank you very much for joining us. I am Ray Guarendi with Father Kevin Fete. God bless you. God keep you, and we'll get together again next time on "What Catholics Really Believe."

Ss. Peter & Paul Church
West Bend, IA

Episode 8 Study Questions

A - Why should I come to a priest to have my sins forgiven? I can go straight to God.

1. If a person goes to God with a contrite heart and asks Him to forgive their sins, God will forgive them. But having done so, what does the person not expressly hear from God?

2. Conversely, if a person goes through the rite or reconciliation and confesses their sins to a priest, under what condition would their sins not be forgiven?

B - God doesn't give men the power to forgive sins. Only God can forgive sins.

3. Quote a verse from the Bible where Jesus gives the Apostles the power to forgive sin. (John 20:23, Matthew 16:19)

4. What two religious rituals, other than confession, do some non-Catholic Christians require be performed by a minister? Why must these rituals be performed by a minister?

5. When we sin, (a) other than God and ourselves whom else do we sin against? And (b) who represents that other entity from which we need to seek forgiveness?

6. In Matthew 9:6-8, although it is Christ who does the healing and proclaims that the lame man's sins are forgiven, the author ends this passage with the words "[the people] were in awe and glorified God who had given such authority <u>to men</u>." In terms of confession, what is the significance that Matthew wrote this passage decades after the Resurrection of Christ?

7. In a broad sense, does Jesus ever say we should forgive the sins of others? If so, in what context is His direction? (Matthew 5:10-12, 22-26, 39-47; 6:12)

8. According to Jesus, if we do not forgive the sins of others what consequence can we expect? (Matthew 6:14)

9. What does Jesus say when He passes on His authority to forgive sins to the Apostles? Quote it. (John 20:21-23)

10. In John 20:21-23 Jesus breathes on the Apostles. What is the other place in the Bible that this happened, and what was the context? (Genesis 1:2)

C - Jesus only gave power to forgive sins to his Apostles, no one else.

11. What two prophecies of Christ related to the forgiveness of sin, could have been interpreted as pertaining only to the first generation, but clearly have been interpreted by most Christians as applicable until Christ returns? (Matthew 28:19, John 16:13, James 5:16)

12. What early Church Fathers, in the first 300 years, understood that confession and penance were necessary parts of a Christian's life?

D - The Catholic Church teaches that to be forgiven you don't have to be sorry for your sins; you only have to go through the mechanics of going to Confession.

13. Even if the priest cannot tell if you are sincere in saying you are sorry for your sins, what part does sincerity of heart play in a valid confession?

14. When should a priest <u>not</u> forgive the sins of someone who confesses?

15. What does the term "METANOIA" mean, and how is it significant if the priest is to absolve you from your sins?

16. *Confession* is not just so you can recite your sins, but a place where you can profess what?

17. What is the purpose of *penance*?

18. What does the term *reconciliation* mean? In Confession with whom are we being reconciled?

19. How does the Sacrament of Reconciliation help prevent sin?

20. There are two reasons we may be motivated to avoid sin. Both are valid, but one is greater than the other. What is the BEST reason? What is the LESSER reason?

Imagine Being There

Holy Rosary Church
Minneapolis, MN

9. Mary I

Who Mary Is

DRG: Father Fete, when I was on my journey as a non-Catholic Christian, I listened to the misunderstandings, the misperceptions, the accusations and sometimes the ill will against what the Catholic Church teaches. People would say:

> It's not Scriptural. It's not historical. The early Church didn't think that. The early Christians didn't believe that. Or even, It's not logical.

So, I began to search out the answers for these arguments myself, and that has been part of the seed for this series. But one Protestant convert to the Catholic faith said this:

> There were three obstacles in my coming to the Catholic Church. In the end, there were three obstacles that fully remained—Mary, Mary and Mary.

I would have to say, in the non-Catholic world, probably one of the biggest struggles to understand the Catholic Church is her relationship with Mary — I'm going to say a phrase here that causes problems—"The Mother of God."

FKF: Theotokos — Mother of God.

DRG: Do we worship Mary, Father? You know what the accusations are—"You Catholics worship Mary. I'm not going into any idolatrous church that worships Mary."

Do we worship her, Father?

FKF: That is the misunderstanding and the false claim.

DRG: The mother of all misunderstandings maybe?

FKF: No pun intended there. But what you have here is the question of how do you use these words: "worship," and the other word, "prayer". You say, "Oh! We don't pray to anybody but God alone." Well, how are you using these words?

Worship: Catholics would <u>not</u> worship Mary. Catholics do not worship any of the saints. The word that we would use, the better word is venerate.

DRG: **Honor.**

FKF: Or honor. Now that word, <u>honor, is a great word</u>, because we were told by God to honor people. Most specifically two people we are told to honor: our father and our mother. Venerate your mother. Now this is important for us, because <u>did Jesus not himself follow the commandments</u>?

DRG: **Perfectly.**

FKF: Perfectly, so He would have <u>honored his mother</u>, Mary.

DRG: **Perfectly.**

FKF: He would have venerated his mother, Mary.

DRG: **Perfectly.**

FKF: And as Christians, are we not to emulate the example of Jesus?

DRG: **Of course we are.**

FKF: Therefore, we have to venerate Mary.

DRG: But you Catholics get carried away.

FKF: We get carried away?

DRG: You elevate her to a position equal to Jesus. You elevate her to a position far beyond anything Scripture says that she is. And furthermore, the cult of Mary didn't come along until several centuries later when people started to get scared of Jesus Christ, because He has just too much majesty. We had to have a softer version of approaching Him, so, "Let's go talk to His mom. We won't go straight to the big guy. We'll talk to His mom." That's what you Catholics do.

> **THEOTOKOS**
> A term that means "Mother of God" and refers to Jesus's mother, Mary. It was canonized by the Council of Ephesus (A.D. 431) in defense of Mary's divine maternity, against Nestorius, who claimed that Mary was only the mother of the man Christ.

FKF: Again, that is a claim that people make.

DRG: That's <u>not</u> what Catholics do?

FKF: Let's just start with this <u>claim</u> that the veneration of Mary was not done in the early Church but started much later.

If we want to look at the "cult" of Mary, let's go to Luke's Gospel and start at the very beginning. What do you find in there? You have this great proclamation at the beginning of the Gospel with the Angel Gabriel. What's the Angel Gabriel talking to Mary about? The angel starts talking to Mary about "blessed are you..."

DRG: "...among women." The angel says:

> *Most blessed are you among women, and*
> *blessed is the fruit of your womb. (Luke 1:42)*

By the way, Father ...

FKF: Hail Mary?

DRG: Yes. "Hail!" Basically that greeting is a very technical term, which almost always is only spoken to royalty. And to have an angel speak such a royal term to a peasant Jewish girl is next to unthinkable.

FKF: This proclamation: "...the Lord is with you." That's just a real <u>strong</u> proclamation. And it's interesting for us as Catholic Christians. Sometimes people

Sacred Heart Cathedral
Davenport, IA

talk about the prayers that we have and one of the prayers is the "Hail Mary!" Listen to that prayer. I'll just say it real quickly,

> *And coming to her, [Gabriel] said, "Hail, favored one. The Lord is with*
> *you." (Luke 1:28)*

That's the beginning of the *Hail Mary* prayer.

DRG: That's the Angel Gabriel speaking.

FKF: That's the angel. <u>It's Scripture</u>. It's the Word of God being quoted.

DRG: We're not honoring Mary with our <u>own</u> words. These are <u>God's words</u>, aren't they?

FKF: Yes. These are God's words, and we have people say, "How do you come up with these ideas in these prayers?"

We are Bible-believing Christians. We would never make stuff up.

DRG: What about the rest of the "Hail Mary?"

FKF: "Blessed are you among women."

DRG: "Blessed is the fruit ... "

FKF: "…of your womb, which is Jesus."

DRG: Who said that?

FKF: Elizabeth. When you get to Luke, Chapter 1, what you've got is the greeting of Elizabeth when Mary goes to visit her, and Elizabeth says to Mary,

> *Who am I that the mother of my Lord should*
> *come to me? (Luke 1:43, paraphrase)*

DRG: "Lord," by the way, can be translated "God."

FKF: Yes.

DRG: "Mother of God." These are the words that Elizabeth uses for Mary. "Who am I that the mother of the *Kyrios/* God should come to me?" (Luke 1:43)

Messiah Episcopal
St. Paul, MN

FKF: Yes, which is where we get the word, in the Greek actually, <u>Theotokos</u>, the <u>God Bearer</u>. It's important to understand that term, because in the early Church we had people who had problems with Mary, too. But, more importantly — <u>not</u> because of Mary — they had <u>problems with Jesus</u>. You had people who said,

> Jesus wasn't God. Jesus wasn't divine. Jesus was
> just human. Jesus was just a great prophet.

DRG: Jesus had two natures—as defined by the Church, through the Holy Spirit—one God and one human.

FKF: Mary gave birth to the human, but (in jest) the divine guy jumped in at the baptism or something.

All these different ideas floating around about Jesus was the reason why the statement of Mary being the <u>Theotokos</u>, the <u>God Bearer,</u> the <u>Mother of God</u> —

translated in the way we use the language—was used for her, <u>to emphasize the divinity of Christ</u>.

DRG: **So, "Mother of God" initially came about in answer to a question about Jesus' identity.**

FKF: The issue was "Christological."

DRG: **Not Marian.**

FKF: Not Marian. It's Christological, <u>but the term tells us who Mary is, too</u>.

DRG: **She is the Mother of the <u>whole</u> Jesus.**

FKF: Divine and human, yes.

DRG: **And Jesus is wholly God.**

FKF: The whole Incarnate, Word made Flesh, the Lord.

DRG: **You can't separate the two ideas. She's the mother who was human. She's the mother of <u>Jesus, who was God</u>.**

FKF: Yes.

DRG: **This, then, is the very basis for a misunderstanding. When we call Mary the "Mother of God" people immediately think, "You're saying she was around before God the Father."**

FKF: Or, the misunderstanding that she is the mom of the Trinity—creating the Trinity, giving birth to the Trinity.

DRG: **She's not.**

FKF: She's not, but the people who say you can't refer to Mary as the Mother of God, came out of the people who said, "You can't refer to Jesus as Lord. You can't call Jesus God."

DRG: **So in other words, if you call Jesus. God, by logic you have to call, theologically, Mary the Mother of God.**

FKF: To deny it, to deny Mary is the Mother of God is to deny that Jesus is God.

DRG: **Father, let's say your mother is here. Would she say, "I'm the mother of Kevin Fete in the flesh?"**

FKF: Well, sometimes she would deny it.

DRG: **So she would deny the whole thing.**

FKF: There are times that that would get denied. That was a bad example.

DRG: Sorry about that.

       No, she's the mother of Kevin Fete, the person.

FKF: Yes, the <u>whole</u> person.

DRG: Then it needs to be explicitly stated: <u>Catholics do not worship Mary</u>. There may be individual Catholics who get carried away and who don't understand, but that's true in all aspects of all doctrines of faith.

       The Catholic Church has <u>never</u> taught anybody to worship anybody other than God. Always. Ever, okay?

FKF: Right.

DRG: What about statues?

       You guys have statues in your churches, and I see people kneel in front of those statues. They're praying to those statues. You have statues all over the place. And you don't just have Mary; you have whole bunches of statues.

       Now, explain that.

VENERATE
To pay honor to someone or something, which does not detract from God's glory, but adds to God's glory. Veneration is not "adoration" or "worship" which are activities, within Catholicism, reserved for God alone.

FKF: There are different approaches we could take here, and one of them is that we should, maybe in another show, talk about the whole iconoclastic controversy. That's about having images—images that point us to the real people.

DRG: Images?

FKF: Images in a church and how that got "settled." Again, it goes back to a Christological thing with that settlement. People were saying, "You can't have these images of Jesus. We cannot have these in our church, because it says you shall worship no false images."

DRG: Make no graven images.

FKF: No graven images. And <u>graven</u> is the key word here. Not just images, but graven images—images that lead to death, images that are false, images that are idolatrous in nature.

DRG: Because our Lord commanded - - God <u>commanded</u> - - people to <u>make images</u>. There are seraphim on the ark and the temple is full of images. So, <u>God commanded images</u>.

FKF: The use of images is permitted.

And the images of Christ came about because people saw Christ; they knew Christ. John, some say, was one of the earliest iconographers. John, who was one of the youngest Apostles, with his relationship with Jesus, would remember Jesus. Also, being so young, he lived long past the death and resurrection of Jesus, so he would have been one who wanted Jesus to be remembered in a very personal way and would have started creating these images.

DRG: He didn't have any photos. No snapshots?

FKF: Well, they'd have to <u>paint them</u>, <u>but by very strict rules</u>. One rule was that the images had to be rendered in two-dimensions - - not more true three-dimensions - - in order that the representation of the person not be too real. Their argument was that we were told not to worship <u>graven or false</u> images. The rebuttal argument is that pictures and statues allow us to make an image of the <u>real</u> Jesus Christ, who is both God and man, and not false or graven at all. The statue is a true image to look at and to remember the one who was born of the Blessed Virgin.

Holy Cross Church
Onamia MN

DRG: Why do Catholics kneel in front of statues then, if they're not worshiping them?

FKF: We have a sense of, again, veneration, of <u>honor</u>. We humble ourselves before those we honor.

DRG: Are you praying to the statue?

FKF: Not to the statue. It's an image that reminds us of that person. When you see somebody who's far away from home, and they open up their wallet, and they take out a picture of their kid, and they kiss it, do you say, "Oh, that's a weird person?"

DRG: (jesting) Idolatry!

FKF: They're having a relationship with a piece of paper. That person just kissed the paper.

DRG: I've seen them do it with money. I've seen them do it with George Washington and Hamilton and those guys.

FKF: That's right; they love them. They embrace that. But nobody would be so lost in his or her thoughts as to say, "Oh look! He's got a picture of his wife. He doesn't love his wife. He loves the picture. Maybe they're going to settle down and make some little pamphlets. Who knows what's going to happen here." Now, that's just ludicrous. It's a <u>symbolic reminder</u> of the <u>real love you have for the real person</u>.

DRG: For the Catholic then, we use these things to help focus all of our senses on the reality of God and the holy ones who were in the faith before us.

FKF: Yes, those who have been judged worthy. It's interesting, because we have Gospel versions—the Gospel according to Matthew, Mark, Luke, John. Why do we have their names on them? Why don't we just say the Gospels according to some guys that knew Jesus?

DRG: Or just the Gospel, period. We don't need anything else.

FKF: Or just the Gospel versions. Here they are.

But, we remember these people <u>because</u> of what they have done in the faith. <u>And we remember that they are alive</u>. They're still alive.

One of the saddest things I've ever heard was when somebody, who was concerned about us Catholics and why we talk or pray to these saints, said to me:

Why do you talk to dead people?

St. Mary Aldermary
London, England

DRG: Was this a Christian?

FKF: It was a Christian, and I thought, how sad. How sad that someone who professes belief in Christ Jesus, who believes in the power of the Resurrection, would look at the faithful who have died a bodily death and not think that they're alive in Christ Jesus who promised that they would have life.

DRG: But Scripture is real clear. You are not supposed to go to spirits of the dead and try to get information and "conjure them up." Scripture is clear about that.

FKF: Yes, and I suspect that there were people who were also upset with the appearance of Jesus with Elijah and Moses at the Transfiguration:

Why are you hanging out with those guys?

DRG: They're dead.

FKF: They're dead, and they're moving around. That's even worse.

DRG: And getting information from them.

Here's the game plan, Jesus. We talked to Your Dad, and He said ...

FKF: You weren't supposed to do this.

And that takes us into all kinds of different tangents that you don't want to get into.

DRG: You can't; we only have 28 minutes.

FKF: I understand. But there is that sense of moving into this awareness of the saints who have gone before us in faith and who share in the joy of the Resurrection. Some people say:

Well, that doesn't happen until the end, until the end time.

Jesus, when He hangs on the cross, and He has the thieves on each side, what does He say to the one?

DRG: (in jest) "In the end of time you will be with Me in Paradise."

FKF: No. He says, today you will be with Me ...

DRG: Today.

FKF: "Today you will be with Me in Paradise." He doesn't say, "You're going to go down, be a worm farm, and when I come back in glory, I'll come back and get you." He says, "Today you will be with Me in Paradise."

DRG: Okay, Father, here's one:

You Catholics call Mary YOUR mother. You say, "Our Blessed Lady." You call her BLESSED.

DRG: **What's the problem with that?**

FKF: I have no problem with that.

DRG: **Is there any place in Scripture?**

FKF: Not only in Scripture for Mary, but what does Jesus say in the Beatitudes? <u>Blessed</u> are they who — <u>Blessed</u> are they — <u>Blessed</u> are they — There are a whole bunch of <u>blessed</u> people.

DRG: <u>**Blessed**</u> **are you, Simon bar Jonah.**

FKF: How could those made in the image of God, who respond faithfully to the call of God, be called anything but blessed?

DRG: **What about the claim that Mary was just a Jewish peasant woman? Many devout Christian people who are non-Catholic will say she was just—I've heard the word "vehicle" being used.**

Holy Trinity Cathedral
Waterford, Ireland

FKF: Like she was a Chevy truck.

DRG: She was a <u>VEHICLE</u>.

FKF: Hey Mary, I've got a load, drive it on down here.

DRG: **God needed a woman, and He said:**

You, you're pretty holy. You can incubate My Son for nine months and raise Him for the first 30 years. And then, thank you, you're done. Let's go on with the plan of salvation here.

FKF: I have this repeated image of Sanford and Son driving down with a truck, bringing Jesus along.

DRG: **So Mary says:**

...behold, from now on will all ages [generations] call me <u>blessed</u>.
(Luke 1:48b)

I remember one time somebody asked me—this was during my drifting away from the Church:

Who are the only Christian denominations who calls her blessed?

FKF: Yes.

DRG: **We Catholics and ...**

FKF: ...the Orthodox.

DRG: **The Eastern churches.**

FKF: Right. The two traditions that go all the way back to the time of Christ. Maybe there's a reason we're the only two churches that call her blessed.

DRG: **Here's something that was in Time Magazine. I had a friend say this to me just the other day, from Time Magazine. Now, you know you can trust Time for theological discourse.**

FKF: Right. (laughs)

DRG: **My friend says:**

> Time Magazine said "Mary is about to be declared Co-redeemer—Mediatrix of all graces." So all of this mumbo jumbo that you Catholics are saying that you don't worship her, your own Pope and theologians are kind of saying we need to call her Co-Redeemer. We need to make that an article of the faith.

How do you argue with that? Their language is black and white—Co-Redeemer.

FKF: The problem again is language. That's always been a problem when you get into the whole thing of Christ with his divinity and humanity. The translation of words become big problems. And so too, I think the Church needs to look at how it uses terms, not only for the way it's meant by the Church but also how it will be interpreted by people.

CO-REDEEMER

A term that references Mary as someone who is not equal with Christ as Redeemer, but someone who "CO-OPERATED" with Christ to bring redemption.

"Co-Redemptorist," I hear people use that word, or "Co-Redeemer." Those terms don't mean that Mary is the equal of Jesus. Co-Redeemer means that she co-operated in God's plan for redemption of all people.

DRG: **With the Redeemer—not equal to the Redeemer.**

FKF: No, no, not equal.

DRG: **Are you sure she's not seen as our feminine goddess version of Jesus?**

FKF: That's NOT what it's trying to say.

But, in fact, there are a lot of people who would be co-redeemers in the faith.

DRG: **We're called that in Scripture.**

FKF: Yes, anyone who is working with God to help bring about God's plan of salvation is a person who is <u>COOPERATING</u> in the redemption of humanity through the grace of <u>God</u>. That's how those terms are to be taken. The big problem is that people are going to mis-portray what is meant by that, so as to bring scandal to the Church.

DRG: **So the official Church view of that would be, through her own free will—"Let it be done to me according to <u>Your</u> will," she said this to the angel — Mary cooperated with God's salvation plan. And through her, came the Redeemer of the world. She wasn't a robot. It's not that she <u>had</u> to say "yes" because God made it that way, or that God just kind of wired her in such a way that she'd say "yes" automatically. The Church says we respect her free will, correct?**

FKF: She had to have free will.

DRG: **She could have refused?**

FKF: It would not be a loving act if the decision were forced on her. And God is a God of love. That's why God doesn't force those things on

All Saints Anglican
Winnipeg, Manitoba

us. We take them freely or not at all, because that's the only way they can be given in love. If it's not loving, it's against the very essence of God Himself.

DRG: **The Church says that she, of her own volition, said, "I cooperate in whatever You have planned for me."**

FKF: And with that cooperation we see in her an <u>example</u> for all of us. That's why we have pictures and statues of her, of other saints, and of Jesus Himself.

But, people do that with pictures of family members. I go to a lot of people's homes, and one group on this matter that I really respect, because they stay to their sense of conviction, are the Amish. If you look at an Amish doll, there's no face on it. If you go to an Amish home, there are no pictures of the relatives up on the wall because they have this sense of <u>making no images</u>.

But other people that talk down about our images in the Catholic Church, if you go into their homes, they have an image of grandma there. And, I may like their grandma. They may have a good grandma, but I don't know if their grandma is better then Jesus' mom. I mean, the family's grandmother may be a great mom, but I can't rank her better than the mom that Jesus got.

DRG: **But we know what her grandma looks like. We don't know what Mary looks like. So whatever image we're putting up there, we don't know if it is a true image.**

FKF: That's the complaint you're going to get from people. But it's the representation of the <u>goodness</u> of a person who responded to God's call.

DRG: **So Mary is our hero, or heroine.**

FKF: Indeed, yes. And she's a person we look to, because the saints are alive due to the Resurrection. We call upon them and upon Mary.

People say, "Well, why do you do that? They're dead." But, they're not dead if you're a believer in Resurrection…

DRG: **…they're very much alive.**

FKF: People will still say,

> *You shouldn't call upon other people to pray for you.*
> *You can go to God yourself directly and pray.*

I hear that all the time. And yet at the same time these same people will ask me, just before surgery or something important:

> *Hey, Fr. Kevin, would you pray for me?*
> *Remember to say a prayer for me.*

I think, well, why don't you just go to Jesus yourself?

DRG: **You should just tell them, "I can't. There's only one mediator between God and man, and it's not me…"**

FKF: And that's Jesus.

DRG: ...so I can't pray for you.

FKF: But we call upon people to pray for us all the time. We go to our pastors, we go to our friends, we go to our family, and we say, "Pray for me." If we can ask the people here and now who are believers to pray for us, all the more reason we can go to those who have already found eternal life in Christ and ask them to pray for us.

DRG: We're going to get to this in our next show—the Communion of Saints. Let me read to you the earliest prayer that has been discovered on record. It's called the Sub Tuum, Latin for under you, right?

FKF: Right.

DRG: In 250 A.D., this was written.

> We fly to thy patronage, O Holy Mother of God.
> Despise not our petitions in our necessities,
> but deliver us from all danger,
> O most glorious and blessed Virgin Mary. *(Sub tuum)*

DRG: This prayer is older than when the Church officially established the doctrines of the "Trinity," about which all Protestants and Catholics would not even argue.

FKF: Before the Trinity was formally defined.

DRG: Formally defined, yes. Now I have to throw this question at you.

Why do you Catholics call Mary your Mother? Is that Scriptural?

FKF: There's certainly Scripture basis for that. One would be the crucifixion of Christ, when the Apostle John stands at the foot of the cross, and next to him is Jesus' mother, Mary. And Jesus says to John, "This is now your mother," as if to say, "John, change the way you look at her."

> Then he (Jesus) said to the disciple, "Behold your mother." *(John 19:27a)*

Also in Revelation you see an accounting of that.

SUB TUUM
Beneath your compassion, We take refuge, O Theotokos: do not despise our petitions in time of trouble: but rescue us from dangers, only pure, only blessed one.

DRG: Let me read that. Father, this is coming on the heels of — and we'll talk about this more next time — the verse that says,

> A great sign appeared in the sky, a woman clothed with the sun, with the moon under her feet, and on her head a crown of twelve stars. She was with child and wailed aloud in pain as she labored to give birth. (Revelations 12:1-2)

Early Church interpretations have been that this is variously **Mary** or the **Church.** A few verses later it then says,

> Then the dragon became angry with the woman and went off to wage war against the rest of her offspring, those who keep God's commandments and bear witness to Jesus. (Revelation 12:17)

It's talking about the offspring of this woman as us believers.

FKF: The Church, yes.

DRG: Verses like that, I have to admit, I was never shown when I was outside the Catholic Church, in non-Catholic settings.

FKF: And Scripturally, you see a strong sense of the importance of Mary in the plan God had for salvation.

You spoke just a little bit ago about one of the earliest prayers, and you're talking pretty far down the road. But one of the earliest prayers actually is a hymn that's <u>found in the Scriptures</u>. That hymn is, by most Scripture scholars, said to be accredited to Mary, but something that was also proclaimed about Mary <u>by the early Church</u>. That's in Luke, Chapter 1,

> And Mary said: "My soul proclaims the greatness of the Lord; my spirit rejoices in God my Savior. For, He has looked upon his handmaid's lowliness; behold, <u>from now on will all ages call me blessed</u>. The Mighty One has done great things for me, and holy is His name." (Luke 1:46-49)

Mary's Magnificat goes on from there. How could we ever take someone who proclaims the greatness of the Lord and then shun him or her

St. Francis Xavier Cathedral
Green Bay, WI

from our sense of their importance in God's plan of salvation? How could we hide his or her image? How would we rebuke their importance?

DRG: Non-Catholics would say:

> We don't do that. We honor her, and we
> respect her for her rightful position.

But, they would also say,

> You Catholics have this whole theological ball of wax surrounding her. You pray to her. You think she was sinless—without original sin. You sometimes call her Queen of Heaven. Come on, now!

And so you and I, on our next show on Mary, are going to address these things.

FKF: That'd be great.

DRG: And I think, Father, what we'll find is that many of these doctrines that the Church has always protected did not crop up in 1950, or in 1854.

FKF: Or, the Council of Trent.

DRG: That, in fact, these doctrines go all the way back to the beginning; and this devotion to Mary is solely because of who Christ is.

I'll close with this example. If I were a painter, and I painted this wonderful picture of my mother, and you came and just stared at me, I'd say, "No, look at my picture." And you'd reply:

> Oh no, you're the painter, I just want to stare at you, I don't care about that stupid picture.

FKF: Right.

DRG: Or if I were in love with you, and I said, "Hey, I need you to come and meet my family." And you said,

> No, no, I love you. I don't care about your family.

And I'd say: "But I want you to meet my mother." You'd counter:

> I'm in love with you, I'm not really all that concerned with your mother.

FKF: That should cause some folks to think about Mary's importance.

DRG: (to audience) Once again, we just had the briefest of opportunities to scratch the surface on why Catholics believe what they really believe about Mary. We're going to take it again next show. I'll be wearing the same shirt.

FKF: I like it.

DRG: You like it?

FKF: Yeah, I'll wear the same one too.

DRG: This is, "What Catholics Really Believe" about Mary. I'm Ray Guarendi. With me, Pastor Kevin Fete. God bless, God keep you. Walk with God.

Annunciation Chapel
Haverlee, Belgium

Episode 9 Study Questions

Some non-Catholics claim:

A - Catholics worship Mary by praying to her.

1. Why do non-Catholics think that Catholics worship Mary?

2. How do Catholics define "prayer" differently from many non-Catholics?

3. If Catholics do not worship Mary, what word better describes how they think of her, and what does that word mean?

4. What two categories of people does the Bible command us to honor? (Exodus 20:12)

5. How well did Jesus follow the commandment to honor our father and mother?

6. How is "praying to Mary" the same thing as asking a relative or close friend to pray for us?

B - Catholics get carried away and elevate Mary to a position equal to Jesus, creating a "cult of Mary" that is not Scriptural.

7. What two Biblical personages began the cult of Mary by proclaiming her blessed and favored of God? (Luke 1:28-30,42)

8. What person in the Bible makes the proclamation: "Hail, Mary, full of grace"? (Luke 1:28-30)

9. What person in the Bible makes the proclamation about Mary: "Blessed are you among women, and blessed is the fruit of your womb"? (Luke 1:42)

10. What does the Greek word "THEOTOKOS" mean, and why did the Church decide to start calling Mary the "Mother of God"? Were those two titles meant to elevate Mary? If not, then why were the titles given to Mary?

11. To deny that Mary is the mother of God is to deny what other basic tenet of Christianity?

12. Is it possible that some individual Catholics get carried away to the point that they really do worship Mary?

13. In what circumstance, situation, or way does the Catholic Church teach us that Mary should be worshiped?

C - Catholics have statues and idols of Mary. The Bible says you shall have no graven images.

14. What does the term "graven images" mean and how does that commandment differ from the making of "true images"?

15. Why do some Catholics kneel before images of Mary and the saints? Are they praying to the statue or the picture?

16. When a person shows you a picture of their child or grandchild, and maybe even kisses the picture, is the person worshipping the picture? What is the person doing?

D - The saints are dead. Scripture says we are not supposed to conjure up the dead.

17. Why are the names of the authors of the four Gospels in the titles of the Gospels? Why aren't the books titled the Gospels of Jesus Christ?

18. Where in the Bible does it say that the Apostles, Mary, or the saints are dead?

19. Did Jesus conjure up the dead spirits of Elijah and Moses at his Transfiguration? If not, how would you explain what was going on? (Matthew 17:1-6, Mark 9:1-8, Luke 9:28-36, 2 Peter 1:16-18, John 1:14)

E - Catholics call Mary blessed, and the Bible doesn't say we should call her that.

20. List those who Jesus says should be referred to as blessed? (Matthew 5)

21. What had just happened when Mary says that future generations will call her blessed? (Luke 1:48b)

F - The Church is about to declare Mary the co-redeemer, the Mediatrix of all graces, the equal of Jesus.

22. What does the word "Co-Redemptrix" or "Co-Redemptress" mean? Do these words mean she is equal with Jesus?

23. In what ways is Mary our heroine? What did she do, and what does she do yet today that we should practice in our lives?

G - Catholics call Mary their Mother. That is not Scriptural.

24. What are the situations in Scripture that imply that Mary is our Mother? (John 19:27, Revelation 12:17)

25. How does Mary refer to God in her Luke 1:39ff prophecy?

*Joseph supported Mary when Jesus was born in a stable,
and another Joseph helped Mary bury Jesus in a tomb.*

*Guardian Angels Cathedral
Las Vegas, NV*

10. Mary II
Her Relationship to Jesus

DRG: Welcome to "What Catholics Really Believe." I'm Ray Guarendi, a psychologist and lay member of the Catholic Church. With me, Pastor Kevin Fete, pastor of Little Flower Parish in Canton, Ohio.

In our journey we are talking about the common teachings most misunderstood by non-Catholics, Fr. Fete, and sometimes sadly by Catholics. We are talking about Confession and Purgatory and the Eucharist and Mary and Mary. Do you remember the person who said there were three things that blocked him on his final step to the Catholic Church?

FKF: Yes. They were Mary, Mary and Mary.

DRG: So we are attempting to dispel some of the misconceptions and to show Scripturally and historically why the Church's view of Mary is profoundly true. It is not an exaggeration. It is not something that clouds over the importance of Christ. Last show we talked about the "Mother of God."

FKF: *Theotokos*/God Bearer.

DRG: That's a term that bothers a lot of non-Catholics. Give us a quick explanation.

FKF: The term "Theotokos" arose <u>not</u> out of an issue about Mary but out of the nature of Jesus. Was or was not Jesus God? Was He divine or wasn't He divine? Those who said that Jesus was not divine held the position that Mary was the mother of a great prophet, of a human being with no divinity. The other group that said that Jesus was divine—He is the Son of God—by being the <u>Son</u> of God, He <u>is</u> God. Therefore, by Mary's giving birth to Him she was giving birth to one who was divine.

DRG: So the term given by the early Church to <u>protect</u> the teaching of Jesus' divinity was "Mother of God." And, in fact, there is Scripture to support that title. For example, when Elizabeth says,

> *And how does this happen to me, that the <u>mother of my Lord</u> should come to me? (Luke 1:43)*

FKF: " … that the <u>mother of my Lord</u> should come to me."

DRG: "Lord" translates as "God" in the Greek, right?

FKF: Right.

DRG: Okay, secondly the very, very popular misconception: "You Catholics <u>worship</u> Mary." Please dispel that quickly.

FKF: We honor the saints, just as Christ would follow the commandments and honor His mother, so too do we follow the commandment and honor His mother. We do <u>not</u> see her as the bearer of <u>salvation</u>. We do <u>not</u> see her as the one who gives us eternal life. That is what has come to us from the grace of God through the death and Resurrection of Christ.

DRG:

St. Joseph's Cathedral, Sioux Falls, SD

Not true, not true! Your words sound fancy but even your own Pope, and I read this in Time Magazine, you know, that theologically trustworthy journal, that the Catholics are going to make Mary <u>Co-Redeemer</u>.

FKF: (in jest) Yes.

DRG: There you have it, equal to Christ.

FKF: "Co-Redeemer" sometimes gets misinterpreted, as a result of people thinking that Catholics are saying that Mary is the equal of Jesus. But, in this case the prefix "co" just means that she <u>cooperated</u> with God to fulfill the plan that God formed long ago for the salvation of all people.

DRG: So through her free will assent, "Be it done to me according to Thy will," she essentially said <u>yes</u> to God.

FKF: Yes, she was a cooperator in the work of redemption.

DRG: By the way, and we don't have time to get into it in this show, but some of the early Church Fathers referred to Mary as "the cause of our salvation." That's the kind of language nowadays that people would just go: "GASP!"

FKF: They would see that as a red flag.

DRG: Yes, red flag language. But, in fact, the Church Fathers were meaning that Mary's "Yes" was necessary—Christ could only come to us through Mary.

Let's get into a couple of more things, a little more in depth.

You pray to Mary, clearly. What are you doing? First of all those folks—saints in heaven—they can't hear us. There's nothing in Scripture that indicates that they even know we're around. They're with Christ. So therefore, who are you praying to?

Talk about that please.

FKF: First of all, one of the things to talk about, and this isn't just a situation with Mary – although Mary, being one of the great holy ones, certainly would exemplify sainthood. But as Catholics we would talk to all the saints. And we have this idea that we call "the Communion of Saints."

Now, Saint Paul uses the word "saint" in his writings to refer to the Christian believers who were alive at the time, those who are dedicated and committed to the faith. Some people say:

See, saints refers to the living people here on earth.

But, you have to remember, Paul is writing to the first generation. There aren't those believers who have died and gone before him out of his generation.

DRG: Do we have any historical evidence that the early Church believed that this Communion of Saints wasn't just the believers on earth but in fact included those who had gone before? Do we have any evidence of that?

FKF: Actually you have Scriptural evidence. One of the things we talked about before is in the Book of Revelation. If you talk about a revelation, the Book of Revelation has one.

DRG: It's a good revelation.

FKF: Yes, it is. And chapter 5, verse 8, which you know very well…

DRG: That verse describes elders around the throne of the Lamb, our Lord. And it says very wonderfully that the elders were taking the bowls of incense, the golden bowls of incense, which were filled with the prayers of the saints, and taking them to the Lord. It says,

> *Taking the golden bowls of incense, which were the prayers of the saints, and carrying them to the throne of the Lamb. (Revelation 5:8 paraphrased)*

FKF: These were the saints in heaven.

DRG: Those saints are identified a little later in Revelation as including those also on earth, carrying them to the throne of the Lamb. So you have this whole intercessory image.

Now, what about the Transfiguration?

FKF: Again another magnificent place of recognizing that Jesus Christ is the Lord of Life. He is the Way, the Truth and the Life. I talked about that once before, that the saddest thing that I ever had happen was a Christian came to me and said:

TRANSFIGURATION

Jesus took Peter, James, and John to the top of a high mountain. There "his face shone like the sun and his clothes became white as light." Moses and Elijah appeared and talked with Jesus.

Matthew 17:1-9, Mark 9:1-9, Luke 9:28-36, 2 Peter 1:16-18.

> Well, I don't talk to the saints; they're dead.
> I don't talk to those people; they're dead.

We believe in the Resurrection, and we believe that there are those who have been raised up to new life who, on this day, join Christ in Paradise. Christ Himself, as He hung upon the cross says to the one thief, who turns his life over to Christ, "On this day you will be with me in Paradise."

In the Transfiguration what we have is this sense that…

DRG: …the saints are alive.

FKF: Yes! Jesus Christ, who is fully God but also fully human, somehow is going between those who have passed through death to life and those who are still alive in this world.

DRG: Moses and Elijah were the two who had passed through death.

FKF: And He has Peter, James and John with him—those still living. So, you have Jesus— who is fully man and fully God—with His other friends who are fully human, talking to these people who have gone before them in the ways of faith to the next life. What's amazing is that the fully human people see Moses and Elijah as present also.

DRG: When people say,

> Well, there's nothing that indicates they're aware of us.

That's when I love to show them this verse:

> *There will be more joy in heaven over one sinner who repents than over ninety-nine righteous people who have no need of repentance. (Luke 15:7)*

There is more joy in heaven over one sinner who repents. Well, how's heaven supposed to know about that? What do they know about us?

FKF: How can they rejoice unless they know, somehow?

DRG: I'll tell you some of the evidence I like the most. The catacombs that imprisoned many early Christians were found to be filled completely with inscriptions from the very earliest days of Christianity with prayers to the saints, those who have gone before, who have finished the race. Hebrews 12:1 says:

> *...since we are surrounded by so great a cloud of witnesses...(Hebrews 12:1)*

And it refers to these people who have gone before us, the holy ones of the Old Testament.

*Nativity Church
Bloomington MN*

FKF: Yes.

DRG: We pray to Mary. We pray for her intercession. Let me give you a couple of quotes from the early Church Fathers. Once again, from the very beginning, back in the earliest liturgies, we have evidence they prayed to saints. This is from Clement of Alexandria. Clement, A.D. 208.

In this way the true Christian is always pure for prayer. He also prays in the society of angels as being already of angelic rank; and he is never out of their holy keeping. And though he prays alone, he <u>has the choir of saints standing with him in prayer</u>. (Clement of Alexandria, *Miscellanies* 7:12 [A.D. 208])

Or, Jerome. Jerome's a great guy. He was writing here in answer to a heretic's book:

You say in your book that while we live we are able to pray for each other. But, afterwards when we have died, the prayer of no person for another can be heard. But, if the Apostles and martyrs, while still in the body can pray for others at a time when they ought to be concerned about themselves, how much more will they do so after their crowns, victories and triumphs. (St. Jerome, *Against Vigilantius* 6 [A.D. 406])

FKF: That's a great quote, because one of the things that you hear people talking about is this "nonsense idea" of us asking someone who's past death to pray for

St. Mary's Church
Horseshoe Bend, AR

us. Yet, they're the same persons who go to their pastor, to their friends, to their mom or dad and say:

Pray for me, pray for me, pray for me.

And I always think, "Well, if you only need to talk directly to God…"

DRG: There's only one mediator between God and man.

FKF: Jesus Christ.

DRG: The man, Jesus Christ. That's it, you can't pray for <u>anybody</u> if the saints in heaven can't be solicited to pray for us.

FKF: So if there's only one mediator, Jesus Christ, and you want to be consistent and say, "You shouldn't ask the saints to pray for us," then we shouldn't ask anyone on earth to pray for us either.

When you use that word "prayer," — let's define it. When we [as Catholics] say we "pray" to the saints, that <u>does not</u> mean "prayers of <u>worship</u>" but prayers of <u>petition</u>. They are <u>requests</u>, given to those who have passed over, to go to the Father and to offer this petition for us. We do that all the time with people on earth. We say, "You know, Marge is going in for surgery next week. Pastor, please pray for her," because we know we can go to holy ones and ask that they, too, speak to the Father and call upon God's grace in our lives.

DRG: The prayer of a righteous man avails much. That's in James 5:16.

FKF: Sure.

DRG: So, we pray to Mary and to the saints in heaven to pray for us.

Now, there's this title for Mary, "The New Eve." People will say:

> You make a big deal out of Mary, but she is not that prominent in Scripture. She comes up a few times here and there.

Father, if I lay the background for Second Samuel, chapter 6, will you fill it in from Luke 1 and 2 regarding Mary being The New Eve?

FKF: The parallels between the two? Sure.

DRG: In the Old Testament, the Ark of the Covenant was lost in battle. The enemy took it and kept it for a while. Finally, it came back. Several decades later, David conquers Jerusalem and says, "I want the Ark of the Covenant here. I want the glory of God back to us." So he sends to get the Ark. The Ark was kept in the hill country of Judea for three months at the house of a man named Obed Edam. <u>When David saw the Ark he leapt for joy and he said:</u>

> Who am I that the Ark of the Lord should come to me? (2 Samuel 6:9b, paraphrase)

St. Edward's
Seattle, WA

Here, in Luke, chapter 1, we have the angel Gabriel coming to Mary saying,

> The holy Spirit will come upon you, and the power of the Most High will overshadow you. (Luke 1:35a)

The word "overshadow" there is the same exact Greek word used for the Shikinah glory cloud in the Old Testament <u>overshadowing what?</u>

FKF: <u>The Ark of the Covenant.</u>

DRG: Then Mary leaves. Where does she go?

FKF: She goes to visit Elizabeth.

DRG: Where did Elizabeth live?

FKF: In the hill country.

DRG: **The hill country of Judea. How long did she stay with Elizabeth?**

FKF: Well, it says until the third month.

DRG: **Three months. Exactly the time that the Ark of the Covenant was in the hill country. And, what did the baby in Elizabeth's womb do when Mary arrived?**

FKF: <u>He leaps for joy</u>. Just like David leapt for joy before the Ark.

DRG: **And what did Elizabeth say?**

FKF: Who am I that the mother of my Lord should visit me?

> *And how does this happen to me, that the mother of my Lord should come to me? (Luke 1:43)*

DRG: **I had a friend say to me,**

> Those are all coincidences. Luke didn't mean anything by that. Those are all coincidences.

FKF: There are no coincidences with the <u>plan</u> of God. God doesn't have coincidences. God has a plan.

DRG: **If those were all coincidences, I've got a ton of quotes from the early Church Fathers who talk about her as The New ARK, The New Eve. Irenaeus said,**

> What Eve bound, Mary loosed. (Irenaeus, d. circa 200AD: *Against Heresies, Book III*, Ch. 22.)

She's called the New Eve/The New Ark everywhere. What did the Ark of the Old Covenant contain? Do you remember? This is a little Old Testament trivia. I know I'm putting you on the block here.

St. Andrew's Cathedral Victoria, BC

FKF: The Ark of the Covenant contained the law.

DRG: **The Ten Commandments—The Law. It also had Aaron's rod—the budded rod of the first High Priest. And it had the manna. Jesus is called the Word/the Law/the Logos. He's called the great High Priest and He's called the Bread of Life.**

FKF: Yes. The Ark carried the <u>prototypes of Jesus</u>. Mary carried <u>the real Jesus</u>.

DRG: **This imagery of Mary from the Old Testament Ark of the Covenant points to Mary as "The Ark of the New Covenant." Father, read Revelation, chapter 12, verse 1. Just read it out loud. It's one of my favorite verses in all of Scripture regarding Mary. John had just seen the Ark of the Covenant. It was something that no one had seen for 600 years in Jewish history.**

FKF: In Chapter 11 he says <u>he now sees the Ark of the Covenant.</u>

> *A great sign appeared in the sky, <u>a woman</u> clothed with the sun, with the moon under her feet, and on her head a crown of twelve stars. She was with child and wailed aloud in pain as she labored to give birth. (Revelation 12:1-2)*

DRG: **The early Church interpretation of that woman was what, Father?**

FKF: It's the Blessed Mother. It's the one who is the Theotokos, the <u>Christ-Bearer</u>.

DRG: **And John parallels Mary with The Ark of the Covenant immediately.**

FKF: Right.

DRG: **He says, "Here's the Ark"—end of Revelation, chapter 11, and "Now I see a woman"—Revelation 12:1—the very next verse. And later on he talks about how she is the mother of all those who follow Christ.**

> *Then the dragon became angry with the <u>woman</u> and went off to wage war against the <u>rest of her offspring</u>, those who keep God's commandments and <u>bear witness to Jesus</u>. (Revelation 12:17)*

For those who say,

> *You Catholics call Mary the Ark of the New Covenant.*

Well, Scripture does, too. For those who say,

> *You Catholics call Mary your mother.*

Well, Scripture does, too.

FKF: And Jesus relays that, too, at the foot of the cross with the bestowing of the Blessed Virgin to John as John's mother—John, <u>who represents the faithful followers of Christ</u>.

DRG: One more new Eve parallel. You ready?

FKF: Okay.

DRG: In Genesis 3:15, God says,

> I will put enmity between you and the woman, and between your offspring and hers;… (Genesis 3:15a)

He calls Eve what? He says, Eve was called "<u>the woman</u>" before she was called Eve, right? "The woman you gave me made me do this."

FKF: <u>The woman</u>. That's a strong term.

DRG: It is a strong term. Genesis 3:15 says,

> I will put enmity between you and the <u>woman</u>. (Genesis 3:15)

At the wedding feast of Cana, what does Jesus call His mother?

FKF: Well, in our days we almost think of it as in insult. He says, "<u>Woman</u>, My time has not yet arrived."

DRG: <u>At the foot of the cross</u>, what does He call His mother when He says, "Behold your son?"

FKF: <u>Woman</u>, behold your son.

DRG: In what you just read in Revelation, Chapter 12?

FKF: Woman.

DRG: Woman. Is it an accident that John, the author of all three of those quotes, essentially says, "the woman?"

FKF: The woman.

DRG: This is The New Eve. This is the Ark of the New Covenant.

FKF: John picks up that title (Woman) in his Gospel. One of the magnificent parts about that story is it gives us Catholics our sense of Mary, both in terms of the title "Woman" given her there, but also in <u>her actions</u>. That's the last accounting of anything Mary ever says in John's Gospel. And what's the conclusion that John chooses to use as Mary's last words? She takes the guys who are the stewards at the wedding and she tells them to go get the jars of water. And then the last thing she says …

DRG: **Do whatever he tells you.**

> *His mother said to the servers, "Do whatever he tells you." (John 2:5)*

Sankt Marie Kirke
Helsingor, Denmark

FKF: Yes, those are the last words Mary utters in the Scriptures. "Do whatever He tells you to do."

DRG: **Nice piece of intercession, you know? Jesus says to Mary, "My hour is not yet come. I'm not ready to do this yet." And she says, "Oh, okay, you're right."**

No! Like a [good Jewish] mom she says, "Do whatever He tells you."

FKF: You get it done.

DRG: **"You should see what my Son can do. Watch this."**

FKF: Yes, <u>she intercedes</u> for the wedding party and goes to Jesus and says <u>do it</u>. And Jesus, on theological grounds saying, "No, I don't think so," changes His mind, because He's going to <u>honor His mother</u>.

DRG: **Honor His mother.**

FKF: But then the call from Mary—the woman, the New Eve—is, "Look, this is the new Adam. Do whatever He tells you. <u>I'm here to point to Him</u>. I'm here to say Jesus, my son, is the one that you are to follow."

DRG: **We could talk for days, not only on the depth of the Scripture verses regarding Mary, but on the many, many quotes from centuries past, way past, before the Middle Ages. That's when Mary got all her prominence, way back with the early Church Fathers. We don't have time. I want to focus on just a couple more Scripture verses.**

Very quickly, the angel comes to Mary. Gabriel says,

> *Hail, full of grace,… (Luke 1:28, Jerome's Translation)*

That was Jerome's translation. He tried to capture it. If I recall my Greek, the word, "full of grace" there is *kecharitomene*, which essentially has the meaning, <u>you who have been perfected in grace</u>. You're perfect. You're sinless.

FKF: Yes, full of grace.

DRG: Full of grace. You're <u>completely sinless</u>.

FKF: That's right.

DRG: But the interesting thing about that, Father, is do you remember the meaning of the Greek word "hail," which is *chairo*. It is used only with royalty. Has an angel ever addressed anybody like that in Scripture? Has an angel ever addressed a human being with, "Hail"?

> **KECHARITOMENE**
> Greek meaning
> "full or grace" or
> "perfected in grace."
>
> **CHAIRO**
> A Greek word used
> to hail royalty.

FKF: Well, yes.

DRG: Yes?! Who?

FKF: It's MARY.

DRG: Mary, of course.

FKF: But not in any other place in Scripture. And even when you look at the great prophets, or you look at King David, who may be given some great terms but not that kind of proclamation.

DRG: That is fascinating to me, because of the 300 plus appearances of angels in Scripture, it's always the humans who were viewed as lower. This instance, Gabriel's essentially saying <u>to Mary</u>, "<u>You're royalty</u>."

FKF: Yes.

DRG: All right now, one more thing about Mary.

> Just to show you how much you Catholics don't understand the Bible, you say Mary was a <u>perpetual virgin</u>. Scripture clearly says Jesus had brothers and sisters. Mark chapter 6, verse 3.

> *Is he not the carpenter, the son of Mary, and the brother of James and Joses and Judas and Simon? (Mark 6:3a)*

It says He had brothers and sisters. Now how do you maintain that Mary stayed a virgin? Come on, you're going straight into the face of the Bible.

FKF: If you look up that passage, one of the things Jesus doesn't do is to <u>acknowledge</u> them as His brothers either. What does He say?

DRG: Who are my brothers and sisters? (Mark 3:33-34, Luke 8:21)

FKF: Who are my brothers and sisters? He goes on to this theological sense of whoever does the will of My Father is mother and brother and sister to me.

When you look at the sense of what a brother is in those times, you need to look at Jesus going to the temple as a young boy and they lose Him. The reason he gets lost is everyone traveled in big parties. Families were very closely related. The word for brother and the word for cousin were interchanged back then, and kids would be seen as members of a larger family in that way.

DRG: There was no Hebrew or Jewish or Aramaic word for *blood brother*. It was *friend, kinsman, clansman, tribal member*. It was this broad, "We're all kind of brothers here."

FKF: There would be ways to make it clear that this is a blood brother, but that's not what's used by Luke when he writes, "Your brothers and mother are outside waiting for You."

Annunciation Church
Minneapolis, MN

DRG: In the <u>Greek</u> the word *adelphos* is *brother* and, of course, that does mean blood brother. But the counter argument is this: Everywhere the word *brother* appeared in the Old Testament, the translators used the Greek *adelphos* by default.

Yet, there's more evidence that Mary stayed a virgin, besides the fact that all the early Church Fathers said she stayed a virgin. If we had time — well maybe we do have time — I'm going to quote some of the reformers, in a minute.

First this is Augustine, one of the early Church Fathers.

> Surely, Mary would not say, "How shall this be?" (Remember when the angel said, "You'll conceive?") unless she had already vowed herself to God as a virgin. If she intended to have intercourse, she wouldn't have asked the question." (Augustine, *On Holy Virginity*, 4)

Augustine logically looked at this issue and writes, 'If she says 'how can this be,' when she's obviously going to get married, the angel could say, "Mary, you're going to get married, and that's what happens when people get married. They have kids."

FKF: He could have said, "You're going to have a relationship with your husband."

DRG: Now, here's Luther:

> Christ our Savior was the real and natural fruit of Mary's virginal womb. This was without the cooperation of a man and she remained a virgin after that. (Martin Luther, *Sermons on John*, Chapters 1-4, 1539; LW, Vol. XXII, p. 23. Also cf: *That Jesus Christ Was Born a Jew*, 1523, LW, Vol. 45, 199ff)

Calvin wrote,

ADELPHOS

Adelphos [singular] & Adelphoi [plural]: These terms for "brother" or "brethren" are used in the New Testament over 300 times, and refer not only to blood relationships, but about half the time refer to close friends and associates. For example, in 1 John 2:7 the Apostle addresses his letter to the "brethren" (adelphoi). In Colossians 1:2 Paul refers to "saints and faithful brethren" (adelphos). And in Acts 22:13 Luke uses adelphos when telling the story of Ananias's healing of Paul's blindness, "Saul, my brother (adelphos), regain your sight." These are not blood relationships.

Helvitius has shown himself to be ignorant in saying that Mary had several sons because mention is made in some passages of the brothers of Christ. (John Calvin, *Harmony*, Vol. 2 / From Calvin's Commentaries, Tr. William Pringle, Grand Rapids, MI: Eerdmans, 1949, 215; on Matthew 13:55.)

And I could go on and on.

Remember the women at the cross, at the foot of the cross? There are three places where they are identified. If you look across those passages, you will find that Simon and Joseph, identified as the "brothers" of Jesus, are actually sons of Mary, the wife of Cleopas. And Jude, I believe, was also the son of Mary, the wife of Cleopas.

FKF: Right.

DRG: Okay, one more question. Mary objectors will say:

> *Scripture claims Mary had no relations with Joseph <u>until</u> the birth of her son. There's that word <u>until</u>. What are you going to do with that?*

FKF: The word "until" does not mean that after the birth of Christ Mary had relations with Joseph. If someone says:

> *Father Fete, you're not going to get paid a million dollars until you strike it rich.*

St. Joseph's Baraboo, WI

Well, when you strike it rich you still may not have a million dollars. There's no guarantee there.

DRG: The verse I love for the word *until* is 2 Samuel, chapter 6 where it says:

> *And so Saul's daughter Michal was childless <u>until</u> the day of her death.* (2 Samuel 6:23)

FKF: So, I guess after she died she had kids.

DRG: Of course, a lot of times kids will do that to you. I have ten of them, and I'm pretty close to comatose myself.

Okay, I have to ask a couple more questions about Mary, and again, this is just to dispel these ideas that we Catholics give her too much status. Non-Catholics will claim:

She takes away from Christ. Your theology might be that she's not to be worshipped, and your theology might have Scripture verses, but the fact of the matter is Mary takes away from Christ.

Respond.

FKF: Mary doesn't take away from Christ, <u>Mary points to Christ</u>. One of the great forms of art we have in the Church are the icons. If you look at the icons closely, the eyes are considered the windows of the soul. What's interesting is that in most icons, Mary holds Jesus— they're not separate usually, they're together.

DRG: **On her lap, right?**

FKF: Yes.

DRG: **The Ark of the Covenant. That image of *on the Ark -- on the seat*.**

FKF: And some icons show Christ <u>within</u> Mary, *in the Ark*.

DRG: **How far back do these icons go?**

FKF: They go back to the early centuries of the Church. But what you notice in the icons is that the direct eye contact is seldom seen with Mary. The direct eye contact that the

St. Mark's Episcopal Pro-Cathedral Hastings, NE

viewer has is with Jesus. And Mary is looking <u>at</u> Jesus. The reason it's painted that way is that if you look at Mary, you're going to look at what Mary looks at. <u>Mary is the one that leads you to look at Christ</u>.

DRG: **Always pointing to her Son.**

FKF: Yes, <u>always</u> pointing to her Son.

DRG: **Do whatever He tells you.**

FKF: Right.

DRG: I think you used the example of the artist who paints a magnificent picture, and people want to just stare at the artist. The artist is saying:

> No, no, no! I painted this picture to look at. Look at Mary. She's beautiful. She's spotless. She's the carrier of the God-man.

And people are saying:

> No, no, no. I don't want to look at your beautiful picture. I just want to stare at the artist.

So you would then say that even though some Catholics might get carried away...

FKF: Yes, there are those. We've got to be cautious of them.

DRG: And again, people can get carried away and misunderstand any point of teaching, can't they?

FKF: Oh sure. You see it in our own lives. You can look at someone who's your minister, your pastor and say, "Oh, I just love him. He's so great." Well, no matter how good he is, no matter how great he is, he pales in comparison to Jesus Christ Himself. And, we understand no matter how great Mary is, she, too, pales in comparison to Jesus. But that doesn't mean that we reduce how great <u>she</u> is or how much we love <u>her</u>. To do so would be an insult to Christ Himself. That's His mom you're talking about.

DRG: "Honor thy father and mother." He carried out the law perfectly.

FKF: Sure, and we as followers of Christ follow His example. We should carry out the law too, and honor His mother.

DRG: All generations ...

FKF: Shall call me blessed.

DRG: Who are the only people now who really call her blessed?

FKF: The two most ancient of Christian traditions—the Orthodox and the Catholic Church—are those who still adhere to the position of the Scripture and call Mary blessed.

DRG: There is an *end of story* to that convert to the faith who said his three main roadblocks were Mary, Mary, Mary.

FKF: Yes?

DRG: He said once he got into the Church, he realized that <u>Mary</u> helped him <u>understand</u> and <u>worship</u> and be <u>devoted to Christ</u> at a level more deep than anything he'd ever experienced.

(to audience) I'm Ray Guarendi. I'm a psychologist, lay member of the Catholic Church. With me, Pastor Kevin Fete. We could talk about Mary for months and just scratch the surface of the history and the theology and the understanding. But we attempted to do our best to give you a very briefest thumbnail of sketches on what the Catholic Church teaches and believes and why, about our Lord's Mother.

Thank you for joining us. We will be back, God willing. Walk with God. Hold your kids real tight by the hand, too.

Como Park Lutheran
St. Paul, MN

Episode 10 Study Questions

Some non-Catholics claim:

A - We should not pray to Mary or the saints because they can't hear us and there's nothing in Scripture that indicates we should pray to her or the saints.

1. What two categories of people does the phrase "communion of saints" refer to in the Apostle's Creed?

2. For each of the following Scriptures, describe the evidence of saints in heaven praying for and being aware of us – (a) Revelation 5:8, (b) Luke 15:7, (c) Hebrews 12:1.

3. What two early Church Fathers taught that saints in heaven pray for us?

B - There is only ONE mediator between God and man and that is Jesus Christ.

4. How does praying to Mary or any of the saints in heaven <u>preserve</u> the belief that Jesus Christ is the only mediator between God and us? Describe what Mary is and is not when we pray to her.

5. How is asking a friend to pray for us the same as asking a saint in heaven to pray for us?

C - Catholics make too big a deal out of Mary. There is very little about Mary in the Bible.

6. Draw parallels between the Old Testament's *Ark of the Covenant* and Mary as *Ark of the New Covenant*, as described in 2 Samuel 6:9 & Luke 1:43.

   • What was inside the Ark and what was inside of Mary?

   • Where in Israel was the Ark taken by David, and where did Mary go in Luke 1?

   • How long was the Ark in Obededom's house, and how long was Mary at Elizabeth's?

   • How similar was David's behavior and John the Baptist's behavior when the ark or Mary arrived?

7. How does John, writing in Revelation, compare the Ark and Mary? Begin with Revelation 11:19 and continue through Revelation 12:18.

D - Mary was just a vehicle that God used to bring Jesus to Earth. She does not otherwise play a significant role in God's plan of salvation.

8. How did the early Church Father Irenaeus compare Eve and Mary?

9. What is the common title given by Moses to Eve in Genesis 3:15, and what is the common title given to Mary by Jesus in John 2:4, John 19:26, and then multiple times by John in Revelation chapter 12?

10. What were Mary's last words as recorded in Scripture, and to whom was she referring? (John 2:5)

11. To whom does Mary point to as the person to obey? (John 2:5)

12. Of the 300 plus instances of angels appearing to humans in Scripture, which one does an angel address with esteemed favor and unique honor?

E - Mary could not have been a virgin all her life, because the Bible clearly says that Jesus had brothers and sisters.

13. In Mark 6:3 and Luke 8:19-20 the terms for "brother" and "sister" could be translated into contemporary English how — thus indicating that Jesus had no blood brothers or sisters from Mary?

14. What is St. Augustine's argument that Mary had pledged herself to perpetual virginity even before Gabriel came to her as told in Luke 1?

15. What did Martin Luther claim about Mary's perpetual virginity?

16. How did John Calvin describe the intellect of those who claimed Mary had sons and daughters other than Jesus?

17. In Matthew 1:25 it says that Joseph had no relations with Mary until she bore a son. Provide a good argument for why the word "until" does not mean Mary <u>must have had</u> relations with Joseph after Jesus was born.

F - Catholics may claim that they do not worship Mary, but what they do with Mary takes away from Christ's importance.

18. What pictorial evidence in religious art is there that Mary is always pointing to Jesus?

19. What logical argument indicates that admiration of a created artwork reflects the greatness of the artist?

20. Is it possible that some Catholics get carried away and elevate Mary to equal Jesus? Does their error distort what the Church teaches about Mary?

21. How does Mary's "greatness" compare to the greatness of Jesus Christ?

22. If Christ perfectly followed the commandment to honor his father and mother, how should we follow his example?

23. What two Christian Churches still adhere to the Scriptural invitation to call Mary "Blessed?" (Luke 1:48)

"I give you the keys to the Kingdom of Heaven..."

Blue Cloud Abbey
Marvin, SD

11. St. Peter

DRG: (to audience) In this series, we are talking about common misperceptions, erroneous ideas that folks, Catholic and non-Catholic alike, have about the Catholic Church. We are also offering the reasons historically, Biblically, logically, for why the Church has taught these things for two thousand years.

(to Fr. Fete.) St. Peter. Well, you're not St. Peter—didn't want to confuse you, Father.

FKF: I'm not confused. Sure, let's talk about St. Peter.

DRG: St. Peter is one that we revere as Catholics, a saint we revere very much. We recognize that he had great authority and pre-eminence in the Church.

If we're going to establish how important St. Peter is, let me ask you: Do you know how many times his name is mentioned in Scripture, in the New Testament, and who is mentioned second most often, and how many times?

FKF: Well, Peter is by far mentioned the most. I think around 170 times.

DRG: That's pretty good.

FKF: Give or take some.

DRG: That's pretty good. You just kind of conjured that number up?

FKF: Lucky guess?

DRG: Lucky guess. The answer is 195.

FKF: I was a little shy.

DRG: You know who's second?

FKF: Well, the Apostle that Jesus loved most, which would have been John.

DRG: Right. John is mentioned 29 times, and Peter is mentioned 195 times in Scripture. Peter is mentioned 60% of the time that all Apostles are mentioned.

FKF: And then the other 11 make up for the 40% that's left.

DRG: **All right, who is listed first when all the Apostles are listed in Scripture?**

FKF: Peter. Always listed number one.

DRG: **Who's listed last?**

FKF: Judas.

DRG: **Very good. Now, the phrase, "Peter and the twelve" is mentioned several times in Scripture, which suggests that Peter represents the unity of the Apostles.**

FKF: That's right.

DRG: **And that sets up some interesting facts about this unique Apostle. Who is the only Apostle to get his name changed?**

FKF: Peter.

Now there are some that will question that. But there's a difference in just going from a Roman name to a Hebrew name.

DRG: **Like Paul to Saul or Matthew to Levi, but that's not —**

FKF: …an actual change of name to show a difference in the <u>meaning of your existence</u>. That would be Peter.

*St. Joseph's
Hammond, IN*

DRG: **Who is the only one given the keys of the kingdom?**

FKF: Peter.

DRG: **Who is the one given the vision that the Gentiles should be admitted into the Church?**

FKF: Peter.

DRG: **Who is the one who walked on water?**

FKF: Peter alone.

DRG: **Who is the one who gave the first sermon, the first homily to the masses after the Resurrection?**

FKF: Peter.

DRG: From whose boat did Christ preach to the crowds?

FKF: Peter's.

DRG: Who was the first Apostle to enter Jesus' tomb after the Resurrection?

FKF: Uh — Peter.

DRG: Who determined the course of the Jerusalem council [Acts 15]?

FKF: Again, Peter.

DRG: Father, I have an article that provides 50 similar New Testament proofs for the pre-eminence of Peter. You and I could go on forever.

FKF: When you talk about Peter, one of the great places in Scripture that shows the respect given to Peter by the other Apostles is on the day of the Resurrection. You remember Peter and John are racing to the tomb?

DRG: John was the younger guy, so he got there first.

FKF: Peter's older. Peter's winded on this deal.

DRG: He had to take a cab.

FKF: That probably would have been me. But he still would have run a little slow.

DRG: Have somebody get oxygen for Peter.

> **LOCUS CLASSICUS**
> Latin for "the definitive passage" or proof.

FKF: That's right. What's interesting is that John outruns him. John was very close to Jesus. John gets to the tomb first, and the Bible says he stops, and he waits. In all his enthusiasm, in all his excitement, he still stops and waits and lets Peter go in first. That Peter is the one who is to experience the Resurrection before anyone else shows this clear sense of respect for the primacy of Peter even in the fullness of Scriptures.

DRG: Let's go to some of those verses.

For Catholics the *locus classicus* would be Matthew, chapter 16, verses 15 and 18. I'll read this to you, and then you comment.

> *[Jesus] said to them, "But who do you say that I am?" Simon Peter said in reply, "You are the Messiah, the Son of the living God." Jesus said to him in reply, "Blessed are you, Simon son of Jonah. For flesh and blood has not revealed this to you, but my heavenly Father. And so I say to*

you, you are Peter, and upon this rock I will build my church, and the
gates of the netherworld shall not prevail against it. (Matthew 16:15-18)

Notice the parallel in the words:

You are the Messiah, the Son of the living God

and

You are Peter, the Rock.

Then Jesus says,

I will give you the keys to
the kingdom of heaven.
Whatever you bind on earth
shall be bound in heaven; and
whatever you loose on earth
shall be loosed in heaven.
(Matthew 16:19)

That passage—verses 15-19—has
been debated endlessly by many
Protestants and Catholics. The
Catholics would say that is Jesus
telling Peter, "You're the foundation of
the Church. You're the Rock."

FKF: Right.

DRG: **I'm building my Church on this Rock.**

Our Lady of Perpetual Help
Kansas City, MO

FKF: Not just faith. A lot of people want to take the other approach and say the Rock
pertains to the <u>faith Peter was proclaiming</u>.

DRG: **Or, Jesus' confession or Jesus Himself.**

Interestingly enough, I was reading a number of Protestant commentators, and the more
modern ones are saying,

Hey look, in fact grammatically you have to say…

FKF: Rock is rock.

DRG: **Rock is rock, that's right. And their point would be,**

Hey look, Jesus <u>was</u> referring to Peter.

Where they would disagree is they would say,

> Yes, Peter was the rock upon whom Jesus established the Church, but there were no successors after that.

"That's it. <u>You</u> are the Rock, Peter. I'm giving <u>you</u> the authority." And then when Peter died, that <u>didn't</u> continue. Respond to that.

FKF: Well, first of all, it would be kind of bizarre to think that such an authority is given to the first generation with no expectation that it would continue past that generation, especially when Christ makes this promise that "the gates of hell will not prevail" against His Church. So why would He have this safeguard for His Church for the first generation…

DRG: Until Peter is gone.

FKF: And then all of a sudden say, "Well, you're on your own now. <u>We're not going to cover you</u> this way." If anything, you'd think it would have been the <u>opposite</u>. Because you'd say to yourself, "well, all the Apostles knew Jesus personally; therefore, you wouldn't have to single one out for leadership." They can all be great bearers of the witness. But once they start dying off, then you're going to need someone specifically put in charge.

That's an interesting concept, but the opposite of that is true. When all the witnesses are there, still Peter takes the level of primacy. There's this necessity that Peter has to lead the group. Note that it is Peter that the Father revealed Christ's identity to. Why didn't the Father reveal it to all twelve of the Apostles at the same time?

DRG: He said, "You've got the revelation. Blessed are you, Simon Bar Jonah."

FKF: That's right, not all the Apostles.

DRG: Also, "Bar Jonah" is in Aramaic. It means son of Jonah. And that's one of the arguments, that Jesus—99% of scholars believe—didn't speak in Greek. He spoke in Aramaic.

So, He would have said, "You are Cepha (Kepha/<u>Rock</u>), and on this Cepha (<u>Rock</u>), I will build my Church." There was only one word for "<u>rock</u>" in Aramaic; it was "Cepha."

FKF: What about the Greek?

DRG: In the Greek it reads a little different. "You are Rock, <u>Petros</u>, and on this Rock, Petra, I will build my Church." The argument there sometimes is,

> Jesus used two different words for Rock. One means a "big rock," one means a "little stone."

But in the Greek, <u>Petros</u> is the masculine.

FKF: And if you look at the word, too, one of the things that's a little more humorous was that St. Paul and St. Peter, theologically, were united. But there were times they had differences in viewing things. And, if you read one of the times Paul is talking about Peter, he specifically refers to Peter in a way that takes the word <u>rock</u> and implies that he's a <u>rock head</u>, meaning that Peter's a little hard-headed sometimes. So Paul plays on the words to do that.

But, the reason Paul would play on those words is because Paul understands when Christ was talking about Rock, <u>it was applying to Peter. It wasn't applying to the faith</u>. And so, even in that little sense of humor that Paul displays in his own writings, you see that even Paul knows when Jesus said, "You are Rock," He was talking Peter.

St. Peter and St. Paul
Holy Trinity Greek Orthodox
New Rochelle, NY

DRG: When Jesus gave the power to bind and loose, Peter was the only one that He gave that power to by name. Although a couple chapters later in Matthew, Christ does give that authority to all the Apostles.

FKF: Yes, He gave it to all the Apostles…

DRG: …but <u>first</u>, and <u>by name</u> He gives it to Peter. He says what you bind will be bound in heaven and what you loose will be loosed in heaven. That is a very technical, <u>rabbinical way of saying…</u>

FKF: Authority.

DRG: You've got My authority. You're going to be the one in charge. I'm going to give you <u>My authority</u>. My authority to teach, My authority to reprove, My authority to forgive sins, My authority to preach.

FKF: That's right. "You speak for me now." The term we would use in the Catholic Church is the "Vicar of Christ" for the "Pope." In this sense the Vicar of Christ is the person who's sent as <u>Christ's ambassador</u>. This is the person who now does the speaking for Christ and he'll know what to say. Why? Because it's been revealed to him from the Father through the Holy Spirit.

DRG: Now, where'd this idea of the "keys" come from? Does that allude to anything? Peter's the <u>only</u> one who got the keys.

FKF: That's right, and that's what differentiates Matthew 18:18 from what you find
       back in the other passage that you started with (Matthew 16:15-18). Matthew 18
       is dealing with the confrontation and confession of sins within the Church:

> *Amen, I say to you, whatever [sins] you bind on earth shall be bound in*
> *heaven, and whatever [sins] you loose on earth shall be loosed in heaven.*
> *(Matthew 18:18)*

This passage is set off from Matthew 16 where the keys are given to Peter.

A lot of people say, "Well, the keys and the loosening and binding are together."
But for some reason <u>when it comes to all the Apostles, the loosening and binding
is not included with the keys</u>. Only where Christ is talking to Peter about the
loosening and binding are the keys also mentioned.

By the way, the keys are something that comes out of the Old Testament.

DRG: **Isaiah.**

FKF: Isaiah 22 is where you start to get the sense of what the keys represent. It's
       the idea of who has the power to <u>open up</u> the home or <u>close</u> the home. Who's
       been given authority over one finding salvation
       in the sense of being "let in" from the cruelness
       of the world into the security of the Kingdom, as
       opposed to who will be shut out from the security
       of the Kingdom.

> *I will place the Key of the House of David on*
> *his shoulder; when he opens, no one shall shut,*
> *when he shuts, no one shall open.*
> *(Isaiah 22:22)*

St. Margaret Mary's
Omaha, NE

DRG: **It's interesting because that passage was around the
       time of King Hezekiah, and there was a very unworthy
       prime minister, a guy named Shebna. The Lord essentially
       said,**

> *No, you're not going to be prime minister anymore. You're gone, and*
> *we're going to give it over to Hilkiah. He will have the keys, and what he*
> *opens, no one can shut and what he shuts, no one can open. (paraphrase*
> *Isaiah 22:15-25)*

**That was a very common structure of government, especially in the Davidic Kingdom,
which says they're ministers—the Apostles are ministers—you're the <u>prime</u> minister,
Peter. You can actually overrule what they say, or you can let go what they say.**

So, the Keys were passed on. Or did they just stop with the prime minister?

FKF: Oh no, the Keys will <u>always</u> be passed on, especially if you take the literal use of the Keys in the Old Testament. Certainly the necessity is that you passed them on to the next generation. There has to be a worthy successor upon whom you confer this responsibility, because he has this authority now that comes in the Church. As Peter passes on, this responsibility immediately goes to the next guy. And I think, the next one was Clement? Was he the second?

DRG: **Early Church Fathers, Augustine and Eusebius, said the second pope was Linus, then Anacletus, and then Clement was fourth.**

FKF: Fourth, Okay.

DRG: **I wish I would have brought it in, but my wife has this poster...**

FKF: …with the whole history of the papacy?

DRG: **...265 of the Popes.**

FKF: Sorry, I don't have them memorized.

DRG: **You don't have them memorized? I got the first 174, and then I started to get confused about which one was John XXI and John XXII.**

FKF: Ahh, I can get John Paul the second and John Paul the first but back from that, I get lost.

DRG: **The whole idea of the Keys, then, for the Catholic Church would be that <u>Our Lord established Peter as the foundation</u>.**

FKF: Correct.

DRG: **Now in another place, in Revelation, chapter 3 verse 7, Jesus says, "I have the keys."**

> …write this: "The holy one, the true, who holds the key of David, who opens and no one shall close, who closes and no one shall open, says this:…" (Revelation 3:7)

Which is fascinating, because He's giving <u>those Keys then to Peter</u>. Jesus says, "Now <u>you</u> have the Keys," especially after the Resurrection, "You'll have the Keys."

"And, you can pass those Keys on. You're the Rock. I'm going to build My Church on this Rock." And, again to reiterate, even <u>most modern Protestant scholars say</u>,

> You really have to mess up the passage to say that the Rock was anything but Peter.

FKF: Peter, uh huh.

DRG: **So, let's just simply say that Peter has this pre-eminence according to that passage. Let's look at another couple of passages. This is Luke, chapter 22, verse 20. I think I know it by heart.**

> *Jesus said to Simon Peter, "Simon, son of John, do you love me more than these?" He said to him, "Yes, Lord, you know that I love you." He said to him, "Feed my lambs."*
>
> *He then said to him a second time, "Simon, son of John, do you love me?" He said to him, "Yes, Lord, you know that I love you." He said to him, "Tend my sheep."*
>
> *He said to him the third time, "Simon, son of John, do you love me?" Peter was distressed that He had said to him a third time, "Do you love me?" and he said to him, "Lord, you know everything; you know that I love you." (Jesus) said to him, "Feed My sheep." (John 21:15-17*

FKF: Right on.

DRG: **What's He doing there, Father?**

FKF: There are a couple of different interpretations. Some would say that the questioning of Peter three times of "Do you love me?" is to make up for the three times Christ was denied by Peter on the night Christ was arrested.

St. Peter's Cathedral
Kansas City, KS

But others would say that if you look at the Greek language, there are different words for love. And those words are very important, because there's the love you have for friends, there's the love you have…

DRG: *Philia.* The Greek word for "love of friends," right?

FKF: Friendship love, or the brotherly kind of love.

Then you get into *agape* love. Agape would be the <u>kind of love God has</u> for us. And *eros* would be the sense of <u>love you'd have for your spouse</u>, the person that you want to create new life with.

Queen of Peace
Cloquet, MN

DRG: A sensual love.

FKF: Yes. So you have these different terms for love. If you read the Greek, what's interesting is that Jesus doesn't ask the exact same <u>question</u> each time. Jesus is asking questions like, "Do you love me as a friend? Do you love me as a brother?"

DRG: Do you *agape* me? Do you spiritually love me? And Peter's responding with, "You know I *philia*, you," at first. Which is a kind of a friendly, brotherly sort of love.

FKF: What you have there is that Peter is uniquely questioned by Jesus as, "<u>Peter</u>, are you the one <u>Apostle</u> who loves Me in every way that I should be loved?" And Peter shows the depth and the breadth of his love in the answering of those questions and shows himself to be the one that Jesus has the most confidence in. Jesus doesn't have confidence in Peter because Peter's always the <u>brightest</u> guy or because Peter's always the most diplomatic.

No, Peter is the one who is constantly having to call himself back to a spirit of humility. And yet Jesus sees in him this love on all levels that always brings Peter back to be open to <u>allowing God to guide</u> what he's going to do. He trusts that Peter isn't going to go out and set his own agenda and go start his own church or do things the way he wants them personally.

DRG: And, in this passage, Jesus commissioned him. He said, "Take care of My flock." I think the Greek word there for "tend" essentially almost means <u>govern, rule over them</u>.

FKF: Right.

DRG: Administer, take care of this, you're the big guy. You touched on a quote by G.K. Chesterton, the great Catholic apologist. He said,

When Christ at a symbolic moment was establishing his great society, he chose for it's cornerstone neither the brilliant Paul, nor the mystic John, but a shuffler, a snob, a coward – in a word, a man. And upon this rock he has built his Church, and the gates of hell have not prevailed against it. All the empires and the kingdoms have failed because of this inherent and continual weakness that they were founded by strong men; and upon strong men. But the historic Christian Church was founded on a weak man and for this reason it is indestructible. For no chain is stronger than its weakest link. (G.K. Chesterton, *Heretics*, IV)

Jesus was basically saying, Peter, I know what you are, and I choose you.

FKF: And, "<u>You</u> know what you are."

DRG: It wasn't because of Peter's holiness. It was because Christ said I will protect you and, in succession, the Church.

FKF: It's a reminder to us Catholics that a Pope does not have to be a perfect person. A Pope does not have to be someone who is not without character flaws. What <u>protects</u> us from error in the ways of the faith is not the character of the individual but the <u>guidance of the Holy Spirit</u>.

DRG: Well, Father, consider what our Lord told Peter and the Apostles:

> *What you bind on earth will be bound in heaven, what you loose on earth will be loosed in heaven.*

Trinity First Lutheran
Minneapolis, MN

Logically, Christ has to protect His Church, because if He doesn't, you've got men who will be binding goofy things and loosing goofy things. And I can picture God saying up there, "Moses, you know what they concocted now? Now look what I'm bound to." So it would mean that Jesus, in fact, would have to protect His Church; otherwise, they could teach wrong things.

FKF: Which would be counter to the nature of Christ, who is the Way, the Truth and the Life. And One who is the Truth, when He is going to promise that the Truth will be continued throughout the ages, can't set people up with authority to tell the non-truth.

DRG: He has to protect them.

FKF: He has to <u>protect the Truth</u>. He has to <u>guide them in matters of faith</u> and in <u>matters of morals</u>. You see that as you read the Scriptures, which we're going to get into in a little bit in Acts -- the whole issue of circumcision and whether or not that has to happen to be a Christian. What you see is the human Peter with his idea, "Well, you know circumcision is the law. Maybe new Christians should be circumcised." Paul, on the other side, is out there with the Gentiles saying, "Hey, this is nuts! We've got guys that are 40 years old converting to the faith. This ain't going over big."

DRG: **Circumcision is a bit of a roadblock here.**

FKF: This is not on top of the list for people. So what you have is this whole dialogue about it. You have the human Peter and certain prejudices that he brings. He was raised as a person of the Jewish community. He loves the laws of the faith that he was raised in. He doesn't want to cast that aside. So he's tempted to go that way. Yet the interesting thing is, even though people recognize his own personal decisions, what they also realize is he's the leader. And so, whom do they turn to when they convene the Council of Jerusalem?

DRG: **Peter. And after he spoke, it says they were silent, and the debate ended.**

FKF: Right. And what's amazing is that, the view Peter expresses <u>isn't</u> his personal view. The view he expresses is what God calls him to. And that's

St. Mary's Church
Michigan City, IN

what Jesus promised would happen. When he's officially together with the council, when he's speaking officially as the leader of the community, he doesn't mess it up.

DRG: **We need to remember that it's not just Peter, but the Holy Spirit working through him as well as the other Apostles. In Acts 15, verse 8 Peter invokes the holy Spirit, and later the whole council writes:**

> *It seemed good to the Holy Spirit and to us to lay no further burden*
> *upon you. (Acts 15:28 paraphrase)*

DRG: He didn't say, "Well, you know, I checked Scripture, and the Old Testament says very clearly, you have to be circumcised. Genesis 12, it's an everlasting covenant." Peter said, "No, by my authority, guided by the Holy Spirit..." It's the first instance we have of Church government starting to work.

FKF: Yes, this is the first example of the way the Church would work. All of the Apostles are important, so councils are convened <u>with all of them present</u>. Yet, the <u>primacy</u> of whoever is the Bishop of Rome is here. A lot of people just think this is all confined to Jerusalem at that time. But, when you get to the history told about in Acts, we see that different Apostles are covering different territories. And for some reason, it is the one with Rome who takes control and has leadership. We'll look at that later as we look at the Papacy in history.

DRG: Okay, you have two problems. In our little bit of time left, you're going to have to give us a brief answer.

FKF: Okay.

DRG: Galatians, Paul says,

> *I stood up to Peter. I told Peter, "You're leaving, and you're not eating*
> *with the Gentiles here. What are you doing? You said that they don't*
> *have to be circumcised. And now the Judaizers are coming in, and*
> *you're not hanging around with the Gentiles." And Paul said, "I told*
> *him." (Galatians 2:11-14, paraphrased)*

Some people read this Scripture and say, "See, Peter can't have authority, because Paul stood up to him." Answer?

FKF: Again, sometimes discretion is the better part of valor. Even Paul himself has on argument about the meat, because it's sacrificed to idols. Really it isn't sacrificed to anything because the idols aren't real. Therefore, you <u>can</u> eat it, but <u>don't</u> eat it, because of how it's going to look.

DRG: In Acts 16, Luke tells the story about how Paul had Timothy circumcised because Timothy was working among the Jews. You could say to him, "Hey Paul, you yelled at Peter for that."

FKF: "You're doing the same thing." Sometimes it's not a matter of your theology, but a matter of diplomacy.

DRG: Plus, I also think Paul was angry because Peter acted hypocritically, not because he didn't have the authority.

FKF: Again, you can look at the humanity of Peter, find fault with him and make a statement about it. But you cannot look at Peter when it comes to things that are doctrinal and say he messed up. You <u>never</u> see any mess-ups when it comes to actual teaching.

DRG: Jesus will protect for all eternity what His Church teaches to keep it free from error -- in matters of faith and morals.

FKF: Faith and morals.

DRG: We have the briefest of moments. One last stumbling block for a lot of folks: Right after Jesus gives Peter the keys and calls him a rock, He says, "Get thee behind me, Satan." Remember when Peter says, "I'm not going to let you go to Jerusalem and get killed. They're going to kill you there." And Jesus says, "Get behind me, Satan?" People say,

> *Peter couldn't have been so important if Jesus is calling him Satan.*

> *Then Peter took him aside and began to rebuke him, "God forbid, Lord! No such thing shall ever happen to you." He turned and said to Peter, "Get behind me, Satan! You are an obstacle to me. You are thinking not as God does, but as human beings do." (Matthew 16:22-23)*

In the interest of television, you have one minute.

FKF: You get right back to what we started to talk about just a minute ago. When Peter is speaking on God's behalf, his thoughts and words are directed by God. Remember, Jesus had said to Peter, "No mere man has revealed this to you."

When Peter gets off on his own little human track, he goes back to the Jewish sense of what the Messiah was. And as a result, he's clinging to this old sense that this person can't suffer now. Out of his own personal thoughts, he starts to take offense to what Jesus is saying, and he says to Jesus, "You can't do it," because his personal emotions are taking over. He loves Jesus. He doesn't want this happening to him. So again, it's the person, Peter, prone to his human weakness, who has Jesus saying, "Hey, you're not looking at this as God does now; you're looking at it as man does."

DRG: The person Peter.

FKF: Right, the person Peter. But that's not what we teach as the Primacy of the Papacy.

DRG: (to audience) Next time we get together here on "What Catholics Really Believe," we will logically follow this up. What does this pre-eminence of Peter mean for the history of the Church? How does this relate to the Papacy? We will talk about why Catholics have a Pope, where it comes from Scripturally and historically. Did our Lord establish it? Were there bad Popes? And what does that mean?

I'm Ray Guarendi. With me has been Pastor Kevin Fete. Thank you for being with us. Walk with God.

The Crucifixion of St. Peter

Notre Dame Church
Beaune, France

Episode 11 Study Questions

A - In the New Testament Church Peter wasn't any more important than any of the other Apostles.

1. How many times is the Apostle Peter mentioned by name in the New Testament and how many times is the next most often mentioned Apostle?

2. Who is the first Apostle called by Jesus? Who is his brother that was called at the same time? (Matthew 4:18, Mark 1:16, Luke 5, John 1:42)

3. From whose boat did Christ preach to the crowds? (Luke 5:3)

4. When the Apostles are listed by name as a group who is always listed first? (Matthew 17:1, Mark 3:16, Luke 6:14, John 21:2, Acts 1:13)

5. Who is the only Apostle to have his name changed by Jesus to show a difference in the person's status? What was his old name and what was his new name? (John 1:42, Matthew 16:18)

6. Who is the only Apostle to walk on water? How many times does this Apostle jump out of a boat (which represents the Church) as recorded in the Gospels? (Matt 14:29, John 21)

7. Who is the only Apostle given the keys to the Kingdom by Jesus, and what do the keys represent? (Matthew 16:16-19, Isaiah 22:22, Revelation 3:7)

8. When Christ was arrested, all of the Apostles disappear except John and another Apostle, whom the Gospel writers follow and describe in some detail his denial of Christ and his repentance. Who is it, and why do you think all four Gospel accounts include detail about it? (Matthew 26:69-75, Mark 14:66-72, Luke 22:31-34, 22:54-65, John 18:15-18, 18:25-27)

9. When Mary of Magdala found the empty tomb, whom did she first tell? (John 20:2)

10. Although he was not the first Apostle to arrive, who first enters the empty tomb of Jesus, and who was with him? (John 20:6)

11. Jesus only asked one Apostle to feed the lambs and sheep of the early Church. Who did Jesus ask, how many times, and where did it occur? (John 21:15ff)

12. Who led the Apostles in selecting a successor to Judas, and who was elected? (Acts 1:15f)

13. Who is the first Apostle to preach as an evangelist and lead about 3,000 into the Church? As part of what event did this happen? (Acts 2:14-41)

14. Who was the only Apostle given the vision that Gentiles should be admitted into the Church? Describe the vision. (Acts 10)

15. What Apostle was the first to perform a healing, and whom did he heal? (Acts 3:7)

16. Who determined the course of the Jerusalem council, and how? (Acts 15:7-11)

B - The rock upon which Jesus established the Church is Peter's faith not on Peter.

17. Does Jesus give the power to "bind and loose" to "faith" or to "Peter?"

18. What is the logical argument that Peter's authority to bind and loose <u>was</u> passed down to successors and did not stop with Peter?

19. Explain what other situation points directly to Peter as the one person in authority after Christ's Resurrection? (John 21:15ff)

20. In Galatians 2:11-14, Paul makes a point of confronting Peter. What does Paul call Peter in that passage that reinforces what Catholics say is happening in Matthew 16:18-19?

21. What is the significant difference between Christ passing on authority to the Apostles in Matthew 16:18-19 and 18:18-19? To whom is Jesus addressing his words in these two passages?

22. What is going on in Isaiah 22:22 and Revelations 3:7, the two Biblical passages that use the concept of a "key" as a sign of authority?

C - Peter denied Christ three times, how could Jesus trust Peter to lead the Church?

23. In John 21:15-19 what happens between Jesus and Peter that reinforces Peter's call to lead the Church, even after Peter's denial?

24. In John 21:15-19 what are synonyms for the words "feed" and "tend" that suggest Peter was to lead the Church?

D - Popes cannot lead the Church because they are not perfect, like Christ

25. Why is Peter's human weakness evidence that the Church was established by Christ and not by man?

26. What or who protects the Church from making doctrinal errors of faith and morals?

27. Because Peter was fallible as a human, where did he mess up in terms of establishing authoritative doctrine?

Benedict XV (1854-1922)

12. The Papacy

DRG: Today we are talking about the Papacy, something that sticks in the craw of an awful lot of folks, because they don't understand it, or they don't agree with it. They look at the Catholic Church and see it as an institution founded upon a man.

Fr. Fete, last show we talked about Peter, and we felt that we needed to show how our Lord viewed Peter. Can you recap a little bit?

FKF: I think one of the things that we made very clear last time is that when you look at the Sacred Scriptures, Peter takes primacy: The number of times he is mentioned compared to the disciples, the fact that he is the one who is given the task of revealing that Jesus <u>is</u> the Messiah, the Son of the Living God. He's the one that walks on the water. He's the one that is the first to go into the tomb to see that Jesus has been raised from the dead…

DRG: He's the one to tend the sheep. He's the one that presides over the Council of Jerusalem. He's the one who lets the Gentiles into the Church by his proclamation. He's at the top of every listing of the Apostle's names in Scripture. He's everywhere. If this were a show, he'd be the star.

FKF: Right, and he is always looked at as the leader. The other Apostles, and even Paul, certainly show him respect as being the authority figure that you go to before some major decisions are made.

DRG: So he's not just,

> Well, hey, that's Peter and he's — we're all equal,
> and we sort of give a little nod in his direction
> -- but maybe he's a tad bit more equal.

It's not like that?

FKF: No, and one of the things that was real crucial to our discussion last time was what Jesus Christ Himself said. Jesus says,

> *Peter, you're a Rock. Upon this Rock I build my Church.*
> *(Matthew 16:18)*

Then saying,

> *Whatever* <u>*you*</u> *hold bound or hold loose will be bound or loosed.*
> *(Matthrews 16:19)*

We know that's something that's given to <u>Peter in an authoritative way</u>. And something that you don't see given anywhere else to any of the Apostles are the <u>Keys</u> to the Kingdom; they are given <u>exclusively to Peter</u>.

DRG: **Keys, authority, prime minister. Isaiah 22 is clearly where in the Davidic Kingdom there was a head man, the <u>prime</u> minister who was over the other cabinet ministers.**

FKF: Right.

> *I will place the key of the House of David on his shoulder; when he*
> *opens, no one shall shut, when he shuts, no one shall open.*
> *(Isaiah 22:22)*

DRG: **And one thing I'd like to touch upon a little bit more. In Scripture, when a name is changed, when God changes the name of one of His people in salvation history, like Abram changed to Abraham, what does that mean? Is it just kind of like, "Well I don't like my name, 'Raymond.' I think I'm going to change it to 'Ramon.' I want to go down to the courthouse and change my name." That's not what it meant in that culture, is it?**

FKF: No, even from the very beginning of Scripture, if you read Genesis, chapter 2 where people are given the charge of naming the animals, it gives a sense of, <u>in the Hebrew language</u>, the importance of names. <u>Names speak of the essence of something</u>. They're not just labels to identify something to make categorizing them easy.

> *So the Lord God formed out of the ground various wild animals and*
> *various birds of the air, and he brought them to the man to see what*
> *he would call them; whatever the man called each of them would be its*
> *name. (Genesis 2:19)*

DRG: **A name says who you are.**

FKF: <u>Your name is who you are at the core of your being</u>. And if you change your name, you are changing the whole essence of what your role on earth is. So, when Peter's name gets changed by Christ, and he gets called "Rock," it's this sense that, "you have been ordained by God to do this special thing."

DRG: To follow that up, did you know that when our Lord points to Peter and says, "You are the Rock," that archeologically there is no evidence of anybody else being called Peter up to that time. <u>He is the only person in Scripture, other than God, who is personally called Rock</u>.

FKF: Correct.

DRG: Which is fascinating. So, if our Lord said, "Peter's the Rock," if He gave Peter the keys, then what is the natural outgrowth of that? Does it end with Peter? Our Lord needed to establish the Church to get it going, of course. But after 20, 30, 40 years of momentum the Apostles die off and then what? Was everybody equal after that?

Pius X (1903-1914)
Our Lady's Basilica
L'Epine, France

FKF: We talked about that in the last show a little bit, that there's probably more need to have a leader post-death of the Apostles than pre-death of the Apostles. The Apostles all had this directly personal relationship with Jesus Christ Himself. They knew the Way, the Truth and the Life in the flesh. So it would be kind of ludicrous to say. Jesus would establish leadership when the Church is at its most solid state of existence, and yet when the original Apostles—who knew Jesus Christ personally—started to die, then He would leave no way for the Church to have some authority deriving from God—the revelation of what direction to go.

DRG: In terms of leadership, I find it fascinating that in the first chapter of Acts the Apostles replaced Judas.

> *Then they gave lots to them, and the lot fell upon Matthias, and he was counted with the eleven apostles. (Acts 1:26)*

They didn't say, "Now there are only 11 of us. Okay, we'll just do the best we can." It is Peter who spoke and said, "We must replace him." And so they handed on this authority given to Peter, too.

(Peter said,) *"Therefore, it is necessary that one of the men who accompanied us the whole time the Lord Jesus came and went among us, beginning from the baptism of John until the day on which he was taken up from us, become with us a witness to His Resurrection. (Acts 1:15, 21-22)*

DRG: So, Catholics believe that authority resides in the Bishop of Rome, the Pope, papa, father. But non-Catholics don't like that idea. And unfortunately, there are a lot of Catholics who don't like that idea. Their point is that:

Look, I'm going to follow the teachings of Jesus Christ. I'm <u>not</u> going to follow the teachings of some guy, especially one who's not married and who lives 6000 miles away.

Respond to that.

Benedict I (575-579)
St. Mary's, St. Benedict, KS

FKF: I think one of the things we have to remember is the nature of the Church. Consider the four marks of the Church—<u>one, holy, catholic,</u> and <u>apostolic</u>. Those are four terms that give us some great insight about why Christ founded this role of the Papacy to lead the Church — <u>to stay united as one body</u>.

We have a lot of people who say:

Well, I'm going to follow Jesus. I can interpret the Scriptures, I can do what I'm going to do, and I can do it with the guidance of the Spirit.

What's amazing is that so many people who are going to do what they're going to do, by "following the Spirit," <u>start their own congregation</u>. Then somebody else who's "following the Spirit" starts a different congregation because they disagree with the congregation that the Spirit started over there. It's almost as if the Holy Spirit must be <u>schizophrenic</u>, because we've got the Holy Spirit giving one set of directions to this group, another set of theology to that group, and a different teaching to yet another group. That really becomes problematic.

The result is the sense of the Church being <u>one</u> gets nullified very quickly when certain individuals think <u>on their own</u> that they can <u>assume the role</u> of being the authority figure of the community and to be holy. Again, we're prone as people to our own sense of "hearing from God," and we can limit the nature of the Church if we operate out of our own human desires. We see even how with Peter, when he's <u>on his own</u>, he's chastising Jesus, saying, "Oh, You can't go up there. They're going to kill You, Jesus." But to be holy means you have to be open to God, <u>and</u> you also have to have God open to you. So, <u>God specifically gave authority to the role of the person who follows in the steps of Peter, so that holiness can be taken care of</u>. Catholic …

DRG: **Meaning "universal."**

FKF: Universal, worldwide. If you're going to have anything worldwide that has the ability to stand together and to be able to continue, <u>it's got to have somewhere a unifying force</u>. Now we can all say that unifying force is the grace of God. But too often, because of the different ways denominations interpret the Bible and history, the grace of God gets communicated in a way that it can immediately have a separating effect on the people of God.

One of the things that is magnificent, about the Catholic Church, if you watch the Holy Father, is that <u>the Pope has the ability to unify the worldwide Church</u>. Under the Pope's leadership you have this "one, holy, catholic, and apostolic church."

DRG: **<u>Apostolic</u> means our roots go back all the way to the Apostles.**

FKF: Yes, back to the Apostles. Why would it be going back to the Apostles? Why would the Church need to be Apostolic? The reason is because <u>the Apostles, all of them, got their authority from Jesus Christ</u>.

DRG: **He breathed the Holy Spirit on them. He gave them the power to bind and loose. He said, "You've got My authority."**

FKF: One of the things we have to understand is, not just the importance of the role of the Pope, but of all the Apostles. All who are bishops today have <u>direct apostolic succession</u> to the original Apostles.

DRG: **You said that historically you can trace the succession of, say, the present bishop of the Youngstown, Ohio diocese, Bishop Tobin, all the way back to the Apostles?**

FKF: All the way back, yes. And there's a specific way of passing that authority on to the next generation.

DRG: **Yes, that's the question. Because other people would say:**

> Well, our Protestant churches have apostolic succession, too, because we are preaching the <u>pure</u> gospel.

But the Church would say, "No. This passing on of <u>authority</u> is through the laying on of the hands, which is very Scriptural." Paul talks about it. The Church, and only the Catholic (and Orthodox) Church, has practiced this for 2,000 years.

FKF: And when Matthias is brought in, you see there's a link. They don't just take anybody who's preaching the Word.

DRG: **And he's a smart guy.**

FKF: Yes, he is. He's well educated in the faith, and yet he doesn't just walk up and anoint himself the new Apostle. You don't have some guy named Chuck come out of the crowd and say:

> Hey, I'm Chuck. I'm pretty well read, went to Hebrew Union, understand this stuff pretty well, listened to Jesus, got it all down. Therefore, I'll be the next Apostle because I feel the Spirit called me.

That wasn't the way it worked. The way it worked was God called people to ministry, but it was <u>discerned through those who were already the Apostles</u>.

DRG: **In other words, the Apostles alone had the authority to pass on that authority.**

FKF: Right.

DRG: **If somebody broke off from them and said:**

> I don't agree with what you're teaching. I'm going to go over here. And since I, too, was given that authority, then I'm just going to give that authority to somebody else.

They couldn't do that.

FKF: Right. And the question is, how much authority do you really have? Myself as a priest—most people don't realize this—I am not a person who possesses the fullness of priesthood. To possess the fullness of priesthood you have to be a bishop. You have to be one of the successors of the Apostles.

DRG: **Direct line.**

FKF: Direct line. And you have to be a bishop because being a bishop gives you the ability to celebrate the fullness of the Church's life in the Sacraments. I do not have the authority to pass the line on.

DRG: Only the bishops?

FKF: Only the bishop does. Only a bishop can ordain the next person to serve as bishop or priest.

Boniface I (418-422)
St. Mary's
Kickapoo IL

DRG: And this is not the Catholic Church's concocted way to maintain its power grip. It is because it is being faithful to the way our Lord set things up in Scripture and as has been passed on through the ages.

FKF: Yes, it's part of the Church <u>being Apostolic</u>. The Church is Apostolic because this methodology of choosing the leadership of the faith community comes to us directly from the Apostles <u>who were chosen specifically by Christ</u> and given authority from Christ.

DRG: Now we need to clarify some of the common misconceptions about the Papacy. For example, well you know, <u>there were some bad popes</u>. There were popes who had mistresses. There were popes who were crooks. There were popes who may not even have loved Jesus. They were just purely in it for the power. And, fortunately, anybody who knows history knows, thank God, that of the 265 popes, that's only been a handful.

The vast majority of popes were very holy men. As a matter of fact, Father, I think 33 of the first 34 popes were martyred.

FKF: Put to death.

DRG: Now, if in fact you're a Roman, and you want to squash this new religion, you go after the head. They knew who to go after. They knew the Bishop of Rome was the pre-eminent figure.

FKF: Oh sure.

DRG: **So what about these bad popes?**

FKF: Well again, we even see in the Scripture with Peter that there is a tendency sometimes to cling to our human weakness rather than to avail ourselves of the fullness of God's grace. As a result of that, there are times when Peter isn't always making the right decisions.

DRG: **Like the time when he said, "I swear to God I don't know Him"?**

FKF: Yeah.

DRG: **I always use that example with people. I ask, "What would you say if you found out that in history there was a pope who came out publicly and said, "I swear that I am not a Christian, I don't know Jesus Christ, and I don't want to have anything to do with Him." And they say, "Well that would prove that pope is 'bad' for me." Then I say, "Well, you're talking about Peter."**

FKF: That's right. What's interesting, though, is that any time Peter is asked something personally, he is prone to either get it very right or very wrong on his own. Anytime he's asked something that is to be <u>prophetic</u>, something that is to be a <u>proclamation of faith</u>, he <u>never</u> misses it. He always gets it right.

DRG: **But that's <u>not</u> because he's so brilliant. Why is that?**

Athanasius & Pope Sylvester (314-335)
St. Joseph's, Baraboo, WI

FKF: That's because of the grace of God that is guiding the Pope and what the Pope is going to say. It fulfills what Christ said when He said to His Apostles that He would be "with you always," until the end of time, and that His Church would not have "the gates of hell prevail against it." (Matthew 16:18)

DRG: **Hold on a second. You said something that's real prone to misunderstanding.**

God is protecting the Pope in what he would say. Does that mean that the Pope can just make some proclamation on any matter—economics or government? Or, the Pope can come out and say:

> I think that in Scripture we need to add three more books. I think I'm inspired by God to say we need to add three more books, the book of Fate, spelled "Fete", and 1 and 2 Hesitations.

Can he do these things?

FKF: No, he can't. And that is one of the misconceptions -- that everything the Pope says is infallible.

DRG: **That's a misconception?**

FKF: It's a great misconception that everything the Pope says Catholics claim is infallible. That is <u>not</u> the teaching of the Church. That has <u>never</u> been the teaching of the Church. The Church teaching is, <u>when the Pope specifically chooses to make a proclamation *ex cathedra*, which means "from the Chair of Peter"</u>…

> **EX CATHEDRA**
> A doctrinal proclamation from the Chair of Peter, or the authority of the papacy.

DRG: **From the <u>Chair of Peter</u> …**

FKF: …and we'll get into that term "chair" in a little bit here, because I think it's a magnificent chair. But, when he makes a proclamation that he says will be infallible, and it specifically deals with matters of faith and matters of morals…

DRG: **…when he speaks to a deposit of the faith that Christ left His Church…**

FKF: That's right. He's saying, "This is an essential truth. This is the doctrine of the Church. This is from God." <u>That's when he is speaking infallibly</u>.

DRG: **And he can't change anything that has historically been taught "from the Chair of Peter" over the past 2000 years.**

FKF: Correct. Anything that's been taught <u>doctrinally</u> cannot be changed

DRG: **Doctrinally. But disciplines can change, of course.**

FKF: That's right. Disciplines and practices in the Church can change, but not doctrine.

DRG: So, in terms of the Pope coming out and saying, "Revelation is no longer closed. In fact, there may be five or six more books that we can add to the Bible. We're not sure. We're looking at it."

FKF: He can't do it.

DRG: He can't do it, and what if he would?

FKF: He wouldn't be able to.

DRG: So the Bishops, the worldwide Bishops in concert would simply say, "You can't do that?"

FKF: Well, he wouldn't be able to even …

DRG: He doesn't have the authority.

FKF: He doesn't have the authority, and the reality is there's been no pope in history that's ever tried.

DRG: That's fascinating.

FKF: There's never ever been a pope, no matter how bad he's been, no matter how evil he has been.

DRG: He didn't teach error.

FKF: There's never been a pope that proclaimed a Church teaching that turned out to be fallible.

DRG: That's where a lot of people have a common misconception about the Papacy, Father. I hear folks who say:

> How can I believe that the Catholic Church is protected by God when in fact over the centuries its taught <u>this</u> doctrine one century, and it's taught a contrary doctrine the next. The Catholic Church has changed its mind on this and that.

But they're referring to various Church "practices" or "disciplines" that have changed from cultural to culture and era to era, right?

FKF: It's hard to know about what they're referring to.

DRG: But on matters of faith and morals—the deposit that Christ left us—the Church has never said: "Homosexuality is okay," and then, "Homosexuality is not okay." Or, "You do have to be baptized," and then at another time, "You don't have to be baptized." Or, "You can lose your salvation -- you can't lose your salvation."

FKF: Sure.

DRG: There was one pope—I believe it was Sixtus. Interestingly enough, he was, I guess, an arrogant kind of guy, and he commissioned his own Scriptural translation. He wanted to put out a better Bible. But he didn't like what the scholars did, so he said, "Well, I'm going to do it." It was very bad, and many of the people around him, the Bishops, said, "This is bad." So he backed off. Then he re-thought it. He was set to release it, and there was great turmoil in the Church at that time because they were saying, obviously if he does this, he's putting out a kind of an "errant" form of Scripture.

You know what happened to him? He was in good health, but he contracted a brief illness and died suddenly — because he was set on releasing Scripture that would have been an errant translation.

Pius XII (1939-1958)
Queen of All Saints Church
Chicago IL

FKF: One of the things to remember is that most of the people who have been popes throughout history relied also on the work of the Church Councils. They worked in harmony, in conjunction with the Council of Bishops. We have a belief that the Holy Spirit indeed does work with the bishops as they gather together and convene a council. Even our brothers and sisters of the Orthodox Church understand the nature of the council and the need for all the bishops to gather together from time-to-time to consult one another and listen to the Holy Spirit.

So, the major changes in our Church, when we change disciplinary practices and things like that, often times come from the Councils, not from the Pope himself. But being the Bishop of Rome, when all of the Bishops are called together, he's there. And even in the early Church, when the Orthodox were still a part of the same Catholic Church that we are a part of, that was the way things were done: by the calling of the Councils. The Patriarch of Rome was always given primacy. He was always considered the first among equals.

The Eastern Orthodox Church, even today, that doesn't accept papal infallibility, would still say they can't count their Councils as Councils when all their patriarchs are together because they know they're missing the prime patriarch who has to be there. The Patriarch of Rome has not been there since they broke off from the Church. So they only recognize the first seven Councils as Ecumenical Councils because the Bishop of Rome was at those, whereas in the Councils after that which the Orthodox Church has gathered together, the Bishop of Rome hasn't been there.

DRG: Briefly, give me a couple of things that the Councils, through the guidance of the Holy Spirit, have crystallized for us that we now take for granted in our faith.

FKF: The biggest would be, and its something that we spoke about earlier in another show, the Council of Nicaea in 325 A.D. That whole sense of the nature of God being Father, Son, and Holy Spirit — God is Three-in-One/Trinity. They solidified the doctrine of the Trinity and resolved the issue of the relationship of humanity and divinity both residing in Christ Jesus.

DRG: That He was God, fully and completely.

FKF: Right.

DRG: Some people don't realize that doctrine had been challenged.

PAPAL INFALLIBILITY
Refers to *Ex Cathedra* pronouncements only on issues about faith or moral teaching.

FKF: Oh, certainly. It was a big, big dispute in the early Church — the nature of Christ. So the Council did get together, and under the guidance of the Pope — the Pope who calls them together — these things were resolved. A lot of people have the misconception that the Council of Trent (1545-1563) "made up" a lot of stuff after the Protestant Reformation.

The reality is, however, that the Council was called to articulate the faith that has always been held throughout the ages. Even the whole idea of the Pope's infallibility comes out of the first Vatican Council.

DRG: In 1870.

FKF: Yes, it did not come from a pope. You don't have the Pope calling the Pope infallible. It came from the Council.

The pope didn't say, "I'm going to make an infallible statement here. My infallible statement is, I'm infallible." <u>It came out of a Council</u>. It came out of a gathering of the bishops united together saying that this first among equals, this Patriarch of Rome, the Pope, the Bishop of Rome. <u>This is the person who, when given matters of faith and morals and proclaims them *ex cathedra*, proclaims them in infallible fashion</u>.

Clement I (92-99)
Holy Cross Church, Liege, Belgium

DRG: It's interesting, too, that for the Councils, one of the things they determined was what constituted <u>Scripture</u>. The councils decided, "This is our Bible."

A lot of non-Catholics don't realize that. They don't even think about where the Bible came from.

FKF: Right.

DRG: I want to take you in a different direction just before we have to stop.

One of the biggest objections against the Papacy is the idea that a pope heading the Church <u>was a medieval invention</u>. The Papacy, so the idea goes, is something that gained in power, it gained in pomp, it gained in circumstance, and it really wasn't seen until about 400-600 A.D.. But, let me read from some of the early Church Fathers. This is Ignatius around 110 A.D.. Ignatius, remember, was a disciple of the Apostle John.

> To the Church in Rome, which holds the presidency in the place of the country of the Romans, worthy of God, worthy of honor, worthy of blessing, worthy of praise, worthy of success, worthy of sanctification, you have envied no one, but others you have taught. You are a credit to God. You deserve your renown and are to be congratulated. You deserve praise and success. You rank first in love, being true to Christ's law and stamped with the Father's name. (Ignatius of Antioch, *Letter to the Romans* 1:1 [A.D. 110])

This was Irenaeus, in the second century. He was Bishop of Lyon, France.

> Having founded and built the Church, the blessed Apostles entrusted the Episcopal Office to Linus, who is mentioned by Paul in the epistles to Timothy. Linus was proceeded by Cletus after him. In the third place from the Apostles, fell to Clement. (Irenaeus, *Against Heresies* 3:3 [A.D. 189])

So, it went Peter, Linus, Cletus, Clement, in succession. He also says,

> We will point out here that the succession of bishops of the greatest and most ancient Church known to all, founded and organized at Rome by the two most glorious Apostles, Peter and Paul; that Church which has the tradition and the faith which comes down to us from the Apostles; this Church because of its superior origin; all churches must agree, that is all the faithful in the whole world, and, it is in her that the faithful everywhere have maintained the Apostolic tradition. (Irenaeus, *Against Heresies* 3:3 [A.D. 189])

Leo XIII (1878-1903)
St. Joseph's, Hammond, IN

Then there is Eusebius, a Church historian. He says,

> The good and gracious providence of God which watches over all things, guided Peter, the great and mighty one among the Apostles, who because of his virtue, was the spokesman for all others to Rome. (Eusebius, *History of the Church*, 2,14,6, 300 A.D.)

On and on it goes, talking about the primacy of Rome, Peter's successors. It's everywhere, Father. You'd have to ignore the testimony of the early Fathers, looking to Rome for guidance, looking to Rome to essentially maintain the unity of all of this.

We have about two minutes to cover **Ex Cathedra**, <u>"from the Chair."</u> Are you familiar with the verse in Matthew, chapter 23, verses 1 through 3, where Jesus talks about the Scribes and Pharisees, and He says they sit on the Chair of Moses? Do you remember what Jesus said about them?

FKF: Not word for word.

DRG: Okay, here it is, then.

> *The scribes and the Pharisees have taken their seat on the chair of Moses. Therefore, do and observe all things whatsoever they tell you, but do not follow their example. For, they preach, but they do not practice. (Matthew 23:2-3)*

He said do everything they tell you to do ...

FKF: But not what they do.

DRG: But not what they do. They have <u>authority</u>. Sometimes they don't act right, but they <u>still</u> have the authority. And He recognized that even in the scribes and Pharisees.

FKF: Most people don't know this, but the word "cathedral" comes from the word *cathedra*, "the Chair." The <u>cathedral</u> is the place where the Chair is located. And there are a lot of people who don't like this idea of the Chair of Peter. They don't like this idea of the Chair of the Bishop. And yet they have the Cathedral of Life, the Cathedral of Tomorrow, the Cathedral of This, the Cathedral of That. But, that term — <u>cathedral</u> — is a proclamation of the belief that the Pope speaks from the Chair of Authority.

DRG: It's a great comfort for us as Catholics, because, if Christ would allow His Church to teach error, then we wouldn't know what to believe. We would all have to try to figure it out ourselves, become the final authority and say, "I sure hope that pope was right. I sure hope that bishop was right."

<u>If our Lord didn't protect His Church, we would all be floundering.</u>

FKF: Yes.

DRG: (to audience) We Catholics believe that He has protected His Church for 2000 years. I'm Ray Guarendi, with me, Pastor Kevin Fete. Thank you very much for joining us. God be with you. Walk with God into eternity.

Episode 12 Study Questions

Some non-Catholics claim:

A - Peter is equal with the other Apostles; the Bible doesn't give him special treatment.

1.   Other than Peter, whom in the Bible had his name changed by God, and what was the change's significance? (Genesis 17:5)

2.   What is the importance of a name; what does it communicate? (Genesis 2:19)

B - Even if Peter was in charge of the Church while he was alive, there was not a successor.

3.   Why, logically, is it important for Peter and the others to have successors?

4.   What event reveals that the Apostles believed they needed successors? (Acts 1:26)

5.   Who was it that declared successors were needed? (Acts 1:15, 21-22)

C - There is no reason to obey a man who has never been married and lives 6,000 miles away.

6.   What are the four marks of the Church? (CCC 750)

7.   For each of the four marks of the Church, what is one logical reason why there must be only one head, or leader?

8.   Under what psychological condition could the Holy Spirit give different doctrinal directions to different groups?

9.   What position in the Church has the authority to ordain a priest or a bishop? (CCC 1538)

D - The pope can't be infallible because some of the Popes were bad men, and they did and said things that were wrong.

10.   List two things Peter said that were wrong, but were not doctrinal proclamations. (Matthew 26:70, Galatians 2:11-14)

11.   What did Jesus promise the Church about the truthfulness of its teachings? (Matthew 16:18, John 16:13)

12.   What are the limits of the Pope's infallibility? (CCC 891)

13. Which popes proclaimed a doctrine that was later deemed wrong?

14. In terms of evil popes with authority, what is the logical significance of Matthew 23:1-3 where Jesus describes people in authority whose lives are bad examples.

15. What does the term "Ex Cathedra" mean, and what are some church buildings called that come from this term?

E - Over the centuries the Church, through its popes, have changed and reversed doctrines.

16. What doctrines of the Church were changed or reversed by a pope?

17. Do popes or councils come up with most doctrines?

18. What Christian doctrines were decided at the Council of Nicaea in 325 A.D.?

19. What council declared that the Pope could make infallible proclamations only about faith and morals?

F - The papacy was a Medieval invention.

20. What early Church Fathers articulated the preeminence of the Bishop of Rome, and in what years did they write?

21. Other than St. Peter, how many other popes took the name "Peter"?

A Transformation To Look Forward To

First Presbyterian Church
White Bear Lake, MN

13. Purgatory

DRG: Father, I was reluctant to even do an episode on Purgatory, because I've heard from folks who say:

> The Church doesn't even teach Purgatory any more. I haven't heard anything from the pulpit. That's an old teaching, and this whole idea it being some place where you go and you pay for your sins is something that we don't talk about much any more.

So, do we even need to do this show?

FKF: I think we do. As you started out, you were reluctant to do Purgatory, I suspect most of us are going to be reluctant to do Purgatory.

But I think the problem that usually comes with the issue of Purgatory is a <u>semantic problem</u>. It's a matter of the <u>words</u>. I don't know of any Christian people, regardless of denomination who don't believe in a time of Sanctification or Purification. While some people might not like to use the <u>word</u> Purgatory, the <u>concept</u> of what Purgatory is about is universal to Christians.

DRG: So, many non-Catholics would call it, at the end of life, a final rush of Sanctification, or the Lord would do what he needs to do to purify us to be ready for heaven.

FKF: Correct.

DRG: Well then, here's the argument. <u>What is Purgatory</u> ? People say:

> Catholics concoct all kinds of stuff. This Purgatory thing is just this huge doctrine that the Catholic Church has <u>made-up</u> over the centuries.

Distill Purgatory here, if you can.

FKF: The first thing you have to deal with is space and time. We have a tendency, because we are people forced to live in space and time, to translate our sense of what Purgatory is into those terms — space and time.

DRG: So, I'm sitting around in Purgatory getting toasted, looking at my watch, saying, "Oh, I've got another year and a half. That guy just left after three months."

FKF: But what we really need to do is look at Purgatory in the sense of our inward being, being transformed, and <u>being made worthy to be in the presence of God</u>. Scripture tells us that you can't be in the presence of God if you're not perfected in the ways of the Lord. Revelation says nothing with sin shall stand before a holy God [Rev. 21:27]. So those who have sin (e.g. you and me) need to be prepared. One who has sinned, even though they are sorry for the sin they've committed, still needs to be, wants to be prepared to meet God.

*St Jean Church
Troyes, France*

DRG: I recall the Catholic Catechism has about a page on Purgatory. That's about it.

FKF: It's about, I think, three sections.

DRG: Three sections? Summarize them.

FKF: First of all, you have the sense of Purgatory's necessity. Secondly you have the sense that there is some pain involved, but not necessarily in the sense of burning or frying.

DRG: Just some kind of discomfort involved in the purification.

FKF: Yes, and that discomfort can be the discomfort of being made aware of the suffering that came to other people's lives by our sins.

DRG: My wife has this idea that Purgatory will be for us, at the judgment seat, when we finally see ourselves actually as God sees us. Completely and totally with everything within us that is <u>not</u> God-like.

FKF: Scripture talks about <u>everything will be made known</u>, everything will be laid bare, out in front of the whole of all of creation.

DRG: I've got the quote.

> *Therefore, whatever you have said in the dark shall be heard in the light and what you have whispered in private rooms shall be proclaimed upon the housetops. (Matthew 10:27 paraphrased)*

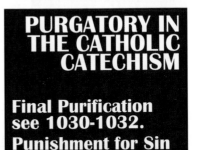

PURGATORY IN THE CATHOLIC CATECHISM

Final Purification see 1030-1032. Punishment for Sin see 1472.

FKF: I think part of Purgatory is, then, not only our sins being made visible and revealed to all, but <u>even to ourselves</u>.

DRG: That's got to be ugly.

FKF: Oh, yes.

DRG: I don't want to have to look at me and say, "Oh, that's the kind of stuff I did."

FKF: And, "That's the kind of effect that I had on others as a result of my sins."

DRG: Okay, so we get the purification.

The Church teaches it is some form of purification that God ordains for us in order to be cleansed. Plenty of Scripture verses imply this:

- *We shall see Him as He is [1 John 3:2]*
- *Nothing with sin shall stand before a holy God [Revelations 21:27]*
- *I shall know fully, as I am fully known. [1 Corinthians 13:12]*

Without being objectively holy, completely sanctified, we can't be in heaven.

FKF: That's right.

DRG: There is some discomfort in being purified, and the Lord talks about that. We'll touch on some of those verses. But what about the third part in the Catechism, the part about how prayers can help?

FKF: In the <u>third part</u>, the Catechism says that <u>we pray for those who are in need of purification</u> from the effects of their sins. That would definitely be something that we as Catholics should participate in.

DRG: So, I can pray for you in Purgatory while I'm on earth. The Church teaches through the Communion of Saints, a doctrine that's two thousand years old, that those in Purgatory are my brothers and sisters whom I can pray for, also -- for their well-being.

FKF: Right.

St. Paul's United
St. Paul, MN

DRG: Then, here's a problem. Where's Purgatory in the Bible?

FKF: Well, one could equally question where is the Trinity in the Bible? Now certainly Jesus says, "Go baptize in the name of the Father, Son and Holy Spirit" [Matthew 28:19]. So you could say, well see, that's it. But the actual word, Trinity, the whole formulation of that idea, that's not specifically and explicitly stated in the Scriptures. So too, one could look at the Scriptures and say there is this <u>sense of Purgatory without using the word</u>. It doesn't have to be explicitly stated. We have a lot of things that we adhere to in our faith that aren't explicitly stated in the Scriptures, yet nonetheless are supported by the Sacred Scriptures.

DRG: So the concept is there?

FKF: Correct.

DRG: Next, let's go through some of these verses and explain how our Lord, through the Scriptures, gave us the idea that we will be purified and held accountable for our sinfulness. Before we do that, just briefly clear up what Purgatory is not. You get all kinds of nutty ideas, people thinking they know what Purgatory is. Non-Catholics especially don't understand it.

FKF: One thing Purgatory is not: it's not a third state of eternal existence.

DRG: I wasn't good enough for heaven, I'm not bad enough for hell ...

FKF: Kind of like the minor leagues. I hope He calls me up to the majors soon.

DRG: I'm in the bush league, you know.

FKF: Yeah. But I might be here forever.

That's one of the things it's <u>not</u>. It <u>is</u> this time of <u>going to</u> the attainment of living eternal life in heaven.

DRG: The saints used to talk about that. They said one of the joys of Purgatory, even though we are being cleansed and purified, is the anticipation of being fully united with God.

FKF: And that may also be part of the <u>pain</u> of Purgatory <u>that anticipation that's not yet fulfilled</u>.

DRG: I've heard a prisoner talk about it that way. If you're in prison, and you know next week you're being released, the closer you get to that release date to be with your family and your friends, the more agonizing that time becomes because you know where you want to go.

FKF: That's right, those are longer days.

DRG: Purgatory is also <u>not</u> the idea that you <u>get a second chance</u>. In other words, you rejected Christ here, and you go to Purgatory. He comes down and says, "Now look, I gave you 72 years on earth, and you still didn't accept Me. So, now I'm going to give you one more shot in Purgatory."

It's not that?

FKF: If you are a person who has made the choice that would be a damnable choice, then damnation is your inevitable result. You can't get out of it at that point. It's not a last shot at believing.

DRG: Let me read you some Scripture verses. This is 2 Corinthians 5:10.

> For we must all appear before the judgment seat of Christ, so that each one may receive recompense, according to what he did in the body, whether good or evil. (2 Corinthians 5:10)

This one is Luke 6, verse 38.

> For the measure with which you measure will in return be measured out to you. (Luke 6:38)

That is one that always bothered me.

And finally, Matthew 12, verse 36.

> I tell you, on the day of judgment people will render an account for every careless word they speak. (Matthew 12:36)

It's this whole idea of, even though our Lord totally atoned for our sins and redeemed us— He paid the infinite penalty—we still are going to be held accountable for our actions.

FKF: Right.

PURGATORY

The state or condition of the justified as their lives are purified and prepared for heaven. Purgatory has nothing to do with atonement for sins, or giving sinners a second change to enter heaven.

DRG: Is that Scriptural?

FKF: It <u>is</u> Scriptural. One of the things we have to look at is this whole sense of God as a <u>merciful God</u>, *and* this whole sense of God as a <u>God of justice</u>. A lot of times people sense conflict there. How can God be a God of mercy *and* be a God of justice? People may think that if he's a God of mercy and will forgive, then He can't be <u>just</u>. That's because sometimes justice entails a certain punishment — a punishment that makes them aware of the severity of what they've done...and the need to reform from it. They may find themselves wanting to be brought back into reconciliation.

So, this sense of <u>Purgatory</u>, this sense of atonement, this sense of being <u>sanctified</u> helps us to understand that the <u>God of justice and the God of mercy</u> simultaneously interact. The God of justice says, "You have to account for what you've done." The God of mercy says, "In your accounting is where you find the mercy." Those two can parallel one another, rather than being a contradiction to each other. They actually become <u>totally intertwined</u> with one another and support one another in the unfolding of God's divine plan of salvation.

St. Stephen's Church
Stevens Point, WI

DRG: More Scripture support for Purgatory can be found in 2 Maccabees, chapter 12. That is not a book that non-Catholics accept as Scripture.

However, we've talked about that on previous shows and in the history of the Christian Church, Maccabees was accepted in every Council as Scripture.

But even if you don't accept it as Scripture, Maccabees provides a clear view of how the Jews saw things at that time, correct?

FKF: Correct.

DRG: **In Maccabees it says,**

> *It is a holy and wholesome thought to pray for the dead that they might*
> *be loosed from their sins. (2 Maccabees 12:46 paraphrased)*

During the Reformation Martin Luther expressed his opinion that Maccabees and other books didn't belong in the Biblical canon. Scholars debate that one of the reasons Martin Luther's theology wouldn't allow the idea of a Purgatory was because, in his mind, Christ paid the full price for all penalty whatsoever, temporal or not! But that's not Scriptural. In the Old Testament, didn't David lose his son because he sinned? Remember, the prophet Nathan told him? (2 Samuel 12)

Then Moses, the poor guy, led the Israelites all over the place, and one time he doesn't do what he's supposed to do, God says, "You're not going into the Promised Land." [Deuteronomy 32:19]

FKF: You may get people who say:

> Well, that's Old Testament. That's before the Christ event.

But even today in our world, even before we die, there's still suffering because of sin. If Christ atoned for all sin, then all of the pain of sin shouldn't be constantly inflicted upon us.

That's one of the reasons some of my friends who are Jewish say they don't believe that Jesus Christ is the Messiah. Because if He were the Messiah, all sins would be atoned for, and all then would be at peace in the world. But the reality is that the death and Resurrection of Christ Jesus <u>is</u> the focal point of all of history. You may think I'm referring to BC and AD, which puts Christ in the middle of the historical plane.

DRG: **B.C.? Isn't that a comic strip?**

FKF: (laughter) The historical plane, is unfortunately, the only place where a lot of people think. We need to go to the vertical plane and realize that Christ's death and Resurrection rises above history, so that what is before and after focuses in, like a funnel, into the Christ event. Therefore, when you take these Old Testament passages, <u>they're just as relevant</u> as the New Testament passages.

DRG: **I've got New Testament passages.**

FKF: Share them with us, Ray.

DRG: **This is 1 Corinthians 3:12-15.**

> *If anyone builds on this foundation with gold, silver, precious stones, wood, hay, or straw, the work of each will come to light, for the Day will disclose it. It will be revealed with fire, and the fire (itself) will test the quality of each one's work. If the work stands that someone built upon the foundation, that person will receive a wage. But if someone's work is burned up, that one will suffer loss; the person will be saved, but only as through fire. (1 Corinthians 3:12-15)*

Many of the early Church Fathers said that is a Scripture that points to this idea of Purgatory where we will be sanctified, finally, fully, completely to be with God.

FKF: Now what would you say, though, to someone that says,

> Okay. Ray, what we're talking about here though is the fire of hell. Anywhere else in Scripture that we find that sense of fire, or that sense of Hades, it's hell.

DRG: **First Peter. It's one of those verses that confuses people, where Saint Peter says:**

> *Jesus went and preached to the spirits in prison. (1 Peter 3:19)*

Remember the Apostle's Creed? "He descended into hell."

FKF: Some say "hell," some say "the dead."

DRG: **So where did He go? I mean, where were these people? They may not have been in Purgatory, but it certainly indicates there was another place. And what is that place in the Old Testament, Sheol, right? Sheol, or in Greek it means Hades. What was that?**

FKF: It's a place of purging, a time of being purified.

DRG: **You waited in that place?**

FKF: Yes.

DRG: **It was a place for the righteous who were waiting for the Messiah.**

FKF: But again, don't put it in a sense of time or space, or a sense of this long, or this room. Put it in a sense of a transition in one's existence from the old life of sin — that is now brought into new life through faith — but nonetheless has to account for its sinfulness.

DRG: **So if somebody says, "Where's Purgatory in the Bible?" you can say, "Well, Sheol, the Hebrew word -- and Hades, the Greek word, are basically parallels.**

FKF: And will there be a time when Sheol or Hades gets thrown away?

DRG: Yes, Revelation, as a matter of fact. Revelation, chapter 20, verse 11. I'll go right to it. This is an interesting passage. This is John writing:

> *I saw the dead, the great and the lowly, standing before the throne, and scrolls were opened. Then another scroll was opened, the book of life. The dead were judged according to their deeds, by what was written in the scrolls. The sea gave up its dead; then Death and Hades gave up their dead. All the dead were judged according to their deeds. (Revelation 20:12-13)*

So now you've got Hades giving up these people. And it goes further:

> *Then Death and Hades were thrown into the pool of fire. (This pool of fire is the second death.) (Revelation 20:14)*

FKF: So Purgatory can't be the lake of fire. It can't get tossed into itself.

DRG: **What about this thought?**

> Purgatory was developed by the Catholic Church. It wasn't around in the early days of Christianity and the Church. This is something that got built up and added on just like the Catholic Church does with so many things.

What would you say to that?

FKF: Two things. Number one is that the <u>term</u> Purgatory did come about over time. But the <u>concept</u> did not. The concept was with us forever, from the beginning of the Church's foundation, which is Jesus Christ.

Trinity Lutheran
Minneapolis, MN

Number two is that you find that the concept of Purgatory is in the early Church because you see evidence in the catacombs of people praying for the dead.

DRG: All over the place, right?

FKF: Yes, and if they're in heaven, <u>why</u> would they pray <u>for</u> them? And, if they're in hell, it would be <u>useless</u> to pray for them. That only leaves a third possibility: that there is this moment of sanctification, purification, of atonement that happens at the moment of our death — this thing we've come to call Purgatory.

DRG: I read about the Mourners Kaddish. It's the Jewish process of praying for the dead for 11 months after their death. Now that's still done by Orthodox Jews today, and it was very much a part of the temple worship in Jesus' time.

FKF: Yes.

DRG: Jesus never said to the Jews:

> You people got it all wrong. You're praying for these dead people. Forget it. They're either in heaven, or they're in hell.

He never corrected this, and for something that large to be a mistake, He never came out and said, "Hey look, you're wrong."

St. Patrick's Cathedral, Thunder Bay, Ontario

FKF: When it's over, it's over.

DRG: It's over. You're done, you're either going to be in one place or be with Father.

He never said that.

The other interesting thing is that we do have many early Church Fathers who talked about Purgatory. Let me read you a just a few of them ...

FKF: Even before you get to the Church Fathers though, one of the interesting stories I find in Scripture, would be the story of the raising of Lazarus from the dead. I always had this question of where was he? Where was he for those four days when he was dead? Was he in heaven and then Jesus raised him and brought him back? If he was, you'd think Lazarus would have been mighty upset to be brought back.

DRG: Like he was thinking: "Hey! I liked it where I was."

FKF: Then the question is, was he in hell when Jesus brought him back? To say:

Well, He couldn't do that and then give him a second chance.

So, there is this sense that the one who is dead can still be brought to this life because the final judgment hasn't been finished. Now you might say:

Well, Lazarus is a special circumstance.

But consider this whole sense of judging. Christ in Matthew, chapter 12 is talking about the sins against the Spirit, and He says,

This is one sin that will not be forgiven in this age or in the age to come.
(Matthew 12:32 paraphrase)

DRG: Age to come. Yes, what is this age to come?

FKF: If this sin can't be forgiven in either age, why wouldn't He just say this is a sin that can never be forgiven? But to say "this age or in the age to come" leaves open the possibility…

DRG: …that there are sins that can be forgiven in the age to come.

FKF: So you take those teachings by Christ, and then you understand why there's a foundation for the early Fathers of the Church to lead to where you were going with their writings.

DRG: This is one of the earliest bishops of the Church, the Bishop of Hieropolis. His name is Abercius. He said he wanted this put on his tombstone:

Standing by, I, Abercius, ordered this to be inscribed. "Truly, I was in my seventy-second year. May everyone who is in accord with this and who understands this, pray for Abercius." (Epitaph of Abercius, [A.D. 180-200])

Second century… I have, as usual, just tons of these early Church Father quotes, but I'll just give you some of them. This was Tertullian in the early two-hundreds.

We offer sacrifices for the dead on their birthday anniversaries. (Tertullian, *The Crown* 3:3 [A.D. 211])

This is Cyprian. He was a bishop in Africa, in the two-hundreds, also.

It is one thing, tortured by long suffering for sins, to be cleansed and to be purged by fire. It is another to have purged all sins by suffering. It is one thing to be in suspense until the sentence of God on the Day of Judgment. It is another to be at once crowned by the Lord. (Cyprian, *Letters* 51[55]:20 [A.D. 253])

In other words, basically on this earth, we can suffer enough so that we may not need so much final purification.

That there should be some fire even after this life is not incredible, and it can be inquired into and either be discovered or left hidden whether some of the faithful may be saved, some more slowly and some more quickly in the greater or lesser degree in which they loved the good things that perish, through a certain purgatorial fire. (Augustine, *Handbook on Faith, Hope, and Charity* 18:69 [A.D. 421])

Sweetest Heart of Mary Church, Detroit, MI

The early Fathers, all over the place, like Augustine, wrote about this whole idea that we're going to need a final cleaning up. We're going to need the final Sanctification because we're not fit to be with God when we leave, at least not most of us.

FKF: Yes.

DRG: Maybe the martyrs or the living saints would be.

Here's something I want to read to you. This is fascinating. <u>Not all Protestants don't believe in Purgatory.</u> This is C.S. Lewis,

Of course I pray for the dead. The action is so spontaneous, so all but inevitable, but only the most compulsive theological case against it would deter me. And I hardly know how the rest of my prayers would survive if those for the dead were forbidden. At our age the majority of those we love best are dead. What sort of intercourse with God could I have if what I love best were unmentionable to Him? (C. S. Lewis, *Letters To Malcom: Chiefly on Prayer*, 20.7-10)

And I have another great quote from him.

I believe in Purgatory. If I remember it rightly, the saved soul, at the very foot of the throne begs to be taken away and cleansed. It cannot bear for a moment longer with its darkness to affront the light. Our souls demand Purgatory, don't they? Would it not break the heart if God said to us, "It is true, my son, your breath smells and your rags drip with mud and slime. But we are charitable here and no one will criticize you with these things. Now, come on in." Shouldn't we reply, "Excuse me, Sir, if there's no objections, I'd rather be cleansed first?"

"It may hurt, you know."

"Even so, Sir." (C.S. Lewis, *Ibid*)

So you have a great mind like C.S. Lewis basically saying that the Catholic Church, in its teaching of this over the two millennia, was faithful to the theological case and history.

One more question: Indulgences.

Indulgences, as they relate to people in a purgatorial state, involve this whole idea that we can do things to help these people who are suffering in Purgatory.

Now come on. Please! Weren't those things even sold in medieval times?

INDULGENCE

An indulgence is a remission before God of the temporal punishment due to sins whose guilt has already been forgiven, which the faithful Christian who is duly disposed gains under certain prescribed conditions through the action of the Church which, as the minister of redemption, dispenses and applies with authority the treasury of the satisfactions of Christ and the saints. (CCC 1471)

FKF: First of all, that's one of the great misconceptions about the Church. Indulgences were not sold. You did have people who would make contributions, in memory of someone. The contributions, though, were their earnest way of showing that they had a great love of God, a love of the promise of mercy and a love of the person who had died.

DRG: **So the Church didn't say, "Okay, for 50 bucks we'll knock off three days in Purgatory. We got a special today, the blue light special, the Purgatory special. Give me a one-hundred bucks, and we'll get your kid out of there."**

FKF: There were some people who, maybe of a less educated ilk, would have put things in terms of "days." But, <u>that was never the teaching of the Church</u>. There was never this day/time program of, "Okay, you get 50 days off, 30 days off. With good behavior you can get this." There wasn't a plea bargaining system with God.

DRG: **An <u>indulgence</u>, then, is a way of me helping the body of Christ?**

FKF: Certainly. What's really important for us Christians to remember, as we talk about how Christ's death and resurrection paid for all things, is this reality — that through the Christ event, we have become the body of Christ. Therefore, we see many times where Paul and others speak about sharing in the suffering of Christ and how sharing in that suffering brings glory to God; and how suffering allows us to participate in what Christ did. So we continue to do what Christ did, as the body of Christ.

DRG: **We share in His sufferings, for the good of all of us.**

Two minutes left, and I have two questions. To the thief on the cross Jesus says, "This day you will be with me in Paradise." There. He didn't go to Purgatory.

FKF: Again there is this whole sense of always reducing things to days. We put it into terms we understand here but not necessarily terms that really apply to the afterlife where there is no time and space.

DRG: **Okay, there is no "time" to explain, but basically, Purgatory (in the case of the thief) could have taken place in an instant, as far as we know.**

FKF: Right.

DRG: **Second question. Here's a Scripture "quote:"**

To be absent from the body is to be present with Christ.

There, how would you answer that? Because that destroys the whole case for Purgatory.

FKF: If you look at that Scripture -- well, you won't find that in Scripture.

DRG: **WHAT?**

FKF: That, ahh... "quote," <u>misquotes</u> Saint Paul. It actually says:

> *…we know that while we are at home in the body we are away from the Lord… we would rather leave the body and go home to the Lord.*
> *(2 Corinthians 5:6-8)*

In fact, where that misquote comes from is actually the part of Scripture that all Catholics use for the vigil service of a person's funeral.

DRG: So Paul didn't say, "To be absent from the body is to be present with Christ."

FKF: Right. People have to manipulate the Word of God to get it to say that.

DRG: Fascinating, Fr. Fete. Thank you.

(to audience) And thank you for joining us on "What Catholics Really Believe." I am Ray Guarendi. With me, Pastor Kevin Fete. Again, God willing, we will visit and talk about other areas and teachings and doctrine of the Church. Why Scripturally and historically we believe these things. Until then, walk with God, and hold your kids real tight by the hand.

St. Leo's Church
Casselton ND

Episode 13 Study Questions

A - Catholics concoct all kinds of stuff, and this Purgatory thing is something the Catholic Church made up over the centuries.

1. Because nothing with the stain of sin shall stand before a holy God, what is the purpose of Purgatory, or purgation?

2. Describe how Luke 12:3 relates to our sins and the end of our lives.

3. What is revealed to those in Purgatory that will likely cause psychological pain, if not physical pain as well?

4. What two things is Purgatory NOT?

5. What do the souls in Purgatory anticipate that could bring both pain and joy simultaneously?

6. Some people argue that if Jesus' death and resurrection really had defeated sin and brought forgiveness to the human race, there would be peace and an absence of war. What basic concept of the human condition does that argument misunderstand, and how does Purgatory resolve the misunderstanding?

7. If Purgatory is not necessarily a physical place or time, what is it?

B - Purgatory is not in the Bible.

8. What Christian doctrines, other than Purgatory, are not explicitly explained in Scripture but are accepted by most Christians and were formulated by a Church council?

9. From what two paradoxical attributes of God does Purgatory arise? e.g. God is both ____ and _____.

10. What did Jews of the Old Testament understand about atoning for the dead, and how does this relate to Purgatory? (2 Maccabees 12:44-45)

11. Describe in your own words how Paul's description in 1 Corinthians 3:12-15 of the judgment relates to the concept of Purgatory and not to hell.

12. After Jesus died and before He ascended to heaven, the *Apostles Creed* says He descended to the dead (hell). What are other Biblical terms for where Jesus went, and how <u>may</u> that place relate to Purgatory? (1 Peter 3:19)

13. Before death and Hades can be cast into the lake of fire and eternal punishment, what does Revelation 20:11-15 say will occur, and how does it possibly relate to Purgatory?

14. Why does Fr. Fete believe that Lazarus was in Purgatory before Christ brought him back to life?

15. How do Christ's words in Matthew 12:32 possibly relate to Purgatory?

C - Purgatory was invented by the Catholic Church centuries after the early Church.

16. What evidence is there in the Roman catacombs that Purgatory is an Early Christian Church concept?

17. The Jewish *Mourner's Kaddish,* or *Prayer for the Dead* does not mention the dead but only the greatness of God, yet what was and still is its purpose in <u>Orthodox</u> Judaism? How long should it be prayed by the children after a parent dies? (Research. Be aware that some "less than Orthodox" Jews may not teach the same thing.)

18. What early Church Fathers believed in Purgatory and praying for the dead?

D - Buying an indulgence is the corrupt idea invented by the Catholic Church that buying an indulgence could get a relative or friend out of hell.

19. What are the two consequences of sin?

20. What is an Indulgence?

21. For what kind of punishment can indulgences not be obtained? (CCC 1471-1473)

E - No modern day Protestant theologian believes in Purgatory.

22. How did Protestant theologian C. S. Lewis understand the importance of praying for the dead in Purgatory?

F - Jesus promised the one thief who died on a cross next to him: "Today you will be with me in paradise." That proves that there is no Purgatory, because the thief went straight to heaven.

23. Human beings live in a temporal world bounded by time and space. When we enter eternity what will be different about time and how will this difference affect our perception of Purgatory?

G - The Scripture that says: "To be absent from the body is to be present with Christ," destroys the whole concept of Purgatory.

24. You won't find the above quote in the Bible. What does Paul actually say and mean in 2 Corinthians 5: 6, 8?

There Will Be A Test

Parish Church
Schellenberg, Liechtenstein

What Catholics Really Believe

ANSWER GUIDE

1 JESUS
Answers

A1) Fr. Fete explains that Peter, endowed by the Holy Spirit, said to Jesus, "You are the Messiah." Jesus confirms this but because titles can be misunderstood Jesus tells his Apostles not to talk about it. Using titles for Jesus doesn't do Him justice. The Church took hundreds of years to look at the person of who Christ is. Catholics would conclude that Jesus is both fully human, fully divine. He is the Son of Man, the Son of God. He is the Messiah. He's the Savior through whom we find salvation.

A2) The Church's teaching gives to Jesus the following titles: Jesus (meaning "God saves"), Redeemer, Savior, Messiah (literally, "anointed"), Christ (Greek for "Messiah"), Lord (Greek: Kyrios), Jesus Christ, Son of God, Son of David, Son of Man, Messiah-King, and God the Son.

A3) Catholics confess that Jesus is the only Son of God, eternally begotten of the Father, God from God, one in being with the Father. For our sake He was crucified. On the third day He rose again. He is the incarnate God, the Word made flesh. He suffered and died for us, and ascended to heaven to sit at the right hand of the Father. He will come again to judge the living and the dead.

B4) Catholics believe that regeneration, or being "born again" occurs at baptism (normally performed in infancy), according to John 3:3-5 ("born of water and the Spirit"; cf. Titus 3:5: "washing of regeneration"; 1 Corinthians. 6:11; Acts 2:38, 22:16; 1 Pet 3:21). "Personal Savior" is not Biblical language, but Catholics, like Protestants, believe in communion with Jesus and the indwelling Holy Spirit (CCC 729-730) with somewhat different terminology. For example, near the end of every Mass, the whole congregation says: "Lord, I am not worthy to receive you, but only say the word and I shall be healed."

B5) To call Jesus our friend requires that we do what He commands (cf. Luke 6:46-49), including serving others and laying our lives down for our friends and for Jesus.

C6) The "altar call" for many Evangelical Protestants, is a heartfelt commitment to Jesus Christ to be His disciple, made in front of the church at the "altar." Many evangelicals believe that this moment of repentance and commitment is the same as "getting saved" or being "born again" (regeneration).

C7) Catholics approach the altar at Mass every week, and believe that through the Eucharist they receive Jesus physically into their bodies. Earlier, through faith, they received Christ into their hearts spiritually, and at the altar, through the Eucharist, they become part of the Body of Christ, literally. Thus it is a continual re-commitment to the Lord and to service to Jesus as His disciple.

D8) Dr. Ray counted the name of Jesus at a recent Mass 37 times. The Gloria in the Mass gives one an idea of how central Jesus is in the Catholic liturgy:

> **Glory to God in the highest, and peace to his people on earth. Lord God, heavenly King, almighty God and Father, we worship you, we give you thanks, we praise you for your glory. Lord Jesus Christ, only Son of the Father, Lord God, Lamb of God, you take away the sin of the world, have mercy on us; you are seated at the right hand of the Father, receive our prayer. For you alone are the Holy One, you alone are the Lord, you alone are the Most High, Jesus Christ, with the Holy Spirit, in the glory of God the Father.**

E9) Catholic churches use crucifixes instead of empty crosses because Paul wrote that "we preach Christ crucified" (1 Corinthians 1:23) and that this was "the power of God and the wisdom of God" (1 Corinthians 1:24). By the same reasoning, a Protestant could be asked why they have in their home a baby Jesus in a manger at Christmas-time, since He is now in heaven and no longer a baby. Catholics want to meditate on the crucifixion, by which salvation was made possible.

F10) The promise is eternal life in heaven. The conditions mentioned in these verses are obedience to the commands of Christ, good works done in His name, endurance till the end (Hebrews 6:11-12), following the "holy commandment" (2 Pet 2:21), faith and belief in Jesus (John 1:12, 5:24, 10:31; 1 John 5:11-12), hope (Hebrews 6:18-19), and God's electing call (John 10:27-29). Acts 1:25 proves that even an Apostle (Judas) can possibly fall from salvation.

F11) Catholics believe that we can be assured of the promises of Scripture: God's mercy and love and desire that all be saved. We can rest in Jesus' knowledge of who are His and who are not. Jesus will render to each man according to his works (Matthew 16:27; Romans 2:5-13) and acceptance of the grace necessary for salvation (John 3:36). Good deeds are pleasing to God and help us grow in sanctity. Those who go to hell do so of their own free will and choice, not due to God's predestination.

F12) Based on God's promises and mercy, we can have joy and peace even in this life. If we live a life of service, charity, willingness to suffer, and desire to become closer to God, we can have a moral assurance that we will be saved in the end by God's grace. The Bible teaches that certain sins, continually committed, can exclude a person from heaven (1 Corinthians 6:9-10; Gal 5:19-21; Ephesians 5:5; Rev 22:15). If we examine ourselves fully and conclude that we are free of grave (mortal) sin committed with full consent of the will, then we can rest in the hope of salvation.

G13) Guilt is an aspect of conscience, which is in turn given to us by God as an aid in determining good and evil and right courses of action. Man can hear God through his conscience (CCC 1777) and so guilt can be a guiding voice that will help deter acts of evil and evil thoughts. "The verdict of the judgment of conscience remains a pledge of hope and mercy" (CCC 1781). The Bible, prayer, gifts of the Holy Spirit, wise persons, and the Church all help properly form the conscience (CCC 1785).

G14) A covenant is a sort of pact or contract or agreement between a greater and a lesser. So, for example, God made covenants with Noah, Abraham and David. It is binding on both parties. Whatever God promises, He inevitably brings to pass, in His providence and omnipotence.

2 BIBLE
Answers

A1) The Bible says: All scripture is inspired by God and profitable for teaching, for reproof, for correction, and for training in righteousness, that the man of God may be complete, equipped for every good work. (2 Timothy 3:16-17)

A2) The Catholic Church "forcefully and specifically exhorts all the Christian faithful" to "frequent reading of the divine Scriptures" because "ignorance of the Scriptures is ignorance of Christ."

A3) When studying the Bible, the Church cautions that interpretation should not be contrary to received Catholic doctrines. Catholics and other Christians ought to read the Bible with accompanying prayer, so that "a dialogue takes place between God and man" (CCC 2653). Reading the Bible is like listening to God.

A4) There are over 25,000 different kinds of Christian groups in the United States, each one claiming that the Holy Spirit led them through the Bible alone to a different truth. This is evidence that either: (a) one group is telling the truth, and the other 24,999 are lying, or (b) the Holy Spirit is schizophrenic and telling each group something different, or (c) there are sincere intentions but honest misunderstandings, or (d) the different groups are clinging to an authority figure's interpretation and not the Bible alone.

B5) No, for the Church "teaches only what has been handed on to it." The Magisterium of the Church is not superior to the Bible, but rather, its guardian (CCC 86). The Church venerates Holy Scripture "as she venerates the Lord's Body" (CCC 103). The Catholic Church believes that inspired Scripture has God as its author, and (far from being "created" by the Church, or inferior to it), has "been handed on as such to the Church herself" (CCC 105). Study of Scripture is, indeed, "the very soul of sacred theology" (CCC 132). The Canon of Scripture was authoritatively proclaimed by the Catholic Church. The Gospels "are the heart of all the Scriptures." (CCC 125)

C6) The Scriptures that imply that the Church and its councils, and not individuals, should be the final arbitrators of how Scripture should be interpreted include:

> **I will give you [Peter] the keys of the kingdom of heaven. Whatever you bind on earth shall be bound in heaven; and whatever you loose on earth shall be loosed in heaven. (Matthew 16:19)**

> **When the Spirit of truth comes, he will guide you [disciples and, by extension, Church leaders] into all the truth; for he will not speak on his own authority, but whatever he hears he will speak, and he will declare to you the things that are to come. (John 16:13)**

Acts 15 records the proceedings of the Jerusalem Council (more on that in D10 below).

2 Peter 1:19-21 explains that Scripture cannot merely be a "matter of one's own interpretation."

C7) The Church teaches that interpretation of Scripture requires knowledge of the rules for proper interpretation of Scripture ("hermeneutics"), and an understanding of the four senses of Scripture: literal, allegorical, moral, and anagogical (CCC 115-118). The Holy Spirit is necessary to fully understand the teachings of the Bible. The intentions of the Biblical authors must be considered, as well as the overall context of the entire Scripture. Scripture must be interpreted within "the living Tradition of the whole Church" (CCC 113), and with the "analogy of faith" (internal coherence of the truths of faith) in mind (CCC 114).

C8) Jesus taught that His teaching was to be authoritatively passed on by His disciples. In turn, they would be closely identified with Him:

> **He who hears you hears me, and he who rejects you rejects me, and he who rejects me rejects him who sent me. (Luke 10:16)**

This authority was especially concentrated in Peter, the leader of the disciples, and hence, the young Church:

> **And I tell you, you are Peter, and on this rock I will build my Church, and the powers of death shall not prevail against it. (Matthew 16:18)**

The powers to "bind and loose" (disciplinary and doctrinal authority, from a Jewish rabbinical term) given to Peter in Matthew 16:19 are also expressly given to all the disciples in Matthew 18:18.

D9) The first authoritative and binding proclamation of the Canon of Sacred Scripture was given by the councils of Hippo in 393 (St. Augustine's hometown) and Carthage in 397. Pope Innocent I confirmed, by his authority, the decisions of these councils in 405.

D10) The Jerusalem Council (Acts 15) was a meeting of "Apostles and elders" (15:2, 4, 6, 22) and "the whole Church" (15:22). This council issued a proclamation binding on all Christians (16:4), under the guidance of the Holy Spirit:

> **For it has seemed good to the Holy Spirit and to us to lay upon you no greater burden than these necessary things: that you abstain from what has been sacrificed to idols and from blood and from what is strangled and from unchastity. If you keep yourselves from these, you will do well. Farewell. (Acts 15:28-29)**

Paul and Silas even proclaimed this decision as part of their missionary activity (Acts 16:4). This, then, provides an explicit Biblical model of how Church government and authority ought to function.

D11) The Jerusalem Council was quite contrary to the Protestant principle of *Sola Scriptura*, or "Bible Alone" [as the only infallible authority] because it involved human cooperation in interpreting the Bible, and this group effort was indeed infallible (Acts 15:28) and binding (according to the Apostle Paul himself) upon all Christian believers (Acts 16:4). This historical fact alone (part of inspired revelation) is quite sufficient to refute Sola Scriptura. Interpretation of the Bible must occur within the Church, as a result of its deliberations in council (bishops and elders), not simply as a function of the "priesthood of scholars" or private interpretation (2 Peter 1:19-21) or denominational relativism.

D12) Genesis 17 records the covenant between God and Abraham (by extension, with the Jews, or Hebrews), which established circumcision as a sign of this covenant. If this Scripture were all that we had, then circumcision would still be a required rite today. The Jerusalem Council, however, declared that circumcision was no longer necessary, especially for Gentile (non-Jewish) converts to Christianity. Baptism was to become the new "rite of entrance" into the Church or the New Covenant, and St. Paul drew a parallel between circumcision and baptism (Col 2:11-13). This development proves that the Bible alone is not enough for doctrinal clarity and certainty. The Church must be centrally involved in interpretation and application of old truths in new situations.

E13) Jesus wanted people to worship from the heart (Mark 7:6). That is what He contrasted with the dead traditions of men. Worship from the heart included obedience to God's commands and good deeds that are the inevitable fruit of true communion with God (Amos 5:11-24; Jeremiah 17:24-26; James 1:26-27).

E14) Sacred Tradition has a number of characteristics. (1) It was passed down by the Apostles to the Church. (2) The bishops, as successors of the Apostles, then preserved the "deposit of faith". (3) Sacred Tradition can be traced back historically to Jesus and the disciples. (4) The Holy Spirit (John 16:13; Acts 15:28) guides the Church in protecting this Tradition. (5) This living Tradition can be developed and applied in different ways as time goes on (Acts 15:29). (6) It is always consistent with Scripture. (7) Sacred Tradition comes from the same "divine well-spring" as Holy Scripture (CCC 80). (8) Bishops and the Pope, and ecumenical councils, in the Magisterium of the Church, as a "servant" to Holy Scripture (CCC 86) pass down, preserve, and guard this Sacred Tradition. (9) All people in the Catholic Church share in the perpetuation of Sacred Tradition (CCC 91-93), and are brought as a whole to an unfailing knowledge of it. All these elements together constitute Sacred Tradition, whereas traditions of men lack one or more of them.

E15) Christian Traditions that are not mentioned in the Bible include: (a) Worship in a church building (never mentioned in the New Testament); (b) the word "Trinity" (the concept is present but not the word); (c) the canon of Scripture itself (the Bible does not have its own Table of Contents); (d) worship on Sunday rather than Saturday (application of the Sabbath principle without explicit Biblical teaching); (e) the Nicene and Apostles Creed and other such statements of belief, that codify Christian beliefs, are traditions that all Christians accept and yet are not in Scripture itself.

E16) Bible verses that state that we should accept Sacred Traditions in addition to written traditions include:

> **But there are also many other things which Jesus did; were every one of them to be written, I suppose that the world itself could not contain the books that would be written. (John 21:25, 16:12, 20:30; Acts 1:2-3)**
>
> **So then, brethren, stand firm and hold to the traditions which you were taught by us, either by word of mouth or by letter." (2 Thessalonians 2:15, cf. 1 Corinthians 11:2; 2 Thessalonians 3:6; Col 2:8; 2 Tim 1:13-14, 2:2)**

F17) No, the Church does not teach anything that is contrary to Scripture because the Church is guided by the Holy Spirit (CCC 78-79). Sacred Tradition is always closely bound with Sacred Scripture (CCC 80). Apostolic succession guarantees the purity of this Tradition (CCC 81, 83), as do the bishops in union with the Pope (CCC 85).

F18) "God communicates to man gradually" and "by stages" (CCC 53). The complete revelation "has not been made completely explicit" and the Church must "grasp its full significance" over time (CCC 66). The Church (just as in the Jerusalem Council of Acts 15) is a guide in the application of this development of doctrine and increased understanding of the received truths of divine Revelation.

3 SCRIPTURE & TRADITION
Answers

A1) It takes about three years to hear the core or essence of the whole Bible if one attends only Sunday Mass.

A2) It takes about two years to hear the core or essence of the whole Bible if one attends Sunday Mass and Daily Mass.

A3) Catholics could be unaware of the Scripture that they are exposed to in the Mass because they do not pay proper attention to the Mass, fall asleep, "tune out" repetitious elements, lack interest in the Bible itself, are unwilling to follow the Church's urging of much private reading of Scripture, or they are in mortal sin.

B4) Some twenty to thirty years after Pentecost, Paul's epistles were the first books of the New Testament written.

B5) The New Testament canon of Scripture was first collected at the Council of Hippo in 393 and Council of Carthage in 397. St. Athanasius was the first Church father to list all 27 New Testament books together, in his thirty-nineth festal letter in the year 367. ("festal letter" = the letter relates to a festival of the Church)

B6)   The Church proclaimed the canon of Scripture closed at the Council of Trent.

B7)   The Catholic Bible has 73 books compared to 66 in the Protestant Bibles.

B8)   The deuterocanon ("second canon") are what Catholics call the additional books they include that Protestants don't.

B9)   Dr. Ray states that the deuterocanon was authenticated when Pope Innocent ratified the decisions of the councils of Hippo and Carthage in 405, in his Letter to Exsuperius, Bishop of Toulouse. The Council of Florence (1438-1445) and Council of Trent (1545-1562) also made pronouncements.

B10) Generally, teachings are further defined as doctrine when they are seriously challenged by those who do not accept them. The Church then examines and defends the historical teaching in greater detail and makes solemn dogmatic pronouncements regarding the precise nature of the doctrines.

B11) It is an incoherent and implausible view which contends that the Holy Spirit led the early Church to the correct canon of the New Testament, but at the same time, were misled as to the correct Old Testament books. The fathers accepted the Septuagint (Greek translation of the Old Testament) and it included the deuterocanon. It is ironic that a belief-system holding that Scripture is the only infallible authority, necessarily has to rely on infallible Church tradition and authority to even know what that Scripture consists of.

C12) The two kinds of traditions are disciplinary and dogmatic. An example of the former would be abstaining from meat on Fridays. Disciplines can change according to local custom or liturgical practice. A dogmatic Tradition, on the other hand, has to do with a doctrinal teaching of the faith, such as the Holy Trinity, the Immaculate Conception of Mary, or the infallibility of the Pope.

C13) Two traditions that Protestants hold include Sola Scriptura, or the idea that Scripture is the only final and infallible authority in Christianity — which is nowhere taught in Scripture — and the abbreviated canon of Scripture (only 66 books vs. the Catholic 72).

C14) The importance of Sacred Traditions in understanding Christianity was stated by Early Church Fathers, including:

> As I said before, the Church, having received this preaching and this faith, although she is disseminated throughout the whole world, yet guarded it, as if she occupied but one house. She likewise believes these things just as if she had but one soul and one and the same heart; and harmoniously she proclaims them and teaches them and hands them down, as if she possessed but one mouth. For, while the languages of the world are diverse, nevertheless, the authority of the tradition is one and the same. (St. Irenaeus, *Against Heresies* **1:10:2; A.D. 189**)

> It is needful also to make use of tradition, for not everything can be gotten from sacred Scripture. The holy Apostles handed down some things in the Scriptures, other things in tradition. (St. Epiphanius, *Medicine Chest Against All Heresies* **61:6; A.D. 375**)

> The custom [of not rebaptizing converts] ... may be supposed to have had its origin in apostolic tradition, just as there are many things which are observed by the whole Church, and therefore are fairly held to have been enjoined by the Apostles, which yet are not mentioned in their writings. (St. Augustine, *On Baptism, Against the Donatists* **5:23[31]; A.D. 400**)

C15) New Testament passages that support the importance of traditions in passing down a correct understanding of Christianity include: 1 Corinthians 11:2; 2 Thessalonians 2:15, 3:6; 2 Timothy 1:13-14, 2:2 (cf. synonymous use of "gospel": 1 Corinthians 15:1; Gal 1:9; 1 Thessalonians 2:9, "word of God": Acts 8:14, 1 Thessalonians 2:13, "holy commandment": 2 Pet 2:21, and "the faith": Jude 3).

C16) New Testament passages that refer to Old Testament traditions not found in the Old Testament include: Matthew 23:2-3: "Moses' seat"; 1 Corinthians 10:4: the "rock" that followed the Israelites (cf. Ex 17:1-7; Num 20:2-13); Jude 9: the archangel Michael disputing with Satan about the body of Moses; Jude 14-15: a prophecy of Enoch, possibly from the apocryphal book 1 Enoch (1:9); 2 Timothy 3:8: Jannes and Jambres as the names of the magicians who opposed Moses (see Ex 7:8 ff.).

C17) The truth and authenticity of the Church's teachings and Biblical interpretation are protected by the Church; specifically the Pope and the bishops (by virtue of apostolic succession). The Pope can write encyclicals and other dogmatic writings for the whole Church; the bishops can make pronouncements that apply in their jurisdictions, and bishops united with the Pope in ecumenical councils can make binding statements of Catholic doctrine.

D18) Change has happened over the centuries because the Church increases in understanding. Doctrines are better understood and develop. The canon of Scripture was itself a developing tradition. The infallibility of the Pope was another.

The custom of eating meat on Fridays (as a binding practice) was a disciplinary matter that could be changed. Priestly celibacy also developed as the norm in the Latin western rites. The Bible indicates something like development of doctrine, too (John 14:26, 16:13; 1 Corinthians 2:9-16; Gal 4:4; Ephesians 1:10; 4:12-16). The Church is called the "Body of Christ" (e.g., Ephesians 1:22-23), and is compared to a seed that grows into a tree (Matt 13:31-32). Seeds and bodies grow and expand.

D19) One can find Biblical evidence for distinctly Catholic doctrines. For example, celibacy was urged as a preferential state of life by Jesus (Matthew 19:12) and St. Paul (1 Corinthians 7:7-38). We have seen references to authoritative Tradition above. The Real Presence of the Eucharist is plainly taught in John 6. Very early Church fathers such as St. Polycarp and St. Ignatius report what was believed by the Church in its earliest days.

If we find no record of distinctive Protestant doctrines, that have departed from received Tradition, then we can assume that they were not present in the early Church, and were later corruptions or novelties.

D20) The Pope has no authority to change doctrines that are firmly entrenched in Tradition. He must build upon what was already present in the apostolic deposit, given by Jesus to the Apostles. Development of doctrine does not involve any essential change from what came before. He can only make infallible and binding what is already widely believed by the faithful.

4 EUCHARIST, I
Answers

A1) Physical objects are mostly composed of the space between atoms, which are composed of protons, neutrons, and electrons.

A2) Electrons are always moving. The Austrian physicist Erwin Schrödinger, in the 1920s, contended (quite successfully) that electrons are three-dimensional waveforms, as opposed to particles.

A3) Electrons constantly move at velocities approaching the speed of light.

A4) Physical senses (without the aid of sophisticated microscopes, accompanied by even more complicated theories of physics and mathematics) cannot enable us to comprehend the fundamental properties of matter and therefore give us an inaccurate understanding of an object's actual nature or real substance.

A5)   What "appears" to be so, may not be that way at all. Objects that appear perfectly at rest are in fact, partially moving at velocities close to the speed of light. Likewise, what appears to us as bread and wine can in fact be the Body and Blood of Christ, made supernaturally present in the consecrated elements (formerly bread and wine), according to the teaching of Jesus Christ Himself. The same Jesus who could travel through walls in His glorified body (John 20:26; cf. 1 Corinthians 15:51-53). According to modern physics and quantum mechanics, such things are literally possible, even in a purely physical realm. So why is there any inherent difficulty in believing in transubstantiation ("change of substance")?

A6)   The Bible describes supernatural objects with "phenomenological" language (the language of appearances and simple observation). In the previous example of Jesus walking through walls, the Bible doesn't attempt to delve into twentieth century particle physics; it simply says "The doors were shut, but Jesus came and stood among them ... " (John 20:26). Likewise, the Bible refers to "this [what appears to be bread] is My Body" (Luke 22:19-20), and Paul equates bread and wine with the "Body and Blood of the Lord" that can be profaned in an irreverent receiving of the Eucharist (1 Corinthians 11:27-30; cf. 10:14-22).

A7)   The Church claims that the Eucharist is the Body, Blood, Soul, and Divinity of Jesus Christ, made present in a unique sacramental fashion. The "accidents" (bread and wine) retain their same properties, but the substance has supernaturally changed.

B8)   If we could have looked through a microscope into Mary's womb at the embryo of Jesus Christ we would have perceived a <u>human</u> cell because the attributes of the incarnate God cannot be ascertained by conventional methods of physical or scientific observation. Although reason (scientific observation) in cooperation with faith (enlightened by supernatural revelation by Jesus and the prophets) can confirm and attest to the supernatural. Jesus wanted people to accept who He was by faith. Hence, Jesus says to "doubting Thomas" after the latter had put his hand in the wound in His side: "Have you believed because you have seen me? Blessed are those who have not seen and yet believe" (John 20:29).

B9)   Those who did not have doubt or serious sin and spiritual "blindness" (John 9:39-41) often regarded Jesus as God, in faith (a faith confirmed by physical observation). For example, the blind man healed by Jesus, who worshiped Him (John 9:35-38), and "doubting Thomas," after Jesus appeared to him (John 20:28). The ones who were blind assumed that He was not only just a man, but also a quite sinful one (John 9:24; cf. Matt 12:22-27, 38-42).

B10) Humans do not recognize God because of lack of faith and its relationship to reason, resulting in excessive doubt and cynicism. Signs, wonders, and miracles (and by extension, "scientific proof") do not suffice for many hard-hearted people anyway:

> **... If they do not hear Moses and the prophets, neither will they be convinced if some one should rise from the dead. (Luke 16:31)**

In John 6, we see that unbelief and lack of faith and skepticism kept "many of his disciples" (6:60) from believing in the Real Presence in the Eucharist, and actually forsaking the Lord (6:66), because it was a "hard saying." Jesus appealed to His ascension, which was an even greater, and more visible miracle (6:62), thus seemingly implying: "if you can't believe this miracle, how, then, will you be able to believe in that one; yet you will see that with your own eyes."

B11) We can use faith, in cooperation with reason, to confirm the sure word of revelation, and thus perceive what is of God. We can also use our internal God-given sense of the holiness that Jesus exhibited in His life, and the trustworthy reports of those who were eyewitnesses of His glory (Luke 1:1-2; Acts 1:1-3). (See the previous three answers, also.)

B12) Nothing whatsoever is wrong in using natural law to explain the super natural! Faith and reason work together to explain what is true. We can utilize that which we know and understand in order to comprehend (by analogy, parallel, or extension), supernatural things that are mysteries to us. Jesus did the same, by using agricultural metaphors in His parables, to reveal the truths of spirituality. Our Lord even compared the unwillingness of the Pharisees and Sadducees to use the same reasoning they used with regard to natural meteorological events of the weather, and apply it to spiritual matters:

> **And the Pharisees and Sadducees came, and to test him they asked him to show them a sign from heaven. He answered them, "When it is evening, you say, `It will be fair weather; for the sky is red.' And in the morning, `It will be stormy today, for the sky is red and threatening.' You know how to interpret the appearance of the sky, but you cannot interpret the signs of the times. An evil and adulterous generation seeks for a sign, but no sign shall be given to it except the sign of Jonah." So he left them and departed. (Matthew 16:1-4)**

C13) Jesus uses extremely literal language in John 6:51-58 to refute the objection that the Eucharist is simply symbolic:

> I am the living bread which came down from heaven; if any one eats of
> this bread, he will live for ever; and the bread which I shall give for the life
> of the world is my flesh.

> The Jews then disputed among themselves, saying, "How can this man
> give us his flesh to eat?" So Jesus said to them, "Truly, truly, I say to you,
> unless you eat the flesh of the Son of man and drink his blood, you have
> no life in you; he who eats my flesh and drinks my blood has eternal life,
> and I will raise him up at the last day. For my flesh is food indeed, and my
> blood is drink indeed. He who eats my flesh and drinks my blood abides
> in me, and I in him. As the living Father sent me, and I live because of the
> Father, so he who eats me will live because of me. This is the bread which
> came down from heaven, not such as the fathers ate and died; he who eats
> this bread will live for ever."

If this were intended as mere symbolic or figurative language, it seems that it was
the least likely to convey that meaning, of any language imaginable. How could it
be stated any more literal than this? How Jesus reacted to the doubts of the hearers
(see B10 above), also reinforces this interpretation.

C14) In the early second century (before A.D. 110), St. Ignatius of Antioch held that
"the Eucharist is the Flesh of our Savior Jesus Christ." (*Letter to the Smyrnaeans*, 7,
1) In the middle of the same century, St. Justin Martyr distinguishes the Eucharist
from "common" bread and drink and calls it "both the flesh and the Blood of that
incarnated Jesus." (*First Apology*, 66, 2) A little later, St. Irenaeus writes, "The bread
over which thanks have been given is the Body of (the) Lord, and the cup of His
Blood." (*Against Heresies*, 4, 18, 4 / 4, 33, 2; cf. 4, 18, 5) St. John Chrysostom speaks
of the priest as the representative of God in the Mass, exercising solely His power
and grace, in order to "transform the gifts" which "become the Body and Blood of
Christ." (*Homilies on Judas*, 1, 6) Elsewhere Chrysostom equates the Eucharist with
Christ's "blood-stained" Body, "pierced by a lance." (*Homilies on 1 Corinthians*, 24)
St. Augustine, the greatest of the Fathers, writes that "Christ was carried in His own
hands, when, referring to His own Body, He said 'This is My Body.'" (*Explanations
of the Psalms*, 33, 1, 10)

St. Augustine expressly sanctions adoration of the consecrated Host:

> He took flesh from the flesh of Mary ... and gave us the same flesh to be
> eaten unto salvation. But no one eats that flesh unless first he adores it ...
> we do sin by not adoring. (*Explanations of the Psalms*, **98, 9**)

C15) Catholics believe that this promise is the literal physical presence of Jesus because
right before He said this (Matt 28:20) Jesus also urged His disciples to "observe

all that I have commanded you". The Eucharist was precisely what Christians do (in obedience to the command at the Last Supper) to bring remembrance to Jesus' presence on earth; and not only remembrance, but Real Presence. Paul said that in observing the Eucharist, we "proclaim the Lord's death until he comes" (1 Corinthians 11:26). John 6:53-54, 58 intimately connects the Eucharist with both spiritual and eternal life. John 6:56 makes reception of the Eucharist a necessity for Jesus to "abide" in believers, and vice versa (cf. John 14:23, 15:4-7).

C16) Objections of cannibalism show that the early Christians were taking Jesus literally (John 6; Last Supper utterances about the bread and the wine being His Body and Blood). But the pagans (like the skeptics who disbelieved in John 6) did not understand the distinction between physical cannibalism and a spiritual, sacramental Real Presence.

C17) These verses involve the intimate connection between the incarnation and the Eucharist (both entail physical presence of God Himself). Catholic convert Thomas Howard elaborates:

> **Sacrament, recalling and presenting the Incarnation itself, is not so much supernatural as quintessentially natural, because it restores to nature its true function of being full of God ... Indeed heaven and earth are full of His glory. Nature is the God-bearer, so to speak ... In the Sacrament, bread, which is already a metaphor, is taken and raised to a dignity beyond mere metaphor ... one step away from the Incarnation itself... It is a scandal. God is not man, any more than bread is flesh. But faith overrides the implacable prudence of logic and chemistry...**
>
> **This mystery ... may be held only in faith, even though it, like the Incarnation, Resurrection, and Ascension, exists quite apart from faith, "out there" in the real world.** (*Evangelical is Not Enough*, **Nashville: Nelson, 1984:110-112**)

In fact, bread and wine becoming Body and Blood is such a natural process that it happens every time we sit down for a meal and consume bread and wine. The Incarnation is the greater miracle. So, if we can accept the Incarnation, the miracle of the Eucharist should be easier to accept.

D18) This objection may be refuted by citing the judgment of Protestant Church historians, who themselves do not believe the Catholic doctrine on the Eucharist (hence cannot be accused of bias in favor of patristic support for the doctrine), yet accurately report what the Fathers believed. For example, the well known Protestant historian Philip Schaff has written:

The doctrine of the sacrament of the Eucharist was not a subject of theological controversy .... till the time of Paschasius Radbert, in the ninth century ...

In general, this period, ... was already very strongly inclined toward the doctrine of transubstantiation, and toward the Greek and Roman sacrifice of the mass, which are inseparable in so far as a real sacrifice requires the real presence of the victim ...

[Augustine] at the same time holds fast the real presence of Christ in the Supper ... He was also inclined, with the Oriental fathers, to ascribe a saving virtue to the consecrated elements.

Augustine ... on the other hand, he calls the celebration of the communion 'verissimum sacrificium' of the body of Christ. The church, he says, offers ('immolat') to God the sacrifice of thanks in the body of Christ. [*City of God*, **10, 20**]

(*History of the Christian Church*, **v.3, A.D. 311-600, rev. 5th ed., Grand Rapids, MI: Eerdmans, rep. 1974, orig. 1910, 492, 500, 507**)

D19) Luther stated:

It is enough for me that Christ's blood is present; let it be with the wine as God wills. Before I would drink mere wine with the Enthusiasts, I would rather have pure blood with the Pope. (Early 1520s; in Paul Althaus, *The Theology of Martin Luther*, **translated by Robert C. Schultz, Philadelphia: Fortress Press, 1966, 376; Luther's Works, [edited by Jaroslav Pelikan] 37, 317**)

The glory of our God is precisely that for our sakes he comes down to the very depths, into human flesh, into the bread, into our mouth, our heart, our body. (In Althaus, *ibid.*, **398;** *Luther's Works*, **37, 71 ff.**)

... Zwingli, Karlstadt, Oecolampadius ... called him a baked God, a God made of bread, a God made of wine, a roasted God, etc. They called us cannibals, blood-drinkers, man-eaters ... even the papists have never taught such things, as they clearly know ...

For this is ... how it was accepted in the true, ancient Christian church of fifteen hundred years ago ... When you receive the bread from the altar, ... you are receiving the entire body of the Lord; ... (*Brief Confession Concerning the Holy Sacrament*, **September 1544; Luther's Works, 38, 291-292**)

D20) The Church's belief in the Real Presence of Christ in the Eucharist was reinforced by the famous symbol of the fish, and depictions of three of Jesus' miracles related to food: the feeding of the 5,000 with fish and bread, the banquet of seven disciples by the Sea of Galilee with the raised Jesus, and the miracle of the wedding at Cana (changing water into wine).

5 EUCHARIST, II
Answers

A1) The only person who can be responsible for the miracle of Jesus' true presence in the Eucharist is Jesus Himself! If that is how He decided to miraculously become physically present again, after His earthly sojourn, then we can hardly object, seeing that it is not much different in essence than the Incarnation itself: God becoming man. On the other hand, if it is false doctrine, no priest could "conjure" up Jesus' presence, because they are dealing with the omnipotent God, and He is not to be trifled with or manipulated.

A2) Credibility is lent to the Church's Eucharistic claim because Christians believe that the Holy Spirit continues to guide His Church, and preserve it from error (what Catholics call "indefectibility"). See Matthew 16:18; John 14:26, and 16:13.

A3) There was universal acceptance (with but a few notable exceptions) that the consecrated host and wine were the true Body and Blood of Christ for nearly 1,500 years after Christ's Resurrection, until the Protestant movement in 1517.

A4) According to Dr. Ray, 75 years after Luther died there were as many as 200 different interpretations of Christ's words, "this is My body."

A5) The concept of transubstantiation is mentioned by St. Justin Martyr, in his First Apology (circa: 100-165 A.D.), 66:5 (complete; emphasis added):

> **And this food is called among us [*eucharistia*] [the Eucharist], of which no one is allowed to partake but the man who believes that the things which we teach are true, and who has been washed with the washing that is for the remission of sins, and unto regeneration, and who is so living as Christ has enjoined. For not as common bread and common drink do we receive these; but in like manner as Jesus Christ our Saviour, having been made flesh by the Word of God, had both flesh and blood for our salvation, so likewise have we been taught that the food which is**

blessed by the prayer of His word, and from which our blood and flesh by transmutation are nourished, is the flesh and blood of that Jesus who was made flesh. For the Apostles, in the memoirs composed by them, which are called Gospels, have thus delivered unto us what was enjoined upon them; that Jesus took bread, and when He had given thanks, said, "This do ye in remembrance of Me, this is My body;" and that, after the same manner, having taken the cup and given thanks, He said, "This is My blood;" and gave it to them alone.

A6) In the Early Church, to reject the true presence of Christ in the Eucharist rejects the authority of the disciples and Apostles, who passed down what had been given to them in the apostolic deposit:

> **He who hears you hears me, and he who rejects you rejects me, and he who rejects me rejects him who sent me. (Luke 10:16)**

A7) "Show Me."

A8) Martin Luther continued to strongly hold to the Real Presence and had very sharp disagreements, enough to break fellowship and unity with other Protestants, like John Calvin and Zwingli, who denied it (see Episode Four, answer D19).

B9) Non-Catholic Christians say they would accept as evidence (for the true presence of Christ in the Eucharist) data provided in the inspired word and revelation of the Holy Bible.

B10) Melchizedek, priest of God Most High, prefigures Christ and the priesthood when he blesses Abram in Genesis 14:18-20 by offering bread and wine before the prayer of blessing, as Christ offered up his Body and Blood, and as the Catholic priest does in the consecration of the bread and wine to become the Body, Blood, Soul and Divinity of Christ.

Psalms 110:4 and Hebrews 7:1-28 speak of a new order of priests, a priesthood, that would be inaugurated with Christ. And it would be similar to Melchizedek who never served before the Mosaic altar, but was yet a priest.

When we trace the origin of this back, we find some very interesting things:

> **And Melchizedek king of Salem (Jerusalem/peace) brought out bread and wine; he was priest of God Most High. (Genesis 14:18)**

> **And on the day when you wave the sheaf, you shall offer a male lamb a year old without blemish as a burnt offering to the LORD. And the cereal offering with it shall be two tenths of an ephah of fine flour mixed with oil, to be offered by fire to the LORD, a pleasing odor; and the drink**

> offering with it shall be of wine, a fourth of a hin. And you shall eat
> neither bread nor grain parched or fresh until this same day, until you
> have brought the offering of your God: it is a statute forever throughout
> your generations in all your dwellings. (Leviticus 23:12-14; cf. also
> Hebrews 5:6, 10; 6:20; 7:1-28)

> The LORD has sworn and will not change his mind, "You are a priest for
> ever after the order of Melchizedek." (Psalm 110:4:)

B11) The Old Testament priest presided over and performed ritual sacrifices of bulls and
other things, in order to atone for the sins of the people.

B12) The Last Supper was actually a Passover meal, in which lamb and bread and wine
were consumed, and was for the purpose of the people remembering how God
had physically delivered them from bondage in Egypt. Jesus used this symbolism
to introduce the notion of the Eucharist: now bread and wine were to be
transubstantiated into His Body and Blood and His followers would be spiritually
delivered by His sacrifice as the "lamb of God, who takes away the sin of the world"
(John 1:29). And they were to remember this in the Eucharist henceforth, just as the
Jews observed the Passover rite in remembrance.

B13) When Christ lifts up the bread, He says, "This is My body" – as opposed to "this
represents My body" or "this contains My Body" or "My Body is present with, in,
and under the bread", or "this is a symbol to help you remember My Body," etc.

B14) None of Christ's words can be reasonably interpreted as only symbolic. The closest
(so some believe) is "do this in remembrance of me." But in the Hebrew mind the
concept of remembrance did not imply that it was a mere recollection or mental
image or pleasing nostalgia, but rather the reality being made present here and now,
just as the Jews regarded the Passover meal.

B15) St. Augustine said that Jesus held His own Body: "Christ was carried in His own
hands, when, referring to His own Body, He said 'This is My Body.'" (*Explanations
of the Psalms*, 33, 1, 10)

B16) Jesus related the cup of wine to the covenant between God and His people:

> For this is my blood of the covenant, which is poured out for many for the
> forgiveness of sins. (Matthew 26:28)

> And he said to them, "This is my blood of the covenant, which is poured
> out for many." (Mark 14: 24)

B17) The Blood of Christ represents bulls, rams, and lambs, used in ritual sacrifice, for atonement. Revelation 7:14 and 12:11 refer to "the Blood of the Lamb [Jesus]."

B18) Celebrants at the Passover meal have to completely eat the lamb, and bread and wine.

B19) The significance of Malachi 1:11 is that in the New Covenant, the Lamb of God and the cross represent the continuation and development of the Old Testament sacrificial system (which is no longer even being performed by the Jews). This passage refers to the Gentiles "in every place" making pure offerings. But since it is not animal sacrifices, it is reasonable to assume that what is referred to is the sacrifice of the Mass and re-presentation of the sacrifice of Jesus, who was once for all, offered at Calvary. The incense represents the prayers of the Mass.

B20) On a daily basis, 300,000 Catholic Masses are offered in worship to God.

B21) Jesus alludes to His Body or Blood being true food twice very directly (6:55) and eight more times speaking of "eating" and "drinking".

B22) Jesus never alludes to His Body or Blood as being symbolic.

B23) Jesus was teaching that His followers had to eat His flesh and drink His blood (sacramentally) in order to have spiritual and eternal life.

B24) By the time of John's writing (later in the first century), the Gnostic heresy was starting to deny that Jesus had come in the flesh, and indeed, asserted that flesh itself was a bad thing. So, John emphasized the physical and "realist" nature of the Eucharist over the Gnostic false teaching.

B25) In John 6:63 Jesus is contrasting "flesh" to "spiritual discernment," in the sense of "flesh and blood" (or a merely natural human understanding; see, e.g., Matt 16:17 for a clear example of this meaning). He was not referring to the Eucharist, but rather to "the words that I have spoken." "Spirit and life" refers back to His references to spiritual and eternal life as a result of partaking of the Eucharist (John 6:50-51, 53-54, 56-58).

B26) The *epiklesis* (the calling down of the Holy Spirit) prayer reinforces the power of Jesus' words. God's words bring about what they refer to. So when the priest repeats the words of Jesus at the Last Supper (the consecration), they continue to achieve what they did then, and Jesus becomes present through the power of the Word. Hence the relation to John 6:63: "the words that I have spoken to you are spirit and life."

B27) *Anamnesis* means "active re-presentation" according to Greek scholars. It is the opposite of symbolic just as "re-present" (the original thing again) is different from "represent" (one thing symbolizing another). Hence, Paul uses ultra-realistic language. He even states in 1 Corinthians 11:27 that partaking of the Eucharist unworthily is the same as profaning His Body and Blood.

B28) Referring to the word "body" in 1 Corinthians. 11:27-30 as the "body of believers" makes no sense because the language is related to the Eucharist instituted at the Last Supper. Jesus referred to the bread and the wine as His Body and Blood. The "Body of Christ" (the Church) is a completely different sense. So Paul equates the bread and the cup with the Body and Blood of Jesus in 1 Corinthians 11:27. In the next verse, he urges Christians to do a self-examination before receiving Holy Communion.

B29) The disciples do not recognize Jesus until He broke bread (a gesture reminiscent of the Last Supper):

> **When he was at table with them, he took the bread and blessed, and broke it, and gave it to them. And their eyes were opened and they recognized him; and he vanished out of their sight. (Luke 24:30-31)**

The sequence of Jesus first explaining Scripture (the Word) to the disciples on the Road to Emmaus, and then at dinner blessing the bread, parallels the celebration of the Mass beginning with the Liturgy of the Word, followed by the Liturgy of the Eucharist. Notice also, as soon as Jesus blesses the bread his body disappears, but He leaves behind his "presence" in the consecrated bread.

B30) It is when "the Word became flesh" (John 1:1, 14) that God was most fully revealed (John 1:18). As the Incarnation revealed God visibly, so the Eucharist makes Jesus present again and gives us spiritual life, through the same principle of the Incarnation—physical matter conveying grace. In this instance, the eyes of the two disciples were blinded until the moment of the Eucharist, and "then they recognized him." The knowledge is spiritually discerned, but made possible through the instrument of the grace-infused matter (John 1:14) in the Eucharist, the actual Body and Blood of Jesus.

6 BAPTISM
Answers

A1)   The Bible says we are saved by (1) belief in Jesus, (2) repentance followed by baptism, (3) being born of water (baptism) and the Spirit ("born again" derives from John 3:6), (4) by the Holy Spirit, (5) by confessing Jesus as Lord and belief in His Resurrection, (6) by God's desire that all men be saved, (7) as a result of justification by works as well as faith, (8) through the grace of Jesus, (9) by being justified by His blood, (10) by faith in Jesus, (11) by a revelation of the knowledge of God.

A2)   Baptism and marriage both are sacraments. In marriage, two people become joined together and obtain grace in committing themselves to each other in so doing; serving each other and God. Baptism is also joining together God's gifts to the person and entrance into the Christian community, to serve God and fellow Christians and the lost as well.

A3)   Jesus says, "... baptizing them in the name of the Father and of the Son and of the Holy Spirit." (Matthew 28:19)

A4)   Depending on their individual beliefs, non-Catholic Christian groups say we can be baptized by immersion, sprinkling, as an infant, and as an adult after profession of Christian faith.

A5)   These verses link baptism, salvation and sin.

> **Jesus answered, "Truly, truly, I say to you, unless one is born of water and the Spirit, he cannot enter the kingdom of God." (John 3:5)**

> **After this Jesus and his disciples went into the land of Judea; there he remained with them and baptized. (John 3:22)**

> **Do you not know that all of us who have been baptized into Christ Jesus were baptized into his death? We were buried therefore with him by baptism into death, so that as Christ was raised from the dead by the glory of the Father, we too might walk in newness of life. (Romans 6:3-4)**

> **And he said to them, "Go into all the world and preach the gospel to the whole creation. He who believes and is baptized will be saved; but he who does not believe will be condemned." (Mark 16:15-16)**

> **And one Ananias, a devout man according to the law, well spoken of by all the Jews who lived there, came to me, and standing by me said to me,**

> "Brother Saul, receive your sight." And in that very hour I received my sight and saw him ... And now why do you wait? Rise and be baptized, and wash away your sins, calling on his name." (Acts 22:12-13, 16)
>
> For Christ also died for sins once for all, the righteous for the unrighteous, that he might bring us to God, being put to death in the flesh but made alive in the spirit; in which he went and preached to the spirits in prison, who formerly did not obey, when God's patience waited in the days of Noah, during the building of the ark, in which a few, that is, eight persons, were saved through water. *Baptism, which corresponds to this, now saves you*, not as a removal of dirt from the body but as an appeal to God for a clear conscience, through the Resurrection of Jesus Christ, who has gone into heaven and is at the right hand of God, with angels, authorities, and powers subject to him. (1 Peter 3:18-22)
>
> Now when they heard this they were cut to the heart, and said to Peter and the rest of the Apostles, "Brethren, what shall we do?" And Peter said to them, "Repent, and be baptized every one of you in the name of Jesus Christ for the forgiveness of your sins; and you shall receive the gift of the Holy Spirit. For the promise is to you and to your children and to all that are far off, every one whom the Lord our God calls to him. (Acts 2:37-39)

A6) Because Jesus was baptizing people, it is possible to make a strong argument from context that the water referred to in John 3:5 was the water of baptism.

A7) Deacon Ed Blaine writes about the recalling of a Catholic's baptism at their funeral:

> As the body is brought into the church it is blessed with holy water that recalls the waters of baptism. This action reminds us that we who are baptized are baptized into the death and Resurrection of Christ. We who have died with Christ in baptism will rise with him. Immediately following the blessing with holy water, the white pall is placed over the casket. This is an action that is appropriate for the family to perform. The white cloth again recalls the rite of baptism and the clothing with a white garment. A religious symbol may now be placed on the casket. This should be something personal to the deceased; a cross, rosary beads that belonged to the deceased, a prayer book. This symbol remains on the casket during the funeral Mass.
> (http://www.canadced.com/catholic_funeral.htm)

A8) J.N.D. Kelly, an Anglican — who was popularly embraced by American Evangelicals.

B9)   Catholic teaching about infant baptism is reinforced because Acts 2:38b-39a states: "you shall receive the gift of the Holy Spirit. For the promise is to you and to your children ... "

B10) These verses describe: (a) the disciples who rebuked the people for bringing children to Jesus, as if they were not part of the spiritual community; and (b) Jesus who welcomed contact with children and said "for to such belongs the kingdom of heaven." Therefore, it stands to reason that a rite of inclusion into the kingdom and Church like baptism should be extended to infants.

B11) Circumcision of Jewish male infants on the eighth day was the rite of inclusion into the Old Covenant. The similar rite for Christians and entrance into the New Covenant is baptism, for both boys and girls. The boys being circumcised didn't have a clue what the painful practice meant spiritually, yet they were included in the community by virtue of it.

B12) St. Paul says:

> **In him also you were circumcised with a circumcision made without hands, by putting off the body of flesh in the circumcision of Christ; and you were buried with him in baptism, in which you were also raised with him through faith in the working of God, who raised him from the dead. (Colossians 2:11-12)**

B13) The logical inconsistency is that absolutely free grace (according to a certain Protestant strain of thought) means we do nothing whatsoever; therefore, requiring this act of assent and acceptance is arguably contrary with the notion of free grace. God is able to regenerate and infuse with grace an infant whether he or she knows what is going on or not!

B14) In A.D. 248 Origen wrote:

> **Every soul that is born into flesh is soiled by the filth of wickedness and sin. ... In the Church, baptism is given for the remission of sins, and, according to the usage of the Church, baptism is given even to infants. If there were nothing in infants which required the remission of sins and nothing in them pertinent to forgiveness, the grace of baptism would seem superfluous.** (*Homilies on Leviticus* **8:3**)

> **The Church received from the Apostles the tradition of giving baptism even to infants. The Apostles, to whom were committed the secrets of the divine sacraments, knew there are in everyone innate strains of [original] sin, which must be washed away through water and the Spirit.** (*Commentaries on Romans* **5:9**)

B15) St. Irenaeus knew St. Polycarp, who had in turn known the Apostle John and some other Apostles.

C16) One must also "believe" as well as be baptized, and the Biblical notion of "believing" Jesus is also to "obey" Him (cf. John 3:36)

C17) Obedience to Christ is crucial. One classic passage (among many similar ones), is Matthew 7:16-27:

> **You will know them by their fruits. Are grapes gathered from thorns, or figs from thistles? So, every sound tree bears good fruit, but the bad tree bears evil fruit. A sound tree cannot bear evil fruit, nor can a bad tree bear good fruit. Every tree that does not bear good fruit is cut down and thrown into the fire. Thus you will know them by their fruits.**
>
> **Not every one who says to me, 'Lord, Lord,' shall enter the kingdom of heaven, but he who does the will of my Father who is in heaven. On that day many will say to me, 'Lord, Lord, did we not prophesy in your name, and cast out demons in your name, and do many mighty works in your name?' And then will I declare to them, 'I never knew you; depart from me, you evildoers.'**
>
> **Every one then who hears these words of mine and does them will be like a wise man who built his house upon the rock; and the rain fell, and the floods came, and the winds blew and beat upon that house, but it did not fall, because it had been founded on the rock. And every one who hears these words of mine and does not do them will be like a foolish man who built his house upon the sand; and the rain fell, and the floods came, and the winds blew and beat against that house, and it fell; and great was the fall of it. (Matthew 7:16-27)**

D18) The Orthodox Church believes the same. This is important because they can also trace themselves back to the Apostles through apostolic succession. Even the Protestant Lutherans believe similarly to Catholics, as do Anglicans and some Methodists.

7 MORALITY ANSWERS

A1) The Gospels teach that we are saved by grace through faith (see, e.g., John 3:16), yet faith is not disconnected from works. The works inevitably follow. When we love

Jesus we want to show him. Jesus emphasized the supreme importance of works in the Christian life in many passages. For example:

> **Thus you will know them by their fruits. (Matthew 7:20)**
>
> **Not every one who says to me, 'Lord, Lord,' shall enter the kingdom of heaven, but he who does the will of my Father who is in heaven. On that day many will say to me, 'Lord, Lord, did we not prophesy in your name, and cast out demons in your name, and do many mighty works in your name?' And then will I declare to them, `I never knew you; depart from me, you evildoers.' (Matthew 7:21-23)**
>
> **Every one then who hears these words of mine and does them will be like a wise man who built his house upon the rock; and the rain fell, and the floods came, and the winds blew and beat upon that house, but it did not fall, because it had been founded on the rock. (Matthew 7:24-25)**
>
> **For the Son of Man is to come with his angels in the glory of his Father, and then he will repay every man for what he has done. (Matthew 16:27)**

A2)   The Catechism teaches that in the final analysis, man has no right to any merit. Everything we have is received from God. God freely chooses to include man in the work of His grace. Man merely decides whether or not to collaborate with God. Good human actions "proceed in Christ" with "predispositions and assistance given by the Holy Spirit" (CCC 2008).

B3)   Jesus is speaking about those who delivered Him to Pontius Pilate for sentencing and punishment. He said to Pontius Pilate: "he who delivered me to you has the greater sin," which suggests that some sins are greater than others.

B4)   The more we respect a spouse, the more we will do acts of kindness, love, and self-sacrifice. The same applies to our relationship to God. But the principle also applies to the opposite situation of sinning against our spouse. If we say something inadvertently or out of momentary anger, (perhaps because we had a bad day filled with frustration and took it out against them), the wise spouse will take that into consideration and "cut some slack". Likewise, when we sin against God we might often do it without much thought. But if we deliberately sin with full consent of the will, it is a far more serious matter. Even courts of law recognize this distinction by punishing a person more, to the extent that he committed a premeditated crime, (e.g. 1st, 2nd, and 3rd degree homicide.)

B5)   The Apostle John implies that prayer for mortal sin would not be effective, because the person who committed it has to repent before God can restore His grace to him.

It may be that you should go to the person and confront him or her about the sin, as described in Matthew 18:15-20.

B6)   If we see someone committing a non-deadly sin we should pray that God will give the person "life" (grace) and restoration to proper relationship with God.

B7)   The Church calls deadly sins "mortal," and non-deadly sins "venial."

B8)   In the early Church the three sins that were thought to remove salvation from a person if he or she did not repent were: (a) blasphemy, (b) murder, and (c) apostasy.

B9)   In the first three centuries, forgiveness of sin was found by public penance (various penalties or punishments or privations). Public penance was for the purpose of putting a social stigma and shame on sin, so that the person would reform himself and stop sinning. See Biblical examples of this in 1 Corinthians 5:1-5; 2 Corinthians 2:6-11.

B10) Our sins are against the Church at large because the Church as <u>the People of God is supposed to stand out among human beings</u> as a special community of the redeemed, bearing witness to the Good News of salvation. Sin separates us from our brethren in the Church and from the teaching of the Church, and causes non-believers in the world to question whether Jesus is Lord (John 17:23).

B11) (A) Often we think that we are under no laws at all because we are saved by grace through faith, a heresey known as *antinomianism*. (B) Antinomianism is dangerous because grace and the new covenant fulfill and develop the Old Testament system of Mosaic Law, and works are still required in the Christian life (though not able to save anyone by themselves).

B12) In the Old Testament, the moral law worked by the "eye for an eye" principle: if you injured someone's eye, then you would suffer the same as punishment. Jesus gave a much deeper analysis, and looked at what lies behind such crimes, and so He noted that anger is the root cause of murder, and lust is the root cause of adultery. The essence of the sin, in other words, was in the intention or wicked inclination before it is even committed.

B13) At the beginning of Mass we ask God to forgive us our sins by (A) Public acknowledgment of sin (confession), (B) recognition of our sinfulness in our thoughts and (C) words, and in acts of (D) commission and (E) omission.

B14) For a sin to be mortal or deadly: (A) it must be a grave, serious matter; (B) it must be committed with sufficient knowledge and reflection; and (C) it must be committed with a full, deliberate consent of the will.

C15) The Catholic teaching about sin has not changed in any essential way over the centuries. The Church has developed its teaching on sin by: (A) a deeper understanding of sin as time goes by; (B) by its origins and consequences; and (c) how to best prevent it by virtue of the guidance of the Holy Spirit.

C16) Civil divorce is permitted in extreme cases (physical abuse of a spouse or children, etc.), though without any permissible "right" of remarriage. A valid, consummated, sacramental marriage between two baptized persons is indissoluble. An annulment is a declaration that a valid marriage never did occur. Thus, an annulment is fundamentally different from divorce.

C17) Many Christian bodies have sanctioned abortion as a moral choice. They have also allowed more and more "loopholes" for permissible divorce, such as when the spouse commits adultery, and also for remarriage after divorce. Oftentimes, the current teaching of a denomination is at odds with the historic teaching of the same denomination.

In respect to abortion, the Catholic Church teaches that it never is a moral choice, because it is an objective act of murder.

C18) The Catholic Church merely claims to be preserving and passing on what it received: the "apostolic deposit" from Jesus and the Apostles. It is not a democracy inasmuch as its teachings are concerned. They are not determined by majority vote. Nor does its government function by representatives, as secular governments do.

C19) In 1968, it is likely that neither the Church nor medical researchers understood that the contraceptive pill could act as an abortifacient.

C20) The importance and/or consequence of moral obedience are referenced in these verses.

> Matthew 5:22: our anger has very serious consequences; possibly eternal.
>
> Matthew 6:15: our forgiveness of others will determine whether God forgives us.
>
> Matthew 12:36: our careless words (not repented of) will cause us to receive a reckoning on Judgment Day.
>
> 2 Timothy 4:7: perseverance and keeping the faith are crucial for ultimate salvation.
>
> 2 Peter 1:10: our zeal will, in turn, confirm our election and cause us by God's grace to persevere.

> **Matthew 7:21: If we don't** *do* **God's will, it may be that we aren't in the elect at all, and will be damned in the end.**
>
> **James 2:14, 17, 24: faith and works go together. True faith always produces good works.** (C.S. Lewis wrote that faith and works were like two blades of a pair of scissors. No one asks which one is more necessary than the other.)

C21) Moral obedience has two sides. It means we must (A) abstain from sin; and (B) that we have the obligation to obey God's commands.

8 CONFESSION
Answers

A1) The person does not hear the clear statement that they are forgiven, or absolved of their sin.

A2) A person's sins would not be forgiven when they are not truly repentant and resolved to change their ways with regard to the sin they confessed.

B3) Two verses where Jesus gives the Apostles the power to forgive sins are:

> **If you forgive the sins of any, they are forgiven; if you retain the sins of any, they are retained. (John 20:23)**
>
> **I will give you the keys of the kingdom of heaven, and whatever you bind on earth shall be bound in heaven, and whatever you loose on earth shall be loosed in heaven. (Matthew 16:19)**

B4) Two religious rituals that some non-Catholic Christians require be performed by a minister are Baptism and the Eucharist, or Holy Communion. Ministers perform these because they are following the model of the disciples, who were leaders in the early Church.

B5) When we sin we also sin against: (A) The Church and those in it. When we seek forgiveness, (B) priests represent the Church.

B6) Matthew's statement that God had given authority to "men" to forgive sin is significant because this happened before the people knew that Jesus was God, and so it represented men forgiving other men. (Jesus used the term "Son of Man" to describe Himself). The incarnation raised mankind to such a level, so that priests could exercise the same function as representatives of God, who took on human flesh.

B7)   In the Sermon on the Mount, Jesus teaches that we should forgive the sins of others. The overall context is righteousness that proceeds from the heart and is transferred into action; also rejoicing when persecuted, and the possibility of judgment if we don't forgive. (Matthew 5:10-12, 22-26, 39-47)

B8)   If we do not forgive the sins of others, God won't forgive our sins.

B9)   When Jesus passes on His authority to forgive sins to the Apostles he says:

> **"Peace be with you. As the Father has sent me, even so I send you." And when he had said this, he breathed on them, and said to them, "Receive the Holy Spirit. If you forgive the sins of any, they are forgiven; if you retain the sins of any, they are retained." (John 20:21-23)**

B10) The other place in the Bible where God breathed on people is:

> **Then the LORD God formed man of dust from the ground, and breathed into his nostrils the breath of life; and man became a living being. (Genesis 2:7)**

The context was creation and making human beings the highest creature, made in the image of God, and with a soul. (In Hebrew thinking the soul was like the breath, or life force.)

C11) Two other prophecies of Christ that are applicable until He returns are: (A) The command to Baptize (Matt 28:19). (B) The Holy Spirit guiding us into all truth (John 16:13). James 5:16 mentions confession and healing with the command to pray for one another, thus suggesting that as prayer is an ongoing practice among Christians, so should confession and absolution.

C12) Early Church Fathers who understood that confession and penance are necessary parts of a Christian's life include:

A) St. Ignatius of Antioch:

> **For as many as are of God and of Jesus Christ are also with the bishop. And as many as shall, in the exercise of penance, return into the unity of the Church, these, too, shall belong to God, that they may live according to Jesus Christ.** (*Letter to the Philadelphians* **3** [**A.D. 110**])

> For where there is division and wrath, God does not dwell. To all them that repent, the Lord grants forgiveness, if they turn in penitence to the unity of God, and to communion with the bishop. (Ibid., 8)

B) St. Irenaeus:

> [The Gnostic disciples of Marcus] have deluded many women. ... Their consciences have been branded as with a hot iron. Some of these women make a public confession, but others are ashamed to do this, and in silence, as if withdrawing from themselves the hope of the life of God, they either apostatize entirely or hesitate between the two courses. (*Against Heresies* 1:22 [A.D. 189])

C) Origen:

> [A final method of forgiveness], albeit hard and laborious [is] the remission of sins through penance, when the sinner ... does not shrink from declaring his sin to a priest of the Lord and from seeking medicine, after the manner of him who say, 'I said, "To the Lord I will accuse myself of my iniquity"'. (*Homilies on Leviticus* 2:4 [A.D. 248])

D) St. Cyprian of Carthage:

> The Apostle [Paul] likewise bears witness and says: '... Whoever eats the bread or drinks the cup of the Lord unworthily will be guilty of the Body and Blood of the Lord' [1 Corinthians. 11:27]. But [the impenitent] spurn and despise all these warnings; before their sins are expiated, before they have made a confession of their crime, before their conscience has been purged in the ceremony and at the hand of the priest ... they do violence to [the Lord's] Body and Blood, and with their hands and mouth they sin against the Lord more than when they denied him. (*The Lapsed* 15:1–3 (A.D. 251])

D13) Sincerity and true repentance is absolutely essential in order to receive sacramental absolution or forgiveness.

D14) If a priest perceives that the person confessing is just playing around and has not genuinely repented, the priest should not forgive the sins of that person.

D15) Metanoia means an internal change of mind, a change of life, or a change of heart. It refers to an internal conversion. Without it, none of the Sacraments have effect.

D16) Confession is a place where you can profess your resolve to follow God wholeheartedly and to try better, with His help, to avoid sin in the future; particularly the sin confessed.

D17) The purpose of penance is to show that one is sorrowful, and to bring home the point that sin has a cost, and that restitution must be paid to God and fellow believers for the sin. The parent punishes his or her children in order to correct them and set them on a better path. Likewise, penance is for our own good, to reform us before our sins become even worse and more entrenched.

D18) The term reconciliation means being united or back in communion or right relationship with someone. In Confession, we are reconciled with God.

D19) The Sacrament of Reconciliation strengthens our resolve; makes us aware of the harmfulness and penalty and cost of sin, alleviates guilt, frees us from the bondage of sin and its adverse effects, and provides us grace through the sacrament, in order to avoid sin in the future.

D20) The best reason to avoid sin is out of love for and obedience to God and gratefulness to Him for His gifts and mercy. The lesser reason to avoid sin is to avoid suffering and negative consequences for ourselves.

9 MARY, I
Answers

A1) Many non-Catholics think that Catholics worship Mary because they equate all prayer as worship; they collapse all veneration and honor into adoration and worship. Hence if directed towards a creature it is regarded as idolatry, because they equate using a statue as a devotional aid with gross idolatry of a piece of plaster, and because they believe that any praise or honor directed towards a creature somehow detracts from worship of God, and God's uniqueness.

A2) Catholics define prayer as intercession insofar as it is directed towards a saint rather than to God. Asking a saint to pray is indistinguishable from asking a friend on the earth to pray. Protestants, on the other hand, often equate asking a saint to pray with prayer *to* the saint as if all power to fulfill the prayer lies with the saint *rather* than with God.

A3) A better word to describe how Catholics think about Mary is veneration, or giving very high honor to her, rather than adoration and worship, which is proper only when directed to God alone.

A4) The Bible commands us to honor our mothers and fathers.

A5) Luke 2:51 gives an indication of how well Jesus honored his mother and father.

And he went down with them and came to Nazareth, and was obedient to them; and his mother kept all these things in her heart. (Luke 2:51)

A6) If Mary is still alive in heaven and is able to "hear" prayers (as Scripture indicates is the case; see Hebrews 12:1), then there is no essential difference in asking Mary or a relative to pray for you.

B7) The two Biblical people who began "the Cult of Mary" were the angel Gabriel: "And he came to her and said, 'Hail, O favored one, the Lord is with you!'"

And Elizabeth: "and she exclaimed with a loud cry, 'Blessed are you among women, and blessed is the fruit of your womb!'"

B8) The angel Gabriel proclaims "Hail, Mary, full of grace." "Full of grace" is a permissible translation of the Greek *kecharitomene*, which comes from the Greek root *charis*, or grace).

B9) Elizabeth, the mother of John the Baptist, proclaims about Mary, "Blessed are you among women, and blessed is the fruit of your womb."

B10) The literal meaning of *Theotokos* is "God-bearer" but it is more commonly translated Mother of God. The title was designed to highlight the Incarnation and Deity of Christ, by showing that God the Son took on human flesh, and in so doing, had a human mother. The word indicates a very high honor indeed of Mary, yet the emphasis and focus in the mind of those who started using the term was on Jesus Christ, and there is no implication of Mary being equal to or above God.

B11) To deny that Mary is the Mother of God is to deny the Incarnation or deity or divinity of Jesus Christ.

B12) Sure, it is possible that some individual Catholics worship Mary. Anything is possible with fallen human beings. But the Catholic Church does not teach this, and shouldn't be judged based on the behavior of some who are misguided in her ranks who misunderstand Catholic teaching.

B13) The Catholic Church does not teach us to worship Mary; only that Mary is to be venerated and honored.

C14) What was forbidden in the First* Commandment (Exodus 20:4-5) was a "graven image" (one of God), that is, "an idol made of wood or stone." What God was forbidding was idolatry: making a stone or block of wood god. The Jews were forbidden to have idols (like all their neighbors had), and God told them not to make an image of Him because He revealed Himself as a spirit. The KJV, RSV, and

Jewish (1917) Bible versions translate graven image at Exodus 20:4, but many of the more recent translations render the word as idol (e.g., NASB, NRSV, NIV, CEV). Context makes it very clear that idolatry is being condemned. The next verse states: "You shall not bow down to them or worship them ... " (NIV, NRSV).

In other words, mere blocks of stone or wood ("them") are not to be worshiped, as that is gross idolatry, and the inanimate objects are not God. This does not absolutely preclude, however, the notion of an icon, where God is worshiped with the help of a visual aid. The use of images is not in the same category, if they are rightly used. Our Lord and Savior Jesus Christ is described four times in the Bible by the Apostle Paul as the image (Greek: *eikon*) of God. Twice, he uses the word directly of Jesus (2 Corinthians 4:4, Col 1:15), and twice in the sense of Christians being transformed into or conformed to the image of Jesus/God (Romans 8:29, 2 Corinthians 4:4). This changes everything. The Incarnation made images permissible, as long as they were representing Jesus, the "image of the invisible God" (Col 1:15; KJV, RSV).

(* Jews, Protestants, and Orthodox call this the "Second" Commandment. But The Catholic Church includes in in the first.)

C15) Catholics are not praying to the statue or the picture. Statues and photographs are merely visual aids to concentrate one's mind on the person represented.

C16) The person is not worshiping the picture. This is not worship, but remembrance and affection or love, directed towards the one visualized in the photograph or painting.

D17) The books are not titled the Gospels of Jesus Christ in order to bring to mind to the reader that these Gospels were written by eyewitnesses of Jesus.

D18) The Bible doesn't say that they are dead, if by that one means "annihilated; no longer existing at all." They are "dead" only in terms of no longer being alive on the earth, but they are still alive in heaven. One could say they are more alive than those living on temporal earth, because they are living in eternity in God's presence.

D19) Jesus did not conjure up dead spirits. Conjuring up spirits was forbidden in the Old Covenant. This was something entirely different: an example of saints in heaven (Moses and Elijah) being actively involved in happenings on earth. They simply appeared (as far as we can tell from the texts describing the event).

E20) Jesus says the following people should be referred to as blessed: the poor in spirit, those who mourn, the meek, those who hunger and thirst for righteousness, the merciful, the pure in heart, peacemakers, and those who are persecuted and reviled and spoken falsely of.

E21) The Annunciation (Luke 1:28-38) is why Mary says that future generations will call her blessed. She says it when she meets Elizabeth, who had been filled with the Holy Spirit, and who proclaimed that Mary would be called blessed, and John the Baptist leapt for joy in Elizabeth's womb.

F22) "Co-Redeemer" is what many people hear, but the more accurate terms are "Co-Redemptrix" or "Co-Redemptress," which simply mean to "work alongside" not necessarily "equal" at all. For example, in English we have the term "co-pay" (meaning, the person also pays some of the fee along with his insurance company). A "co-pilot" is not equal in rank to the pilot of an airplane, but is a subordinate helper to him. Mary's cooperation in distribution of God's graces is entirely secondary and non-necessary. She participates in this way because this was how God designed things.

F23) Mary's "yes" made the Incarnation possible, and hence helped to make salvation of all who are saved possible. She bore God the Son and raised Him and lived with Him for thirty years. She was without sin and always directed spiritual seekers to her Son. Her heroic sanctity is an extraordinary model for us to try to emulate.

G24) The situations in Scripture that imply Mary is our Mother include: (A) When Jesus is on the cross and He tells St. John that Mary is now his mother and he her son; (B) Followers of Jesus are called Mary's offspring in Revelation 12:17.

G25) Mary refers to God as her Savior. Mary was saved like all of us, but by prevention (the grace of the Immaculate Conception, that allowed her to totally avoid original sin, from which the rest of us need to be rescued). In both cases, God's grace was necessarily required. Hence, Mary could call God her Savior, just as we can. It doesn't "prove" that she was a sinner, only that she certainly would have sinned if this grace had not enabled her to always say no to sin.

10 MARY, II
Answers

A1) The phrase "communion of saints" refers to the "saints" (i.e., Christians) alive on the earth and those who have died and are even more alive in heaven.

A2)   The evidence of saints in heaven praying for and being aware of us includes Luke 15:7, which describes "joy in heaven" when a sinner repents. So inhabitants in heaven are aware of even interior spiritual transformation of persons on earth. In Hebrews 12:1, the saints in heaven are expressly compared to spectators in an arena. Revelation 5:8 informs us that creatures in heaven (thought by many commentators to be glorified human beings, as opposed to angels) possess the "prayers of the saints." If that is so, then somehow the creatures in heaven have been made aware of the prayers, either directly, or communicated from God to them, by angels or by God's power and will.

A3)   Church Fathers Clement of Alexandria (208 AD) and St. Jerome (340-420 AD) taught us that saints in heaven pray for us.

B4)   Asking Mary and the saints to intercede for us to Jesus maintains the centrality of Jesus as the sole answerer of prayer. Mary is, therefore, a "channel" to reach God, not the "final court of appeal," so to speak. Asking her to pray for us no more interferes with the sole mediatorship of Jesus, than asking each other on earth to pray.

B5)   In both cases, someone else is approaching God on our behalf. The only difference is whether they are on the earth or in heaven.

C6)   (A) The presence of God or the Word of God. (B) The hill country of Judea in both cases. (C) Three months in each case (2 Samuel 6:10-12 / Luke 1:39-45, 56). (D) David leapt for joy and so did John the Baptist (2 Samuel 6:14-16; cf. 1 Chronicles 15:29 and Luke 1:44).

C7)   The Ark of the Covenant was mentioned (Rev 11:29) right before the passage about the glorified Mary in heaven in Revelation 12. Phenomena of nature are associated with both: lightning, thunder, earthquake, and hail are mentioned in connection with the Ark, and the sun, moon, and stars are associated with the Blessed Virgin Mary (see also Rev 12:12). "Voices" or a "voice" are another parallel (Rev 12:10). Both are in heaven, in or near the "temple" in heaven.

D8)   Irenaeus wrote: "What the virgin Eve had tied up by unbelief, this the Virgin Mary loosened by faith" (Against Heresies, 3, 21, 10). This patristic motif, emphasized especially by St. Irenaeus, is known as "the second Eve" or "the New Eve".

D9)   The common title given by Moses, Jesus and John is "Woman." Therefore, it is as if Mary represents mankind, or functions as a "second Eve."

D10) Mary's last recorded words were, "Do whatever he tells you" – referring to Jesus.

D11) Mary points to her Son Jesus as the person to obey.

D12) Mary (in Luke 1:28) is addressed with esteemed favor and unique honor. "Hail, O favored one, the Lord is with you!" (RSV) ["Hail, full of grace" in the Catholic version of the RSV].

E13) The terms for "brother" and "sister" could now be translated as "cousin" or "kinsman". The Greek *adelphos* has a very wide range of possible meanings.

E14) St. Augustine wrote:

> Her virginity also itself was on this account more pleasing and accepted, in that it was not that Christ being conceived in her, rescued it beforehand from a husband who would violate it, Himself to preserve it; but, before He was conceived, chose it, already dedicated to God, as that from which to be born. This is shown by the words which Mary spoke in answer to the Angel announcing to her conception; "How," says she, "shall this be, seeing I know not a man?" Which assuredly she would not say, unless she had before vowed herself unto God as a virgin. But, because the habits of the Israelites as yet refused this, she was espoused to a just man, who would not take from her by violence, but rather guard against violent persons, what she had already vowed. Although, even if she had said this only, "How shall this take place?" and had not added, "seeing I know not a man," certainly she would not have asked, how, being a female, she should give birth to her promised Son, if she had married with purpose of sexual intercourse. (*Of Holy Virginity*, **4; translated by C.I. Cornish; http://www.newadvent.org/ fathers/1310.htm**)

E15) Martin Luther claimed that: "Christ ... was the only Son of Mary, and the Virgin Mary bore no children besides Him ... 'brothers' really means 'cousins' here, for Holy Writ and the Jews always call cousins brothers." (*Sermons on John*, chapters 1-4, 1537-39)

> He, Christ, our Savior, was the real and natural fruit of Mary's virginal womb ... This was without the cooperation of a man, and she remained a virgin after that. (*Ibid.*)

E16) John Calvin described the intellect of those that disputed Mary's life long virginity as displaying excessive ignorance and as having an extreme fondness for disputation. Helvidius displayed excessive ignorance in concluding that Mary must have had many sons, because Christ's 'brothers' are sometimes mentioned. (*Harmony of Matthew, Mark & Luke*, sec. 39 (Geneva, 1562), vol. 2 / From *Calvin's Commentaries*, tr. William Pringle, Grand Rapids, MI: Eerdmans, 1949, p.215; on Matthew 13:55)

> [On Matt 1:25:] The inference he [Helvidius] drew from it was, that Mary remained a virgin no longer than till her first birth, and that afterwards

> she had other children by her husband ... No just and well-grounded inference can be drawn from these words ... as to what took place after the birth of Christ. He is called 'first-born'; but it is for the sole purpose of informing us that he was born of a virgin ... What took place afterwards the historian does not inform us ... No man will obstinately keep up the argument, except from an extreme fondness for disputation. (Pringle, *ibid.*, vol. I, p. 107)

E17) The use of "till" or "until" doesn't require or necessarily imply that what occurs after the time described by the word is different from what was the case before. This can be seen from other Biblical examples (1 Samuel 15:35; 2 Samuel 6:23; Matthew 12:20) where the use of the word "until" does not mean "after."

F18) "Madonna" paintings with Mary holding the baby Jesus always make Jesus the central figure.

F19) When we praise a great work of art, it is assumed and understood that it didn't create itself; therefore, praise of the work necessarily becomes praise of the artist who created it.

F20) Error is always possible and actual among proponents of any religious belief. This reflects badly upon Catholic teaching, but the teaching itself is what it is, and remains so, regardless of how someone may distort it. One must judge a religious belief system by its actual dogmatic teaching, not the distortions of its poorly informed and least articulate "adherents."

F21) Mary is like the moon to the "sun" of Jesus Christ. He creates and is the source of the light that she reflects.

F22) We should follow Christ's example by honoring Mary His Mother, since He did.

F23) The Catholic Church and the Orthodox Church still call Mary, "Blessed."

11 PETER
ANSWERS

A1) Peter's name is mentioned more often than all the other disciples put together: 191 times (162 as Peter or Simon Peter, 23 as Simon, and 6 as Cephas). John is next in frequency with only 48 mentions.

A2) (Simon) Peter and Andrew.

A3) Jesus preached from Peter's boat.

A4) Peter's name is always listed first.

A5) Peter's original given name was Simon. Jesus changed it to Peter, meaning "rock".

A6) The Gospels record two accounts of Peter walking on water.

A7) Peter was given the keys to the Kingdom by Jesus. The keys represent authority and jurisdiction over a house, as sort of a "superintendent," or as many Bible commentators have noted, in tracing back this Hebrew concept to Isaiah 22: the power to "bind and loose" and "open and shut."

A8) Peter is the other Apostle who stayed around after Jesus' arrest. In all four Gospels, Peter is emphasized as the preeminent disciple or Apostle. He was also the leader of the Church despite his own weakness and volatility, because his office and power rested upon the divine power of Jesus.

A9) When Mary of Magdala saw the empty tomb she first told Peter and John.

A10) John arrived at the empty tomb first, but allowed Peter to enter first.

A11) Jesus told Peter three times at the Sea of Tiberias to feed those Jesus was going to leave behind. (John 21:1)

A12) Peter led the Apostles to select Matthias as a replacement for Judas.

A13) Peter was the first Apostle to preach as an evangelist. He led 3,000 into the church on the Day of Pentecost, or when the Holy Spirit descended upon the disciples to live inside of them and give them strength, guidance, and power (the indwelling).

A14) Peter was given the vision that Gentiles should be admitted into the Church. He saw the heavens opened and a sort of sheet with all kinds of animals on it. Peter was commanded to eat anything because God had made all things clean. This represented the opening up or expansion of the Mosaic Law and Covenant to include non-Jewish Gentiles.

A15) Peter was the first Apostle to perform a healing. He healed a man lame from birth.

A16) Peter presided over and opened the first council of Christianity, the Jerusalem Council, and laid down the principles afterwards accepted and proclaimed by it. After he spoke, the assembly was silent, and no one contradicted what he said.

B17) Jesus gave the power to bind and loose to Peter. This is one good reason why "petros" cannot refer to "faith" but to a person.

B18) It makes no sense for Jesus to set up authority in the Church only in the first generation, which would then die out and then everyone is on their own. Whatever was set up in the beginning was obviously intended to be perpetual and a model for what came afterwards.

B19) Peter was the predominant shepherd of the Church: a metaphor for authority. He would feed and tend the "sheep."

B20) Paul calls Peter "Cephas," which is Aramaic for "rock" or Peter.

B21) In Matthew 16:18-19 Christ is addressing Peter alone, as preeminent; in Matthew 18:18-19 Jesus is addressing the Apostles collectively. The singularity of Peter in Matthew 16 is highly significant.

B22) In Isaiah 22:22 and Revelations 3:7, the concept of the "key" gives the person an overriding power or ability to "open and shut" (i.e., declare things authoritatively, as binding upon others).

C23) Jesus commissions Peter, to feed and tend the "sheep" or followers of Jesus (Christians).

C24) The synonyms for "feed" and "tend" are "shepherd" (verb), "guide," and "lead."

D25) Peter's weakness is evidence that the Church is established by Christ, because if men without the aid of the Holy Spirit were in charge, they would be weak as reeds, and the Church could not last.

D26) God the Holy Spirit protects the Church from making doctrinal errors.

D27) Peter did not "mess up" in establishing doctrine, because God protected the Church from any such error resulting from the weakness and frailty of men.

12 PAPACY
Answers

A1) Abram's name was changed to Abraham, to represent his position as the father of "a multitude of nations."

A2) A name in the Hebrew worldview stood for attributes or characteristics of the person.

B3)   Offices imply succession. Presidents and prime ministers and kings always have successors. It is no different in the Church. Whatever was established in the beginning was intended to be perpetual.

B4)   The desertion of Judas brought about a situation where the Apostles selected a successor, noting, "Lord, who knowest the hearts of all men, show which one of these two thou hast chosen to take the place in this ministry and Apostleship from which Judas turned aside ... " (Acts 1:24-25). If there was to be no succession, then this wouldn't have happened; all the Apostles would have simply died and that would have been it.

B5)   Peter declared that Apostolic successors were needed.

C6)   The four marks of the Church are One, Holy, Catholic, and Apostolic.

C7)   Here is one logical reason for each of the four marks: *One*: Multiple leaders imply more than one Church, or a Church that is divided. One can have many bishops, but only one preeminent leader, just as there can be a Senate and House with many officeholders, in American government, but just one President. *Holy*: one leader can present one unified doctrine of morality, without contradiction. *Catholic*: the Church is everywhere led by one leader, which unifies it. The word means "universal" or "applicable and accessible in every place." *Apostolic*: succession of a single head of the Church requires a single head at all times.

C8)   The Holy Spirit could give different doctrinal directions to different churches if the Holy Spirit had multiple personalities, and was confused about what was true.

C9)   A Bishop has the authority to ordain a priest or bishop.

D10)   Peter denied that he knew Jesus and acted hypocritically with regard to his conduct with or towards Gentiles.

D11)   Jesus promised that the gates of hell would not prevail against the Church (i.e., the Church would break through the gates and triumph) and the Holy Spirit would guide the Church into all truth.

D12)   The Pope's infallibility is limited to binding proclamations regarding faith and morals.

D13)   None. No Pope has ever proclaimed a doctrine that was later deemed wrong.

D14)   Jesus commanded His followers to obey what the Pharisees taught, but to not imitate how they acted, if and when they were hypocrites (as He often reprimanded them for being).

D15) The term "Ex Cathedra" means, literally, "from the seat"; in the Catholic understanding it means "with the very highest authority" and is the root word of the term cathedral.

E16) No actual doctrines were changed; only certain disciplinary practices have been changed.

E17) Popes or Councils do not come up with most doctrines. Doctrines are developed from what was received from Jesus and the Apostles in the beginning, and later proclaimed as binding, after sufficient reflection and pondering.

E18) The divinity or deity of Christ (He is God incarnate; God the Son); also the Nicene Creed was largely developed at the Council of Nicaea.

E19) The First Vatican Council in 1870.

F20) The preeminence of the Bishop of Rome was articulated by St. Clement of Rome, 80-100 A.D.; St. Ignatius of Antioch, c. 110; St. Irenaeus, between 180-200 A.D., Origen: first half of the third century; St. Cyprian, middle of the third century; and many Fathers in the fourth century.

F21) No popes, other than the first, took the name of "Peter".

13 PURGATORY
Answers

A1) The purpose of Purgatory is to cleanse the sinner for entrance to heaven, where no unclean thing can or shall enter, and for the direct presence of God.

A2) Secret sins unrepentant of, will be known and dealt with and purged at the judgment and/or in Purgatory.

A3) In Purgatory the extent of our sin—e.g. the wickedness, evil, deception, pride, self-centeredness, self-delusion, lusts of the flesh, rebellion against God—will be revealed.

A4) Purgatory is not a "second chance" and it is not permanent.

A5) Souls in Purgatory anticipate meeting God directly and being cleansed.

A6) This argument, that Jesus' death and Resurrection should have brought world peace, underestimates the persistence of concupiscence caused by original sin, and its continuing effects, even in the regenerate and Spirit-filled person. Hence, there is still need to rid ourselves of sin and our attachment to it. Purgatory represents an acknowledgement that some of this remnant of sin will still be present in most people at death.

A7) Purgatory is a condition or state.

B8) Many Christian doctrines are not explicitly explained in Scripture, such as the canon of Scripture, Mary as Mother of God, the divinity of the Holy Spirit, the Two Natures of Christ, the two wills of Christ, and the veneration of images.

B9) Purgatory arises from God's holiness (judgment) and love (mercy).

B10) The Jews prayed for the dead to be "delivered from their sin," thus implying that spiritual growth or cleansing continued to take place after death, a la Purgatory; otherwise, such prayers would have been vain and futile.

B11) 1 Corinthians 3:12-15 clearly is talking about a judgment of the saved, not the damned, since it notes "he himself will be saved" (3:15). This is a testing of men's works; related to merit. That is what the judgment is directed towards; it is not related to salvation or damnation, but of relative "reward" and "loss."

B12) Jesus descended to Hades or Sheol: the place of the dead before His Resurrection. This is similar to Purgatory insofar as it is also a third state besides heaven and hell, and a "waiting place" or temporary abode.

B13) Revelation 20:11-15 seems to distinguish between a judgment of works and one of salvation or damnation, as all are judged, but only some are thrown into the lake of fire (hell).

B14) Fr. Fete believes Lazarus, after he died and before he was raised from the dead, was in Purgatory rather than heaven, because Christ had not yet been resurrected, nor had He ascended into heaven. So the saints up to that time were awaiting those events in order to go to heaven.

B15) In order to be forgiven in the next life ("age to come") there must be a state or condition other than hell (no more forgiveness and utter damnation) and heaven (no sin permitted, and perfect holiness of all inhabitants). Purgatory perfectly fits the bill.

C16) There is evidence in the Roman catacombs of prayers for the departed.

C17) The purpose of the Jewish Prayer for the Dead is for the purification and salvation of a departed soul, for entrance into heaven. It includes the line: "He will give life to the dead and raise them to eternal life." It is prayed by children for their parents for eleven months and then at or near every anniversary of their death.

C18) Tertullian, St. Clement of Alexandria, Origen, and St. Cyprian all believed in Purgatory and the belief was widely held by the fathers by the fourth century.

D19) The two consequences of sin are rupture of communion with God and unhealthy attachment to creatures.

D20) An indulgence is a gracious remission of temporal punishment, which we deserve, as a result of our commission of sins whose guilt has already been forgiven.

D21) Indulgences cannot be obtained for relief from the eternal punishment of sin.

E22) C.S. Lewis wrote:

> **I believe in Purgatory ... Our souls** *demand* **Purgatory, don't they? Would it not break the heart if God said to us, "It is true, my son, that your breath smells and your rags drip with mud and slime, but we are charitable here and no one will upbraid you with these things, nor draw away from you. Enter into the joy"? Should we not reply, "With submission, sir, and if there is no objection, I'd** *rather* **be cleaned first." "It may hurt, you know" – "Even so, sir."** (*Letters to Malcolm: Chiefly on Prayer*, **New York: Harcourt Brace Jovanovich, 1964, 108-109**)

F23) When we enter Purgatory time as we know it will be different.

G24) In 2 Corinthians 5: 6, 8, Paul wrote:

> **So we are always of good courage; we know that while we are at home in the body we are away from the Lord, for we walk by faith, not by sight. We are of good courage, and we would rather be away from the body and at home with the Lord.**

When he wrote, "away from the body", Paul meant following the "flesh" (metaphor for sin and concupiscence) – not that all souls without a body are with the Lord. That would not be true of damned souls, anyway. Also, one attempting to use this argument presupposes that being in Purgatory is somehow away from the Lord. It is not, because all who are in Purgatory are already saved; therefore God is with them; in fact, more so than He is in this present life.